K-POP DANCE

This book is about K-pop dance and the evolution and presence of its dance fandom on social media.

Based on five years of ethnographic fieldwork, interviews, choreography, and participation-observation with 40 amateur and professional K-pop dancers in New York, California, and Seoul, the book traces the evolution of K-pop dance from the 1980s to the 2020s and explains its distinctive feature called 'gestural point choreography' – front-driven, two-dimensional, decorative and charming movements of the upper body and face – as an example of what the author theorizes as 'social media dance.' It also explores K-pop cover dance as a form of intercultural performance, suggesting that, by imitating and idolizing K-pop dance, fans are eventually 'fandoming' themselves and their bodies.

Presenting an ethnographic study of K-pop dance and its fandom, this book will be a valuable resource for students and scholars of Media Studies, Korean Studies, Performance Studies, and Dance.

Chuyun Oh is an Assistant Professor of Dance at San Diego State University. As a Fulbright scholar and former professional dancer, she studies racial and gender identities in performance. She is a co-editor of *Candlelight Movement, Democracy and Communication in Korea*, Routledge 2021.

K-POP DANCE

Fandoming Yourself on Social Media

Chuyun Oh

Routledge
Taylor & Francis Group

LONDON AND NEW YORK

Cover image: Artwork by Ganz (Kyeong Tae Kim)

First published 2023
by Routledge
4 Park Square, Milton Park, Abingdon, Oxon OX14 4RN

and by Routledge
605 Third Avenue, New York, NY 10158

Routledge is an imprint of the Taylor & Francis Group, an informa business

British Library Cataloguing in Publication Data
A catalogue record for this book is available from the British Library

Library of Congress Cataloging-in-Publication Data
A catalog record has been requested for this book

ISBN: 978-1-032-07942-4 (hbk)
ISBN: 978-1-032-07939-4 (pbk)
ISBN: 978-1-003-21218-8 (ebk)

DOI: 10.4324/9781003212188

Typeset in Bembo
by Taylor & Francis Books

For my parent, siblings, and David Choi

CONTENTS

ILLUSTRATIONS

Figures

Table

ACKNOWLEDGEMENT

This book would not be possible without warm-hearted supports of my family, friends, colleagues, mentors, and, most importantly, K-pop cover dancers, fans, and the interview participants from Southern California to Seoul, South Korea who have generously shared their stories with me. Special thanks are sent to dance teams and crews at University of California San Diego, and Midtown Utica Community Center (MUCC), and Chris Sunderlin, the founder of MUCC. I also deeply thank faculty at UC San Diego, Dr. Jin-Kyung Lee, Dr. Dredge Kang, and Dr. Patty Ahn. Your support during the research process truly means a lot to me. I send my gratitude to Routledge book editors Andrew Leach and Stephanie Rogers as well as anonymous book reviewers for their constructive and thoughtful feedback. I appreciate my friends and wonderful colleagues who copyedited this book, including Dr. Kirstie Hettinga, Dr. Amy Guenther, and Dr. Jennifer Ambrose. My special thanks to Dr. Guenther whose generous and thoughtful copyediting has made this book further shine. I am also sending gratitude to faculty and my dearest friends at Performance as Public Practice (PPP) at the University of Texas at Austin where I obtained my Ph.D. My study at PPP has provided me with a cornerstone to continue my academic career – Dr. Charlotte Canning, Dr. Paul Bonin-Rodriguez, Dr. Omi Osun Joni L. Jones, Dr. Deborah Paredez, and especially my former dissertation advisor Dr. Rebecca Rossen – I owe this book to this amazing group of faculty at UT Austin, who has shown me the power of academic research as a form of humanitarian activism. I also thank my dissertation committee at UT, Dr. Youjeong Oh, Dr. Cherise Smith, and Dr. Heather Hindman, for their kind support and consideration. I thank dance faculty from UT Austin to Hamilton College, where I completed my postdoctoral study: Prof. Charles O. Anderson, Prof. Elaine Heekin, Prof. Bruce Walczyk. As this is my first book, I also want to extend my gratitude to faculty at Ewha Womans University in Seoul, where I first opened my eyes to dance theory and philosophy: Dr.

Malborg Kim, Dr. Sang Mi Shin, Dr. Kisook Cho, and Dr. Hei-sook Kim whose thoughtful guidance fundamentally has inspired and changed my pathway as an academic. I also appreciate Asian studies faculty at Hamilton College, who truly helped me when I first shaped ideas for this book: Dr. Thomas Wilson, Dr. Masaaki Kamiya, Dr. Kyoko Omori, Dr. Lisa Trivedi, Dr. Zhuoyi Wang, and more. I send my gratitude to faculty and colleagues at San Diego State University: former PSFA (College of Professional Studies and Fine Arts) Dean Joyce Gattas, Dean Peggy Shannon, Dr. Joanna Brooks, Dr. Kevin Delgado, Dr. Eric Smigel, and my valued colleges and friends including Dr. Huma Ghosh, Dr. Yea-Wen Chen, Dr. Christine Sahin, Dr. Andrew Aziz, and Dr. Minjeong Kim. My gratitude is also extended to Dr. Suk-Young Kim, Dr. SanSan Kwan, Dr. Hyunjoon Shin, and Dr. Clare Croft for their supports. I appreciate brilliant students from Hamilton College, San Diego State University, and University of California San Diego whose genuine love and passion for dancing further motivate my research. I also thank my colleagues and collaborators, Dr. Kyung Hyun Kim, Dr. David C. Oh, Dr. Yong-Chan Kim, and Dr. JongHwa Lee for their continuous support. I share my thanks with members of "Korean/Female/Media Scholar" gather, including Dr. Ji-Hyun Ahn, Dr. Jungmin Kwon, Dr. Ju Oak Kim, Dr. Bohyeong Kim, Dr. Su Young Cho, Dr. Claire Lee, to name a few, for their thoughtful feedback and support. Finally, this book is for my parent, my dearest siblings – Dr. Jai Whan Oh, Sunhyung Ko, Dr. Jeeyun Oh, Yujin Oh (M.F.A.), and Junho Oh (J.D.) and my muse and husband, David Choi (Dai Un Choi). Your courage, beauty, and imperfection is all the love I have.

INTRODUCTION: K-POP DANCE

Fandoming Yourself on Social Media

Introduction

In 2020, I took BLACKPINK's "How You Like That" (2020) cover dance class at LP Dance Studio in Gangnam, Seoul. The instructor was a backup dancer of K-pop singer IU. I bought a one-day coupon, assuming that I could learn the movement in one day as a former professional ballet and modern dancer. The class truly humbled me. After class, I ended up registering for a month. The major challenge was the speed. There were too many small, precise movements, especially in the upper body, condensed into short moments. In the song lyrics, BLACKPINK says, "one, two, three." Each finger counts the number, pointing to the front, upward, and to the side, while switching, crossing, and changing the shape and level of the elbows and forearms differently, walking back and forth in a specific floor formation with confidently swaying hips, and maintaining a dramatic gaze at the mirror. All this happens in approximately one second. I felt I could do it if it was three times slower. No wonder K-pop dance classes on the dance app STEEZY Studio offer slow-down functions. I felt dizzy because of the dense, complicated coordination of the upper-body movements. The enormous front-driven energy I exerted for the face, the intensive gaze and dramatic eye contact, as well as the continuous popping chest movements exhausted me.

Yet, I wanted to do it again. I felt pretty, whatever that means, and sassy like BLACKPINK. I also felt like a musical actress performing a dramatic love story. When I was able to coordinate and do all the movements on time, it was truly cathartic. I noticed that my typical yoga pants for a woman in her thirties did not really fit the dance. On my way home, I bought black jogger pants that looked like those that Rosé wears in the "How You Like That" dance performance video. Interestingly, repeating the "How You Like That" choreography for a month was not boring. It was not only because of the intricate, speedy

DOI: 10.4324/9781003212188-1

coordination that needs days of practice. Instead, it was the constant, very strong visual reminder of BLACKPINK conjured whenever I practiced. The more I repeated, the more I felt like I was BLACKPINK.

K-pop (South Korean pop music) is found in every corner of the youth culture today, including the US. In 2019, *CNN* reported that "K-Pop is now the biggest transnational pop culture phenomenon since hip-hop" (Yang). In December 2020, *Time Magazine* introduced BTS as the Entertainer of the Year, the "the biggest band" worldwide, and "a symbol of youth activism" (Bruner). The youth hear K-pop idols' interviews on the Apple Music 1 radio station on Sunday mornings and watch their favorite idols on shows from the *American Music Awards* to *Ellen*. K-pop albums, merchandise, and miniatures are found from Target to McDonald's across the globe. In February 2020, I attended the Fusion Hip Hop Dance Competition, one of the biggest collegiate hip-hop dance competitions in Southern California, held in La Jolla. Cheered by hundreds of audience members, nearly half of the dance teams danced to K-pop songs, mixing K-pop, hip-hop, and urban dance. Referring to the increasing popularity of K-pop dance lessons in 2021, dance teachers in the UK predicted that K-pop could be "as big as tap or ballet" (Greep).

Since the Korean Wave, or *Hallyu*, began in the late 1990s, the global popularity of Korean pop culture has drawn scholarly attention. K-pop, as the leading force of the Korean Wave, and polished idols' synchronized, spectacular dance routines characterize K-pop dance. Scholars have examined K-pop and K-pop fans' alternative formations of cultural, racial, gender, ethnic, sexual, and linguistic identities against the mainstream Western pop culture (Anderson; Chua and Iwabuchi; Hong; Jin and Hong; Jung, *Korean Masculinities*; Jung, "K-pop, Indonesian Fandom"; Y. Kim; S. Kim; J. Kim; Koeltzsch; Kuwahara; D. Oh; Song; Swan; Yoon). An increasing number of research has discussed K-pop dance practices, cover dance, and digital performance (Käng; Khiun; S. Kim; Liew and Lee; C. Oh, "From Seoul to Copenhagen"; C. Oh, "Identity Passing"; C. Oh, "'Cinderella' in Reverse").

Global K-pop fans not only listen to K-pop but also *perform* it. From cover dances on YouTube, to random dancing in public, to TikTok dance challenges, K-pop dance fandom opens up the democratic possibility of "participatory" digital culture (Jenkins et al. 2). With accessible small electronic devices and cutting-edge technologies, fans' engagement online is as physical as it is virtual, as narcissistic as activist, blurring professionalism and amateurism. K-pop fans' protests overarch LGBTQ rights, Black Lives Matter, the #MeToo movement, anti-racism, and social issues such as mental health and suicide. Some fans' labor is commercialized with monetization and brand deals, infused with neoliberal capitalism and competitive youth culture on social media. LALARY is a multi-ethnic group that started as a cover dance group and officially debuted as micro-celebrities on YouTube in 2019 via Kickstarter. Sienna Lalau choreographed for BTS when she was 19 years old as a "K-pop-fan-turned-celebrity-choreographer," according to *Dance Magazine* in 2020 (Murray). Despite its dance-centric nature and global dance fandom, K-pop dance itself has not yet been fully discussed as an academic subject. As explained in this book, K-pop fan dancers have transgressive potential and challenge the long-standing hierarchy between high and low, critics and artists, liveness and digitalization, West and East, and authenticity and imitation.

This book is about K-pop dance and its fandom on social media. It is based on ethnographic interviews and fieldwork on approximately 30 professional, amateur, and collegiate K-pop dancers and choreographers from 2016 to 2021 in New York and California in the US and Seoul, South Korea. The first part of this book theorizes K-pop dance as what I call *social media dance*, traces its evolution from the 1980s to the 2020s, and explains its distinctive choreography. The second part of the book examines K-pop dance fandom focusing on cover dance. K-pop cover dance is a fan-made music video or short dance clip replicating the original MV[1] choreographies. As the first monograph on K-pop dance, this book attempts to situate K-pop dance as an independent dance genre and academic subject. In the following sections, I first explain the main themes of the book and summarize the methodological engagements: cover dance fandom and identity passing, hybridity and authenticity, and intercultural performance. After introducing the main theoretical approaches that overarch the entire book, I summarize each chapter.

K-pop as Social Media Dance

This book suggests a new framework to understand dance on social media, what I refer to as *social media dance*. Social media dance is a social-popular dance of the global youth on social media. Social media is the smallest but most transnational stage on smartphones and is portable in our pockets. In the twenty-first century, social media has replaced the traditional roles of theatre. In the past, people socialized in ballroom halls, clubs, and backstage. The global youth socialize on social media, a front stage to perform and a backstage to socialize. K-pop is a newly emerging social media dance of the global youth who adapt, distribute, and reproduce dance through participatory social media. Social media is a space in which to idolize, fandoming themselves in a way best exemplified by K-pop cover dancers. Compared to admired professional dances in the theatre or idealized dancer-actors on film who are based on flawless perfection and the distance between dancers and the audience, on social media, the public are the dancers. As Chapter 2 articulates, *gestural point choreography* characterizes K-pop dance. It is short, front-driven, and two-dimensional movements comprised of decorative, sophisticated movements of the waist, arms, chest, fingers, face, neck, shoulders, and hair and is focused on the upper body and face. Gestural point choreography provides a perfect source for fans to play with and idolize themselves and their bodies as dance entrepreneurs on social media. The anecdote shared in the beginning of this Introduction reflects my experience in learning gestural point choreography.

Dancers addressed in this book include a Vietnamese dance influencer in the Philippines (Chapter 1), K-pop idols, performance directors, backup dancers, and choreographers (Chapter 2), BTS as modern dancers (Chapter 3), Latinx, Asian, and white Americans and Korean collegiate dancers in Southern California and Seoul (Chapter 4), white American international students in Japan (Chapter 5), and Thai refugee teen cover dancers in upstate New York (Chapter 6).

The cover dancers in this book go through a process of performing and shaping diasporic identities symbolically, physically, and culturally through their racial, ethnic, and fandom-oriented identifications, as well as geographical locations. I use the adjective "diasporic," not the noun "diaspora," because it describes fans' feelings of belonging and not belonging virtually and physically, instead of actual, permeant diaspora and displacement in geography. Within their experiences of diasporic identity, they identify K-pop dance as a "home" from which they, at least temporarily, see a sense of belonging.

K-pop seems to promote equalitarian space for all. In 2015, Airbnb, the American vacation rental company, collaborated with K-pop singer G-Dragon and invited five fans to stay in his Dukyang studio in Seoul. Its promotion video ends with a promising phrase, "a world where all people can belong anywhere." K-pop fans are often generalized as urban, ethnic minority youth against Western mainstream culture. However, what I found through my research are rather drastic differences among K-pop cover dancers based on "intersectionality" (Collins and Bilge; Crenshaw) –how social circumstances, such as race, ethnicity, class, gender, sexuality, education, age, citizenship, and geography, create an individual's simultaneous marginalization and privilege. As I will further explain in the Introduction, this book uses "identity passing" and "intersectionality" as major theoretical frames to see fans' different experiences in performing K-pop dance based on their sociocultural resources.

Identity is a socially constructed performance. How do K-pop cover dancers experience alternative identities based on different intersectionality? By focusing on various groups of K-pop cover dancers across borders, this book extends the notion of identity passing beyond a Black/White racialized binary. I argue that K-pop dance fandom is more than individual choices; cover dance is a slice of the manifestations that illuminate a structural inequality and (in)ability of identity passing. Their identity passing is directly affected by fans' different intersectionality across races, ethnicities, ages, languages, citizenship, geography, education, and class. Dance fandom also reveals fans' audacious hopes and dreams in the (im)possibility of identity passing – a desire that is stronger than the social structure that privileges the privileged. Their multi-layered privilege and marginalization disclose discrepancies rather than solidarity and reveal a structural irony of fandom – the more fans are marginalized, the more they desire to pass to be like the stars, despite having less chance of obtaining the dream.

This book approaches K-pop primarily as a dance genre. Naming K-pop singers as dancers does not aim to negate their musicality. Instead, the book situates K-pop in the long legacy of dance fandom and dance studies beyond the idol industry. This book is a preliminary study that theorizes the emerging principles of K-pop dance and fandom. As it is not meant to be an encyclopedia, only select cases are addressed. I believe that readers of this book will fill in the gaps as "aca-fans"

(Jenkins et al. xi) and further advance the field of K-pop studies, making a difference beyond academia.

While K-pop appears as a site for an egalitarian platform, mystical fantasy, and youth activism on the global social media stage, it is also a gateway for upward class mobility in Seoul's competitive education market in Korea. If children in the US want to become YouTubers, Korean children's most popular dream for the future is to become K-pop idols. K-pop dance is a mainstream genre that demands systematic training, bodily transformation, and strict and harsh physical discipline. When I visited LP Dance Studio in Gangnam, the wall was covered by posters that proudly displayed the names of students accepted at universities and K-pop agencies or who even debuted as K-pop idols. Through a window, I saw a class for trainees preparing to be idols. They were so dedicated that they appeared somber and desperate. The teenagers took classes one after another, wearing sweats. Only a handful of prodigies will debut as K-pop idols or enter universities as dance majors, but if they succeed, they could be the next cover model of *Time Magazine* and some of the richest idols across the world.

The global popularity of K-pop dance would not be possible without the disciplinary education system in Korea. An expansion of education is the expansion of dance. Education can turn a dance craze into a professional's career and from an individual's unique technique to a globally repeated repertoire with a set formula. As Chapter 2 explains, built on broadcasting backup dancers, street dances, and prodigy education accumulated since the 1980s, K-pop dance trainees in the 2020s learn multiple techniques from an early age at dance academies, agencies, or arts schools. Conservatory schools and community colleges, like Seoul Arts College, offer a "broadcasting dance major," which includes K-pop dance. The name of the major continues the genealogy of backup dance troupes at broadcasting companies beginning in the 1980s. An increasing number of universities offer "K-pop majors" in their academic curriculum. Interestingly, K-pop dance's rigid formula and homogeneity in the local context opens it up to versatile adaptations and diversification as a playful source to re-create the originals in a global context. The manufactured uniformity, the "K-pop body" with a particular makeup, body shape, size, and fashion style, also gives fans a clear recipe to imitate and remake their own version of K-pop dances.

With increased lifespans and manual labor replaced by machines, people are interested in spending time more enjoyably. The accessible, visually pleasing formula of K-pop dance has the potential for lifetime education. As people no longer limit their identity to a fixed geography, K-pop dance's boundary-crossing style can further foster the global economy based on experiences and the service-oriented, diasporic consumption of cultures. We live in a digital world: the metaverse, virtual influencers, virtual real estate, and digital artwork such as NFTs. Like SM Entertainment's Aespa, which is composed of real idols and virtual avatars, K-pop's virtual technology will fuel the AI-driven global cultural industry that does not care whether it is real or virtual as long as it is attractive and monetizable.

Methods

This book takes an interdisciplinary approach, drawing theories of critical cultural studies, popular dance studies, and dance and performance studies. Approaching K-pop as a dance genre can challenge the colonial logic of Western dance as the "canon." Popular and social dance research has diversified dance studies that are focused on concert dance, such as ballet, by encompassing dances in film, commercials, music videos, competition television shows, experimental films, and video games (Borelli; Malnig; Dodds "Values in Motion"; Dodds, *Dance on Screen*; Dodds, *Dancing on the Canon*; Dodds and Hooper). Except for a few pioneering examples (Mezur and Wilcox; Zile), Korean dance is often marginalized due to its non-ties to US citizenship, as compared to Asian American dance. Further, research on dance on social media is scarce, while much research exists for Western mainstream films and television shows. Situating K-pop in dance studies, this book focuses on the newest platform, social media, and diversifies the popular dance scholarship beyond Western concerts and popular dance.

The primary methods used in this book are descriptive analysis and ethnography commonly used in qualitative performance analysis. Using ethnography, this book illuminates K-pop dancers' hidden labor. Although K-pop dance often seems like a sleek, manufactured product or a teenager's hobby, it is built on the generational struggles of dancers and fans' hidden labor, sweat, and tears behind the stage. As a former dancer, I provide an insider's perspective in addition to ethnographic interviews. This book includes close participation-observations and descriptions of dance practices, stage rehearsals, workshops, live public performances, and my performance ethnography and dance experiences with cover dancers.

Emerging from ethnography, performance ethnography uses a creative and theatrical performance to present ethnographic research that can stage the researcher's own body as a performer. Performing autoethnography is a "felt-sensing" action that merges "theory, writing, and performing" (Madison, "Performing Theory" 107) and can illuminate "patterns" (Gingrich-Philbrook 353) of social structures. Combining analyses of ethnographic interviews, staged performances, and (auto)ethnographic writing, this book analyzes the "felt-sensing" processes in K-pop dance since 2016.

Instead of universalizing my personal experience, this book unearths the invisible structure and hidden struggles of K-pop dancers and fans and my limitations as an ethnographer who still believes, despite challenges, that performance can show us a better world. I believe that readers of this book are the next generation of academics whose kind generosity will make the fields continuously evolve until we make a harmonious "utopia" (Dolan 2) not just *in* performance, but also *beyond* it when dreaming ourselves through dance is not a complete mirage.

Approximately 30 dancers participated in this book as interviewees from 2016 to 2021.[2] The participants' ages ranged from late teens to late twenties. Most participants resided in New York City and California in the US and Seoul, South

Korea. While New York and California arguably represent some of the most diverse ethnic and racial populations and urban youth culture in the US, Seoul is the birthplace of K-pop. Participants were recruited in person at K-pop cover dance events and through online flyers and snowball sampling. The book introduces them with pseudonyms. Follow-up interviews were held both in-person and online via email, video calls, and social media messenger. Semi-structured interview questions focused on participants' dance backgrounds and experiences in K-pop dance. Each meeting took 60 to 90 minutes, and transcription ranged from 20 to 25 pages. I interpreted the ethnographic data using theories of the performance of racial and gender identities, intersectionality, and identity passing. Not all cover dancers are K-pop fans, and cover dance itself is an emerging dance genre. This book uses the words K-pop "fan-dancers" and "cover dancers" interchangeably due to the interview participants' strong position as fans as much as dancers.

Theoretical Frameworks

K-pop Cover Dance Fandom and Identity Passing

The first theoretical framework of this book is identity passing. A similar term, fluid identity, implies that an individual has a relatively horizontal spectrum of reshaping their identities. Contrarily, identity passing can be driven by stronger, even blinded passion and sensational feeling to "pass" toward. It can more deeply involve in physical, dramatic, and theatrical transformations, which can better explain embodied fandom. My experience described in the beginning of this Introduction resonates with the K-pop cover dancers who experience alternative identities from a sweltering dance studio to the stage. Sun Jung (2011) mentioned a fundamental drive in K-pop fandom has been to "be like" K-pop singers. K-pop cover dance is the leading force of K-pop dance fandom. K-pop cover dance is a practice of imitation – dancers lip-sync in Korean, wear makeup and dress like K-pop idols, and replicate the original choreography. Identity passing is inevitable in cover dance, and similarity matters more than originality (C. Oh, "From Seoul to Copenhagen"; C. Oh, "Identity Passing").

In performance, the notion of identity passing refers to "crossing racial identity borders as well as to intra/interracial issues of identity and authenticity" (Alexander 377). Identity passing can be applied to other identities, such as gender and ethnicity, when someone tries to be someone else, passing as another identity category, often through theatrical or performative engagements. In the US, the notion of identity passing has been mainly discussed in the Black/white racial discourse (Dyer; Fanon; Piper; Smith). There has been scarce research on identity passing across ethnic minorities beyond the Western context.

This book situates identity passing and imitation in the desire of fandom. Imitation has been devalued in the arts, as compared to genuine authenticity, since Greek philosopher Plato's Cave Theory, which criticizes the arts as a mere imitation of the ideal world. However, every single imitation of a dance movement can be authentic because it reflects the dancer's unique individuality. People unconsciously imitate something or someone that they like. A toddler imitates her mother's language, and a teenager imitates his favorite singer's fashion. The desire to be like someone can lead to a moment of identity passing. When falling in love with K-pop idols, fans imitate them.

When imitating K-pop idols, fans follow the idols' bodies, movements, and dance. Dance is inseparable from a dancer and her body. Unlike other artistic mediums, the body is the medium in dancing; the dancing body (object) is the dance (subject). If social media is driven by the fundamental desire of being recognized and showing off, dance is one of the best ways to showcase a person's charm and body. By adapting, imitating, and idolizing K-pop dance via cover dance, fans are eventually *fandoming* themselves and their bodies.

Although K-pop dance fandom on social media seems a new phenomenon, dance has a long history of fandom. Marie Taglioni, Anna Pavlovna, Vaslav Nijinsky, Isadora Duncan, Martha Graham, Josephine Baker, and Choi Seung-hee, to name a few, whose dancing bodies have mesmerized global audiences from visual artists to civil rights activists, have exemplified dance fandom since the nineteenth century. Dance fandom continues into twenty-first-century concert dance, such as the fandom around ballet dancers Misty Copeland and Harper Watters, who are both now celebrated as "dance influencers" on social media.

Hybridity and Authenticity

Previous research, including my own, has pointed out hybridity as a defining characteristic of K-pop that facilitates fans' adaptations across the globe (Shim; C. Oh, "The Politics of the Dancing Body"). Homi K. Bhabha (2004) defined hybridity as the "almost the same but not quite" status of the colonized culture through the desire to be like the colonizer. Hybridity can revisit and destabilize the essentialized, seemingly fixed Western colonizer's identity (122). K-pop emerged partially in an attempt to "be like" the colonizers under the postcolonial modernity in South Korea influenced by Japan and the US since the 1980s. YG Entertainment's dance trainer and choreographer Lee Jae Wook said K-pop dance combines the strengths of Japanese and Western pop: clear point choreography and trendy style, respectively ("Interviews with K-POP's Hidden Protagonists: Choreographer Lee Jae-Wook & PD Ahn Joon-Young"). It is true that K-pop dance is boundary-crossing across classical and popular dances, such as voguing, pole dancing, tap, jazz, swing, hip-hop, ballet, modern, competition, urban, acrobatics, street, and martial arts, not to mention traditional folk, court, and contemporary Korean dances. K-pop's versatile techniques might reflect what SanSan Kwan (2017) called the "hybrid bodily intelligence" of contemporary Asian dance (45).

As postcolonial studies scholars warned, however, hybridity is everywhere, since all culture is hybridized (Hall; Prabhu). I argue hybridity should no longer define K-pop, at least K-pop dance. First, social media has unprecedently become transgressive across geographical and cultural borders and stylistic boundaries. It has become harder for dancers to survive unless they master all different types of versatile, hybrid dance techniques from Bollywood to ballet, as dancers' racial, ethnic, and national identities become more ambiguous on social media. Second, referring to Asian dance as a hybrid of East and West can be problematic due to the long history of perceived racialized authenticity. The term "hybrid" is predominantly only used to describe non-Western cultures.

If hybridity is the opposite of authenticity, racial prejudice often guarantees the West's authenticity. Performance has a long tradition of white European and American artists' identity passing towards and adaptations of Asian, Middle Eastern, Latin, Native Indian, and African dances. Examples include oriental and belly dance (Shay and Sellers-Young; Wong), hip-hop (Borelli; Osumare), twerking (Gaunt), salsa (Bosse; García, "Displace and Be Queen"; García, "The Great Migration"), tango (Savigliano), Cuban and Black social dances (Monroe), neo-swing (Usner), classical Indian and Bollywood dance (Pillai; Thobani), and K-pop (C. Oh, "Seoul to Copenhagen"). Yet, Western works have been considered "genius" inventions, enabling gender liberation, artistic curiosity, or the explorations of alternative identities through which the ethnic origins are easily erased (Manning 66; Wong 45). Contrarily, artists of color are often criticized for being inauthentic when presenting non-native or non-traditional themes (Dox 35; C. Oh, "The Politics of the Dancing Body" 66; Kwan 39). Within this structure, Asian dancers remain native, exotic, indigenous, and traditional to look "authentic."

When modern themes and inventions belong to the West only, it engenders modern Asian dance illegible (C. Oh, "K-popscape"). Stereotyping Asian dance as primitive neglects the long legacy of Western artists' cultural appropriation and influences of the East/Asia from European ballet to American modern and post-modern dance (Warren). In this framework, the notion of authenticity is racialized; authenticity is reserved for whites as originators, and hybridity is reserved for ethnic minorities. Ethnic minorities' works are expected to remain traditional, otherwise, they are viewed as being a copycat, or at best a hybrid. Racialized authenticity reflects the "representational privilege of [being] white" in performing others (Manning 84–87). This unmarked privilege of whiteness as a universal race guarantees their authenticity in appropriating others (Dyer; Phelan). Thus, as explained in Chapter 2, this book gratefully gives full credit to those who helped shape K-pop dance's initial development. Simultaneously, it also resists a racialized binary that simplifies Asia as a hybrid and the West as the authentic originator.

K-pop Cover Dance as Intercultural Performance

This book approaches K-pop cover dance as an intercultural performance, communication across cultures and peoples via performance, not cultural appropriation. In performing other cultures as an intercultural performance, the notion of cultural appropriation comes to the table. Indeed, a big question surrounding K-pop dance is cultural appropriation. As explained in Chapters 4 and 5, fan-dancers are often concerned about it. When discussing K-pop cover dance in my dance theory class, dance majors often ask, "Isn't it cultural appropriation?" I respond, "Our Dance Division offers yoga, hip-hop, Capoeira, and ballet classes. Where do they come from?" Then students list countries, such as India, Brazil, and Italy, and races, such as African American. I ask again, "Do you consider yourself taking the classes as cultural appropriation?" Typically, they are hesitant to name doing yoga, hip-hop, and Capoeira as cultural appropriation. Nearly none even consider ballet as cultural appropriation.

This book suggests using bodily labor to understand the long debate of cultural appropriation. As scholars have argued, embodiment is essential in defining the ethics of performing other cultures and authenticity (Johnson; Jones). Without dedicated time, training, and bodily endeavor, embodiment is not possible. Dancers learning non-Western techniques for years is not cultural appropriation. It is an education, expanding their boundaries beyond Western conventions. They advance their knowledge about the cultures through repetitive practice and learn histories, origins, and contexts outside the dance studio. Dancers' intentions are often the opposite of cultural appropriation that mocks or temporarily wears other cultures for selfish and commercial displays.

If years of learning dance in academia can excuse dance majors from cultural appropriation, so too can years of learning dance excuse K-pop cover dancers. Based on my fieldwork, the interviewees' knowledge of K-pop often exceeds that of dance critics and journalists. They practice K-pop dance until midnight after school. On a film shooting day, a collegiate K-pop fan-dancer in San Diego told me that he practiced TWICE's "Feel Special" (2019) until he felt like vomiting. YouTube has turned into an online lifelong-learning platform, and cover dancers learning K-pop from YouTube should not be neglected as superficial.

It is necessary to be reminded of race and colonial history in defining the ethics of performing other cultures. Ballet is an "ethnic" dance that reflects cultural roots in multiple countries, from Italy, to France, to Russia, languages used, cultural fauna, and aesthetic symbols (Kealiinohomoku). Ballet keeps evolving like in the cases of Shen Yun, Ballet Hispánico, Ballet Folklorico de Tapatio de San Dieguito, and Dance Theatre of Harlem, to name a few, which all integrate various ethnic and cultural traditions. However, ballet is often considered "universal," meaning, reserved for whites, which implies the hidden assumption that Western colonizers' culture is the canon. Contrarily, a dance done by people of color outside of the West, whose roots connect to those of the colonized, are often racially marked and limited as "ethnic," "primitive," and "traditional," as explained earlier.

Dance cannot and should not be separated from colonial history, but it also exists as an independent physical form with possibilities. A soccer player's skin tone does not affect the number of goals they achieve. Not all Asians are born as martial artists, not all African Americans are good at hip-hop, and not all white people are born as ballerinas. Alvin Ailey American Dance Theater is a great example. Established by legendary African American dancer Alvin Ailey, the company initially had African American dancers to share African-centric aesthetics and roots. With its global success and expansion, the company has white, Asian, and various other ethnic dancers who learn, celebrate, and perform African and African American dance with their yearlong dedication and respect. As explained in Chapter 2, like BLACKPINK's Thai-born member Lisa demonstrates, K-pop dance turns into a de-ethnicized dance genre and is taught globally, like hip-hop and ballet, from social media to higher ed institutions, beyond a certain ethnicity. The global K-pop dance fandom suggests the potential of "embodiment" that can "transcend colonialism" (Borelli 14).

Dwight Conquergood (1985) theorized multiple pitfalls of performing the Other, those groups who have been systematically marginalized since the colonial era. He pointed out superficial appropriation and fascination for selfish pleasure or commercial profits (5). Yet, cold, skeptical cynicism and silence, such as saying, "I am neither black nor female" and refusing to engage in the discussion is even worse because it prevents further progress (8). Conquergood suggested a "dialogical performance," a constant, open-ended, and genuine effort to understand and speak with the Other to make a difference. It can bring "different voices, world views, value systems, and beliefs" together through embodied experiences and collaborative, self-reflective conversations between an ethnographer and the community (Conquergood 9). As fully discussed in this book, I argue that K-pop cover dance is an intercultural performance, and fans' genuine embodied effort reflect Conquergood's model of "dialogical performance."

Chapter Summaries

Chapter 1, "Social Media Dance," theorizes dance on social media by drawing an example from Vietnamese dance influencer Quang Đăng's viral "handwashing dance challenge" on TikTok in 2020. As any dance can be a TikTok dance challenge, the chapter examines structural features of the select case study, which resonates with K-pop as both are social media dance. Based on ethnographic interviews and descriptive analysis of the choreography, the chapter suggests five distinctive characteristics of social media dance: (1) a social-popular dance of the global youth, (2) the public's participation over critics' judgment, (3) TikTokable, homogenized simplicity and transformability, (4) condensed space and time, and (5) face dance.

On social media, the stage gets narrower, the distribution becomes faster and easier, and the dance becomes shorter and facialized with whimsical, capricious, and eye-catching livelihood. Social media dance consists of a clear formula along with literal, front-driven gestural movement. It is a half-body dance emphasizing the front, upper body, and face. When movement is condensed into few seconds on the narrow screen, a conventionally attractive body with a constantly changing charming face is the key to draw the audience's attention. Easy, imitable, playable, and clickable, that is, "Instagrammable" or "TikTokable," content matters more than artistic originality, which signifies a rise of imitation that has traditionally been devalued in history. Social media dance's clear template generates an adaptable homogeneity, which increases participation, individuals' transformations, and thus, measurable popularity. Instead of idealizing or idolizing someone, social media dancers are fandoming themselves initiated by the feeling of "I can do better." A dance influencer's ten-second video on TikTok gets more views than a two-hour masterpiece in the theatre. The number of likes and followers substitutes for an elite arts critic's review in a magazine. Popularity on the internet, often sponsored and monetized, replaces credibility and the approval of gatekeepers and fills the gap of what *The Atlantic* called "the death of the American dance critic" (Mainwaring).

Chapter 2, "The Evolution of K-pop Dance," expands the framework of social media dance focusing on K-pop. It traces the evolution of K-pop from the broadcasting dance troupes in the 1980s to its status of global entrepreneurial capital on social media in the 2020s. K-pop dance history is a history of people – performance directors who failed in their idol careers, trainees who survived harsh competitions, broadcasting company backup dancers and underground street dancers who learned dance from nightclubs to chorus stages, and anonymous foreign dance crews who sell their choreography to agencies. Based on major music programs, music videos, and media coverage of select singers/groups, the chapter discusses advancements in backup dancing formations, the emergence of gestural point choreography, major music agencies' iconic dance styles and gendered choreographies, the establishment of the ideal "K-pop body," and finally K-pop dance as a global investment from IT tech-infused, conglomerate performing arts companies whose virtual, international collaborations exchange dance like a digital file, challenging the previous assumptions on copyright belonging to a choreographer's physical body.

Chapter 3, "BTS: The Modern Dancers," is an in-depth dance analysis of BTS as an example of K-pop dance in the 2020s wherein YouTube becomes the theatre of social media. It categorizes BTS into three categories: modern dancers, male dancers as warriors, and Korean folk dancers. Based on a descriptive analysis of the "Black Swan" (2020), "On" (2020), "IDOL" (2018) MVs and other performances, I argue that BTS extends two-dimensional, front-driven gestural point choreography to three-dimensional, voluminal dance films by expanding the spectrum of space, level – especially their legs, feet, and heads – and the size of the backup dancers. In the official music video for "Black Swan," BTS embodies the symbols of the ballet swan and the modern dance philosophy of conquering their first "deaths." Their performance reveals self-exploration, abstract poetic themes, and emotional and physical vulnerability and strength via the use of bare feet, breath, and a self-centered gaze. The official music video for "On" represents the generational, physical, communal, and egalitarian functions of dance and the legacy of male dancers as warriors who have bridged shamanic rituals with festival and resistance with peace since the prehistoric eras in dances such as hula, Capoeira, and haka. Their performance of "IDOL" at the 2018 Melon Music Awards (MMA) as well as their 2019 performance at the MMA integrated Korean classical dances, such as *Dongrae Hakchum, Pungmul, Buchaechum,* and *Salpuri*. As reflected in shamans' stomping feet in ancient cave paintings and toddlers dancing to Christmas carols, dance has belonged to all. Anyone can dance as long as we have a body, and the bodies are ours. BTS brings us the primordial, democratic capability of dancing with mediated social media technology.

Chapter 4, "K-pop Cover Dance as Intercultural Performance," is an ethnographic study on nine collegiate K-pop cover dancers in Southern California and Seoul, whom I interviewed from 2019 to 2020. Chinese American Olivia is privileged due to her parents' support, young age, educational and performance resources from her prestigious institution, a large dance team, and East Asian race. In her easy moment of identity passing, she believes K-pop is for everyone, and its Koreanness is erased. Latinx Emily, a working-class, self-taught, self-employed, and dark-skinned dancer who graduated from a community college in her late twenties, does not have those institutional supports. Yet, this daunting reality further inspires her dreams to be like K-pop idols. Meanwhile, Korean American Joel sees the racial exoticization and fetishization of K-pop. But Korean Lee Min in Seoul does not even use the word "K-pop" and instead calls it a "song." K-pop is generic, mainstream pop music and not racially marked in Korea, and her dance team neither lip-syncs when performing nor dresses like K-pop idols. Korean international student Jun, who used to believe the "real" American culture was either Black or white, ends up being a member of a K-pop dance team in California through which he experiences a diasporic identity and enters another side of American youth culture via K-pop.

Chapter 5, "A White K-pop Fan-Dancer in Japan," focuses on Aelin, a white American K-pop cover dancer on the same K-pop dance team in Southern California discussed in Chapter 4. Using the framework of what David Oh and I (2022) theorized as "white-expat-fans," the chapter examines her racial, spatial, and fannish identities. She is an Asian studies major and went to a study abroad program in Japan where she was a member of a K-pop dance club. Her mediated, romanticized image of "cute" Japan became different in reality. In Japan, as a white K-pop fan and non-Japanese international student, she faced a sense of marginalization with her language barrier and hypervisibility as a white person. In the club, she thought it was "unfair" and "rude" when she played a less significant role than Japanese students and the primary spoken language was Japanese, which reveals potential linguistic imperialism and her expectation for the preferential treatment of whites. In the US, she does not share pan-Asian ethnic solidarity and worries about "Koreaboo" and "yellow fever" and tries to de-racialize and de-materialize K-pop as a piece of music, detaching it from K-pop idols. Yet, her conflation of Japan and Korea resonates with Orientalism, and her fascination with diversity speaks to "eating the Other" (hooks 39). Nevertheless, like other dancers included in this book, her dedicated passion and embodied effort have the potential to transform cultural appropriation into cultural appreciation.

Chapter 6, "A Refuge for Refugee Teens," analyzes a yearlong performance (auto)ethnography titled *Love Means Love* (2017) with a Karen refugee teen K-pop cover dance crew from Thailand at the Midtown Utica Community Center

(MUCC) in Utica, New York. As an example of "dialogical performance" (Conquergood 9), the piece presents Korean shamanic rituals, K-pop, Christian worship dance, and modern dance with the cover dancers. Analyzing the choreographic process, stage performance, and audience reception of *Love Means Love* and ethnographic interviews with the crew from 2016 to 2018, the chapter discusses how the teens utilize K-pop dance in overcoming trauma, destigmatizing the negative perception of refugees, and negotiating diasporic identities using K-pop as an Asian culture. Applying Friedrich Nietzsche's notion of Zarathustra, a dancer, I argue that their resistant, audacious hope and endless will resonate with the liberatory history of dancers who have fought against oppression and dance bans across the world. The chapter also examines the precarious balance between the aesthetics and ethics of staging performance ethnography. Can dance be a tool to dream an alternative life into reality? K-pop dance is a hope, a refuge, that can make the refugee teens escape from their harsh reality. They build alter egos and stage personae and go through identity passing by imitating K-pop idols' fashion, using stage names that sound Korean, having Korean on their social media, and taking photos holding a Korean flag. Yet, they also combine Karen, white American, and African American urban youth culture, constructing fluid cultural identities.

The Epilogue, "A Home Without Home," is a reflection of my attempt in turning a "failed ethnography" into "an ethnography of failure" (Nayfack 96) despite a successful performance of *Love Means Love* and my yearlong effort to help the teens apply for college as dance majors and participate in global K-pop auditions. As this book centers on dance analysis and K-pop as a formal dance genre, the epilogue delineates the privilege and limitations of an ethnographer and dance researcher and the structural hopelessness for activism that nevertheless coexists with the beauty of dance, and thus, still provides reasons to continue.

Fandoming Dance, Fandoming Yourself

I grew up looking at my mother's black and white photos of her singing and dancing on stage. She used to be a professional singer and dancer, and after marriage, she worked as a voice actress in a national broadcasting company. When I was around five, whenever my mother went out for work, my sister and I opened her closet, wore her fancy dresses, which were as big as blankets to us, colored our nails with crayons sitting in front of her vanity table, and started a "show." Like a runway fashion show, we played multiple roles, walking around our living room, dancing, and swaying our hips in a sassy manner. I desired to be a diva, like my mother, so I performed.

I soon started my ballet training when I was seven years old at the Universal Ballet Academy in Seoul, South Korea and studied at its branch at the Kirov Academy of Ballet in Washington, DC, formerly known as the Universal Ballet Academy. In my first *Nutcracker,* I performed as Clara's friend, wearing a blond wig and lighter skin tone foundation surrounded by Christmas stage props, which was an "exotic" experience as a native Korean. During my early career as a modern dancer, I toured across Austria, Germany, Japan, the US, and Korea, performing many different roles on stage. My stage experiences taught me that people perform not only onstage but also in daily life, like a dancer performing a role on stage. I started performing by imitating others, passing identities, and have gradually transformed into a performance studies scholar who understands identities on paper and tells stories through performances on stage that would otherwise go unheard.

What I discovered from K-pop cover dancers was the passion for identity passing connected to self-extension and discovery and how dance fandom and fantasy can turn into actual, physical labor in life, which I have witnessed from my childhood to being a university professor. By bridging my experience of identity passing on and offstage as a dancer and scholar, this book employs an (auto)ethnographic approach to discover the fundamental desire in learning, performing, and fandoming dance – aspiring to be like the shiny dancers onstage, going through years of discipline and fights against and with ourselves and others, until we become a fan of ourselves that resemble the stars we used to love.

Notes

1 MV is K-pop jargon that commonly refers to a music video.
2 The Institutional Review Board (IRB) at the author's current institution approves this study. Ethical clearances and written permissions were obtained from the participants and their guardians for those under 19.

References

Alexander, Bryant Keith. "Passing, Cultural Performance, and Individual Agency: Performative Reflections on Black Masculine Identity." *Cultural Studies ↔ Critical Methodologies*, vol. 4, no. 3, 2004, pp. 377–404. *SAGE Journals*, https://doi.org/10.1177/1532708603259680.

Anderson, Crystal S. *Soul in Seoul: African American Popular Music and K-pop*. UP of Mississippi, 2020.

Bhabha, Homi K. *The Location of Culture*. Routledge, 2004.

Borelli, Melissa Blanco, ed. *The Oxford Handbook of Dance and the Popular Screen*. Oxford UP, 2014.

Bosse, Joanna. "Salsa Dance and the Transformation of Style: An Ethnographic Study of Movement and Meaning in a Cross-Cultural Context." *Dance Research Journal*, vol. 40, no. 1, 2008, pp. 45–64. *JSTOR*, https://www.jstor.org/stable/20527592.

Bruner, Raisa. "Entertainer of the Year: BTS." *Time*, https://time.com/entertainer-of-the-year-2020-bts/. Accessed January 13, 2022.

Chua, Beng Huat, and Koichi Iwabuchi, eds. *East Asian Pop Culture: Analysing the Korean Wave*. Hong Kong UP, 2008.

Collins, Patricia Hill, and Sirma Bilge. *Intersectionality*. 2nd ed., Polity P, 2020.

Conquergood, Dwight. "Performing as a Moral Act: Ethical Dimensions of the Ethnography Of Performance." *Literature in Performance*, vol. 5, no. 2, 1985, pp. 1–13. *Taylor and Francis Online*, https://doi.org/10.1080/10462938509391578.

Coppa, Francesca. "Women, Star Trek, and the Early Development of Fannish Vidding." *Transformative Works and Cultures*, vol. 1, 2008, https://doi.org/10.3983/twc.2008.044.

Crenshaw, Kimberle. "Mapping the Margins: Intersectionality, Identity Politics, and Violence against Women of Color." *Stanford Law Review*, vol. 43, no. 6, 1991, pp. 1241–1299. *JSTOR*, https://doi.org/10.2307/1229039.

Denzin, Norman K. *Performance Ethnography: Critical Pedagogy and the Politics of Culture*. Sage Publications, 2003.

Dodds, Sherril. *Dancing on the Canon: Embodiments of Value in Popular Dance*. Palgrave Macmillan, 2011.

Dodds, Sherril. *Dance on Screen: Genres and Media from Hollywood to Experimental Art*. Palgrave Macmillan, 2001.

Dodds, Sherril. "Values in Motion: Reflections on Popular Screen Dance." In *The Oxford Handbook of Dance and the Popular Screen*, edited by Melissa Blanco Borelli. Oxford UP, 2014, pp.445–454.

Dodds, Sherril, and Colleen Hooper. "Faces, Close-ups and Choreography: A Deleuzian Critique of *So You Think You Can Dance*." *The International Journal of Screendance*, vol. 4, 2014. http://dx.doi.org/10.18061/ijsd.v4i0.4524.

Dolan, Jill. *Utopia in Performance: Finding Hope at the Theater*. U of Michigan P, 2005.

Dox, Donnalee. "Dancing around Orientalism." *TDR/The Drama Review*, vol. 50, no. 4, winter 2006, pp. 52–71. *MIT Press Direct*, https://doi.org/10.1162/dram.2006.50.4.52.

Dyer, Richard. *White: Essays on Race and Culture*. Routledge, 1997.

Fanon, Frantz. *Black Skin, White Masks*. Grove P, 2008.

García, Cindy. "*Displace and Be Queen: Gender and Interculturalism in Dirty Dancing: Havana Nights (2004)*." *The Oxford Handbook of Dance and the Popular Screen*, edited by Melissa Blanco Borelli, Oxford UP, 2017, 155–165.

García, Cindy. "The Great Migration: Los Angeles Salsa Speculations and the Performance of Latinidad." *Dance Research Journal*, vol. 45, no. 3, December 2013, pp. 125–136. *Cambridge Core*, https://doi.org/10.1017/S0149767712000289.

Gaunt, Kyra D. "YouTube, Twerking & You: Context Collapse and the Handheld Co-presence of Black Girls and Miley Cyrus." *Journal of Popular Music Studies*, vol. 27, no. 3, 2015, pp. 244–273. *Wiley Online Library*, https://doi.org/10.1111/jpms.12130.

Greep, Monica. "Could K-pop Dancing Eclipse Ballet and Tap?" *The Daily Mail*, 19 January 2020, https://www.dailymail.co.uk/femail/article-7904463/K-pop-mania-Industry-experts-claim-Korean-boyband-bigger-tap.html.

Gingrich-Philbrook, Craig. "Autobiographical Performance Scripts Refreshment." *Text and Performance Quarterly*, vol. 17, no. 4, 1997, pp. 352–360. *Taylor and Francis Online*, https://doi.org/10.1080/10462939709366199.

Jenkins, Henry, et al. *Participatory Culture in a Networked Era: A Conversation on Youth, Learning, Commerce, and Politics*. Polity P, 2016.

Jin, Dal Yong, and Seok-Kyeong Hong, eds. *Transnational Convergence of East Asian Pop Culture*. Routledge, 2021.

Johnson, E. Patrick. "Performing Blackness Down Under: Gospel Music in Australia." In *Black Cultural Traffic: Crossroads in Global Performance and Popular Culture*, edited by Harry J.ElamJr. and Kennell Jackson. U of Michigan P, 2005, pp. 59–82.

Jung, Sun. *Korean Masculinities and Transcultural Consumption: Yonsama, Rain, Oldboy, K-Pop Idols*. Hong Kong UP, 2011.

Jung, Sun. 2011. "K-pop, Indonesian Fandom, and Social Media." *Transformative Works & Cultures* vol. 8, no. 1, 2011. https://doi.org/10.3983/twc.2011.0289.

Hall, Stuart. "The Local and the Global: Globalization and Ethnicity." In *Culture, Globalization, and the World-system: Contemporary Conditions for the Representation of Identity*, edited by Anthony D.King, U of Minnesota P, 1991. 19–40.

Hamera, Judith. "Performance Ethnography." In *The Sage Handbook of Qualitative Research*, 4th ed., edited by Norman K.Denzin and Yvonna S.Lincoln. SAGE Publications, 2011, pp. 317–330.

hooks, bell. *Black Looks: Race and Representation*. South End Books, 1992.

Hong, Seok-Kyeong. *BTS 길 위에서* [BTS on the Road]. Across Book, 2020.

"Interviews with K-POP's Hidden Protagonists: Choreographer Lee Jae-Wook & PD Ahn Joon-Young." *Paradise*, 21 Jan. 2017, https://blog.paradise.co.kr/671.

Jenkins, Henry. *Textual Poachers: Television Fans and Participatory Culture*. 20th Anniversary ed., Routledge, 2013.

Jones, Joni L. "Performance Ethnography: The Role of Embodiment in Cultural Authenticity." *Theatre Topics*, vol. 12, no. 1, 2002, pp. 1–15.

Käng, Dredge Byung'chu. "Idols of Development: Transnational Transgender Performance in Thai K-Pop Cover Dance." *Transgender Studies Quarterly* vol. 1, no. 4, 2014, pp. 559–571. https://doi.org/10.1215/23289252-2815246.

Kealiinohomoku, Joann. "An Anthropologist Looks at Ballet as a Form of Ethnic Dance." In *Moving History/Dancing Cultures: A Dance History Reader*, edited by Ann Dils and Ann Cooper Albright, Wesleyan UP, 2001, pp. 33–43.

Khiun, Liew Kai. "K-pop Dance Trackers and Cover Dancers: Global Cosmopolitanization and Local Spatialization." In *The Korean Wave: Korean Media Go Global*, edited by Youna Kim, Routledge, 2013, pp.181–198.

Kim, Ju Oak. "BTS as Method: A Counter-hegemonic Culture in the Network Society." *Media, Culture and Society*, vol. 43, no. 6, 2021, pp. 1061–1077. *SAGE Journals*, https://doi.org/10.1177/0163443720986029.

Kim, Suk-Young. *K-pop Live: Fans, Idols, and Multimedia Performance*. Stanford UP, 2018.

Kim, Youna, ed. *The Korean Wave: Korean Media Go Global*. Routledge, 2013.

Koeltzsch, Grit Kirstin. "Korean Popular Culture in Argentina." *Oxford Research Encyclopedia of Latin American History*, 28 August 2019, https://doi.org/10.1093/acrefore/9780199366439.013.766.

Kuwahara, Yasue, ed. *The Korean Wave: Korean Popular Culture in Global Context*. Palgrave Macmillan, 2014.

Kwan, SanSan. "When Is Contemporary Dance?" *Dance Research Journal*, vol. 49, no. 3, December 2017, pp. 38–52. *Cambridge Core*, https://doi.org/10.1017/S0149767717000341.

LaBoskey, Sara. "Getting Off: Portrayals of Masculinity in Hip Hop Dance in Film." *Dance Research Journal*, vol. 33, no. 2, 2001, pp. 112–120. *JSTOR*, https://doi.org/10.2307/1477808.

Liew, Kai Khiun, and Angela Lee. "K-pop Boot Camps in Choreographic Co-creative Labor." *Global Media and China*, vol. 5, no. 4, 2020, pp. 372–388. *SAGE Journals*, https://doi.org/10.1177/2059436420974935.

Madison, D. Soyini. *Critical Ethnography: Method, Ethics, and Performance*. 2nd ed., Sage Publications, 2012.

Madison, D. "Performing Theory/Embodied Writing." *Text and Performance Quarterly*, vol. 19, no. 2, 1999, pp. 107–124. *Taylor and Francis Online*, https://doi.org/10.1080/10462939909366254.

Mainwaring, Madison. "The Death of the American Dance Critic. Why Are There So Few Mainstream Outlets Covering the Art Form?" *The Atlantic*, 6 August 2015, https://www.theatlantic.com/entertainment/archive/2015/08/american-dance-critic/399908/.

Malnig, Julie, ed. *Ballroom, Boogie, Shimmy Sham, Shake: A Social and Popular Dance Reader*. U of Illinois P, 2009.

Manning, Susan. "Danced Spirituals." In *Of the Presence of the Body: Essays on Dance and Performance Theory*, edited by André Lepecki, Wesleyan UP, 2004. 82–96.

Mezur, Katherine, and Emily Wilcox. *Corporeal Politics: Dancing East Asia*. U of Michigan P, 2020.

Monroe, Raquel. "'The White Girl in the Middle:' The Performativity of Race, Class, and Gender in *Step Up 2: The Streets*." In *The Oxford Handbook of Dance and the Popular Screen*, edited by Melissa Blanco Borelli, Oxford UP, 2014, 182–198.

Murray, Lydia. "Meet Sienna Lalau, the 19-Year-Old Who Has Choreographed for K-Pop Superstars BTS." *Dance Magazine*. 8 January 2020, https://www.dancemagazine.com/sienna-lalau/.

Nayfack, Shakina. "Dancing Communities: Performance, Difference, and Connection in the Global City (review)." *Dance Research Journal*, vol. 40, no. 2, winter 2008, 94–97.

Oh, Chuyun. "'Cinderella' in Reverse: Eroticizing Bodily Labor of Sympathetic Men in K-pop Dance Practice Video." In *East Asian Men: Masculinity, Sexuality and Desire*, edited by Xiaodong Lin et al, Palgrave Macmillan, 2016, 123–142.

Oh, Chuyun. "From Seoul to Copenhagen: Migrating K-Pop Cover Dance and Performing Diasporic Youth in Social Media." *In and Out of Norden: Dance and the Migratory Condition*, special issue of *Dance Research Journal*, edited by Inger Damsholt and Petri Hoppu, vol. 52, no. 1, 2020, pp. 20–32. *Cambridge Core*, https://doi.org/10.1017/S0149767720000030.

Oh, Chuyun. "Identity Passing in Intercultural Performance of K-pop Cover Dance." *Journal of Intercultural Communication Research*, vol. 49, no. 5, 2020, pp. 472–483. *Taylor and Francis Online*, https://doi.org/10.1080/17475759.2020.1803103.

Oh, Chuyun. *K-popscape: Gender Fluidity and Racial Hybridity in Transnational Korean Pop Dance*. 2015. The University of Texas at Austin, PhD Dissertation. Texas ScholarWorks, http://hdl.handle.net/2152/31700.

Oh, Chuyun. "The Politics of the Dancing Body: Racialized and Gendered Femininity in K-pop." In *The Korean Wave: Korean Popular Culture in Global Context*, edited by Yasue Kuwahara, Palgrave Macmillan, 2014, pp. 53–81.

Oh, Chuyun and David Oh. "White-Expat-Fans' Performing K-pop Other on YouTube." *Text and Performance Quarterly*, 2022, pp. 1–22. https://doi.org/10.1080/10462937.2022.2062441.

Oh, David C. "K-Pop Fans React: Hybridity and the White Celebrity-Fan on YouTube." *International Journal of Communication*, vol. 11, 2017, pp. 2270–2287.

Osumare, Halifu. "Global Breakdancing and the Intercultural Body." *Dance Research Journal*, vol. 34, no. 2, winter 2002, pp. 30–45. *JSTOR*, https://doi.org/10.2307/1478458.

Phelan, Peggy. *Unmarked: The Politics of Performance*. Routledge, 1993.

Pillai, Shanti. "Rethinking Global Indian Dance through Local Eyes: The Contemporary Bharatanatyam Scene in Chennai." *Dance Research Journal*, vol. 34, no. 2, winter 2002, pp. 14–29. *JSTOR*, https://doi.org/10.2307/1478457.

Piper, Adrian. "Passing for White, Passing for Black." *Transition*, vol. 58, 1992, 4–32. *JSTOR*, https://doi.org/10.2307/2934966.

Prabhu, Anjali. *Hybridity: Limits, Transformations, Prospects*. State U of New York P, 2007.

"Refugee Dance Project: Love Means Love (2017)." *YouTube*, uploaded by Chuyun Oh, April 17, 2017, https://www.youtube.com/watch?v=5z19y-5Egik.

Savigliano, Marta Elena. *Tango and the Political Economy of Passion*. Routledge, 1995.

Scolieri, Paul. "Global/mobile: Re-orienting Dance and Migration Studies." *Dance Research Journal*, vol. 40, no. 2, 2008, pp. v–xx. *Cambridge Core*, https://doi.org/10.1017/S0149767700000346.

Shay, Anthony, and Barbara Sellers-Young. "Belly Dance: Orientalism—Exoticism—Self-Exoticism." *Dance Research Journal*, vol. 35, no. 1, summer 2003, pp. 13–37. *JSTOR*, https://www.jstor.org/stable/1478477.

Shim, Doobo. "Hybridity and the Rise of Korean Popular Culture in Asia." *Media, Culture and Society*, vol. 28, 2006, pp. 25–44. *SAGE Journals*, https://doi.org/10.1177/0163443706059278.

Smith, Cherise. *Enacting Others: Politics of Identity in Eleanor Antin, Nikki S. Lee, Adrian Piper, and Anna Deavere Smith*. Duke UP, 2011.

Song, Myoung-Sun. *Hanguk Hip Hop Global Rap in South Korea*. Palgrave Macmillan, 2019.

Swan, Anna Lee. "Transnational Identities and Feeling in Fandom: Place and Embodiment in K-pop Fan Reaction Videos." *Communication Culture and Critique*, vol. 11, no. 4, 2018, pp. 548–565. Oxford Academic, https://doi.org/10.1093/ccc/tcy026.

Thobani, Sitara. *Indian Classical Dance and the Making of Postcolonial National Identities: Dancing on Empire's Stage*. Routledge, 2017.

Usner, Eric Martin. "Dancing in the Past, Living in the Present: Nostalgia and Race in Southern California Neo-Swing Dance Culture." *Dance Research Journal*, vol. 33, no. 2, winter 2001, pp. 87–101. *Cambridge Core*, https://doi.org/10.2307/1477806.

Warren, Vincent. "Yearning for the Spiritual Ideal: The Influence of India on Western Dance 1626–2003." *Dance Research Journal*, vol. 38, no. 1/2, summer/winter 2006, pp. 97–114. Cambridge Core, https://doi.org/10.1017/S0149767700007403.

Wong, Yutian. *Choreographing Asian America*. Wesleyan UP, 2010.

Yang, Jeff. "No, Simon Cowell, It's Not Time for UK-Pop." *CNN*, 28 November 2019, https://www.cnn.com/2019/11/27/opinions/k-pop-groups-are-changing-music-a nd-world-yang/index.html.

Yoon, Kyong. *Digital Mediascapes of Transnational Korean Youth Culture*. Routledge, 2019.

Van Zile, Judy. *Perspectives on Korean dance*. Wesleyan UP, 2001.

PART I

K-pop Dance

1

SOCIAL MEDIA DANCE

TikTok Dance Challenges

Introduction

We live in the heyday of dance on social media. Dance competitions and dance influencers' videos on Instagram, dance workout apps, prima dancers' tutorial videos on YouTube, and modern dance companies' snippets of repertoires are familiar to many. Ballet companies embrace Twitter, Instagram, and YouTube with their star influencers, such as Maria Kochetkova, Harper Watters, and Misty Copeland. In the twenty-first century, social media has partially replaced the traditional role of theatres, which used to be spaces used for socializing, entertaining, sharing knowledge, and building aesthetic conventions. Dance on social media circulates on a stage that can be as small as a smartphone screen. It is the *smallest* stage in dance history, even compared to the already "small screen" of television (Dodds and Hooper 94). This stage is mobile in our pockets since the audience can watch a video on-the-go. It does not require the "completed," holistic, and intimate viewing of the theatre (Dodds, "On Watching Screendance" 144). Being distracted, such as liking, sharing, and leaving comments, while watching dance is encouraged because it increases popularity. The social media stage converges amateurism and professionalism; a prima dancer's pirouette is juxtaposed on the same stage with a teenager's twerking.

COVID-19 has further escalated the digitalization of dance. During the pandemic, dance on-screen has been "expanded" (Norman and Zanotti 1). From the Dance Theatre of Harlem to the Martha Graham Dance Company, concert dance has begun to migrate to digital platforms with subscriptions. The internet has become a stage for all genres, not only for professionals but also for the public. The pandemic has taught the public "a new way of dancing in the streets" (K. Wang). Quarantine has restricted the spaces available and the space a body can take up and socialize in, while social media has remained the major source of information and

DOI: 10.4324/9781003212188-3

socializing. Dancing rejuvenates a mood by releasing endorphins and counteracts the detrimental physical and mental side effects from COVID-19 (Hammami et al.; Heyang and Martin).

The popularity of dance challenges during COVID-19 showcased how people cope with quarantine (Klug 7). In times of crisis, socially engaged performances can be both "rituals and entertainments," helping one cope "with what's happened and getting away from the daily grind" (Thompson and Schechner 15). During the pandemic, dance challenges offered a habitual ritual of generational gathering, creating physical activity and social engagement, helping people cope with anxiety, and spreading information. Examples include balcony dancing in Italy, the hand-washing dance in Vietnam, Native Americans' "Jingle Dress Dance Challenge," the Dallas-based father and daughter's "Quarantine Challenge 2K20," and Charli D'Amelio's #distancedance challenge, to name a few.

Dance challenge refers to a user-created short dance that goes viral on social media where other users imitate the dance. This trend can be traced back to fall 2019. TikTok is best known for the #dancechallenge among Millennials and Generation Z, who are both motivated to learn new dance skills through dance challenges (Klug 7). Released in September 2016 by Chinese company ByteDance, TikTok is a music-based social media app tailored to creating and sharing short videos. During the lockdown, the time young users spent on Tik Tok doubled (Kennedy 1070), and TikTok became the most downloaded app in 2020, globally "favored by COVID-19 related social distancing and people staying home" (Klug 7).

As Chapter 3 explains, YouTube is like the theatre of social media; contrarily, TikTok provides an easier, shorter, and more playful way for users to create performances. It has audiovisual editing features, such as sound remixing, speed manipulation, time-warp scan filters, voice effects, facial distortion, emoji stickers, and text. It fosters playful engagement, encouraging the creation of lip-syncs, theatrical snippets, musical performances, short dances, and memes. Users can choose the recording duration, ranging from fifteen to sixty seconds. These embedded technologies encourage amateurs to try dance challenges for a short time, improvising and having fun within a prescribed template without too much of a time commitment.

Previous research has analyzed dance on screens, such as film, television, video game, music video, and YouTube screens (Bench; Borelli; Dodds, *Dance on Screen*; Dodds, "Values in Motion"; Dodds, "On Watching Screendance"; Harlig, "'Fresher Than You'"; Miller; Murphy; Reason and Reynolds). Due to its newness, there is scarce research on TikTok. Further, previous research has primarily focused on Western dance, such as Hollywood movies, American television shows, and Western modern and postmodern avant-garde, experimental dance films. Asian and Asian American dance often remains invisible, or, at best, viewed as "traditional" or "primitive," except for a few pioneering works of Asian dance, including Bollywood and K-pop (Chakravorty; S. Kim; Kwan "Performing a Geography"; C. Oh, "From Seoul to Copenhagen"; Scolieri; Wong).

To fill this gap, this chapter applies the theoretical framework of social media dance to Quang Đăng's "handwashing dance" (#GhenCoVyChallenge). It was one of the most viral TikTok dance challenges during COVID-19 in 2020. The case study extends and illuminates the structural similarities of social media dance. Further, it diversifies the typical trajectory of TikTok dance challenges. TikTok dance challenges are dominated by conventional-looking, amateur white teen girl dancers dancing to American pop songs (Kennedy 1070). As an example of social media dance, many TikTok dance challenges consist of simple "arm and upper body movements" (Jean-Philippe). As young women dominate the trend movements, such as sharp elbow kicks with animated facial expressions. Many of the movements are gendered, such as chest waves, hip-swaying that highlight curved female bodies, and the sensual vibration of flesh from chests to hips.

Contrarily, Quang Đăng, a Vietnamese dance influencer, created the hand-washing dance challenge to a Vietnamese pop song. Made in response to Vietnam's National Institute of Occupational Safety and Health's request, it is a 42-second video that literally visualizes the lyrics on how to avoid the virus by handwashing. Due to its gestural dance with an informative function, it has been widely performed and recommended by UNICEF and health professionals. Đăng lives in Ho Chi Minh City, Vietnam, where his dance studio, Life Dance, is located. His appearance on *So You Think You Can Dance* in Vietnam brought him popularity. He has choreographed for singers, sharing his works on social media.

Extending the notion of "the medium is the message" (McLuhan 107) to social media, I approach TikTok, not as a carrier of messages, but as a stage whose medium specificity alters choreographic features. Each social media app is a different stage that has preferred content types, visual and sonic features, screen shapes and sizes, presentational and interactional modalities, audience engagement, and monetization. Online content can be easily shared and converged across platforms, such as TikTok, Instagram Reels, and YouTube Shorts. Yet, from YouTube to Instagram to TikTok, a dance video tends to become shorter, and the distribution becomes easier and faster as the screen gets narrower.

While some scholars focus on the positive impacts of dance on the internet from YouTube education to mobile technology (Anderson; Li et al.), others criticize it as superficial amateurism and virtuality (Heyang and Martin 11; Martin; Schechner). Indeed, an indiscriminate convergence of styles and easy distribution can engender the uncritical cultural appropriation of dance as a digital file to be copied without ethical responsibilities. Further, although social media seems open to everyone, people with racial and gendered privileges and stereotypical beauty standards – light-skinned, fit white users from developed worlds – more easily dominate the space (Boxman-Shabtai; Gaunt; Guo and Lee).

Nevertheless, dance on social media echoes with what Mark Franko called *participatory dance* that could reshape concert dance as a "radical democracy" (Franko 1). In January 2020, the *Los Angeles Times* coined the term *dancefluencers* (Easter). Dance influencers can make as much as $50,000 per post on Instagram based on their number of followers. They represent different body types, races, ethnicities, and dance techniques that have been historically marginalized. The internet is not accessible to everyone, yet the rise of dance influencers reflects a changing dynamic. Social media dancers' geographic locations, training, genres, and techniques and their racial, ethnic, and linguistic ties become ambiguous. Due to the extended stage and audience pool, social media opens up opportunities for minority dancers whose geographies and styles are outside Western conventions.

This chapter first contextualizes concert dance in theatre, social dance in dance halls, and popular dance on television and movie screens. Then it theorizes dance on social media, what I call *social media dance*, and suggests its five distinctive features: (1) social-popular dance of the global youth; (2) the public's participation over critics' judgement; (3) TikTokkable, homogenized simplicity and transformability; (4) condensed space and time; and (5) face dance. This chapter provides case studies by closely reading the handwashing TikTok dance challenge accompanied by ethnographic interviews with Đăng. It examines the original choreographies, not fans' adaptations, to illuminate shared choreographic structures as social media dance.

I argue that social media dance is a social-popular dance of the global youth on social media. Social media is a front stage to perform, a backstage to socialize, and the smallest but most transnational stage. Social media is a space to idolize, fandoming themselves like K-pop cover dancers explained in the Introduction. Compared to admired professional dances in theatre or idealized dance actors on film based on flawless perfection and distance between dancers and the audience, on social media, the public is the dancers who idolize their bodies. As social media dance, the "handwashing dance" TikTok challenge share structural similarities. They are decontextualized as short moving images as digital files in a condensed time and space. They consist of a clear formula along with literal, front-driven movement. They are half-body dances with an emphasis on the upper body and face. When movement is condensed into fifteen seconds on a narrow screen, charismatic and conventionally attractive bodies with constantly changing faces are the keys to grab the audience's attention. Racial ambiguity is a plus because it makes the videos appeal to a wider audience with extended relatability and transformability.

In addition to the personal charm that nudges the audience to imitate the dance, an eye-catching simplicity that evokes in the watcher an "I can do better" mentality is essential. In social media dance, imitable quality exceeds mysterious artistic originality. A clear template generates an adaptable homogeneity, which eventually increases participation, personalized transformations, and thus, measurable popularity. Social media dance blurs professionalism/amateurism, performers/the audience, and authenticity/imitation, transgressing cultural, ethnic, racial, linguistic, and stylistic boundaries. Its versatile combination of Western and Asian and classical and popular dances suggests a possibility of destabilizing the elitism of Western concert and popular dance.

Concert, Social, and Popular Dance

Concert Dance and Social Dance

Concert dance refers to a theatrical dance presented for the audience in a theatre. Its conventions are inseparable from its primary venue, the proscenium stage, which has been historically reserved for professional dancers. An invisible, imagined wall, called the *fourth wall*, exists in theatre between the audience in the auditorium and performers onstage. This setting not only divides the audience and performers physically, spatially, and emotionally, but it also creates a hierarchy between the two. Dancers are expected to satisfy sponsors' and judges' expectations and to awe the audience. They have the pressure of artistically compensating the audience for the capital spent to watch the show with their sophisticated, admirable discipline and mastery of conventions and foundations, often requiring years of training. Theatre is an exclusive space that requires professional networks, accredited training backgrounds, and sponsorship. Performing in Mariinsky Theatre indicates a dancer's technical and artistic superiority approved by the field at large. While concert dance is often associated with Western dance, such as today's ballet and modern dance, its history can be traced back to ancient performing arts traditions with multiple origins. Proscenium stages for professional artists have existed across the globe from Greece to India and China over the centuries.

Contrarily, *social dance* refers to community members' vernacular dance. It has been performed across the globe without a fourth wall since the prehistoric era in rites of passage, social gatherings, ritual ceremonies, and more. Recreational, participatory ceremonial functions often exceed professionals' aesthetic values. Performers are the audience and vice versa and would willingly pay not to watch but to participate. In the twentieth century US, social-popular dances have often been called dance "crazes" or "manias" (Marshall 3). Ragtime, disco, contradances, waltzes, and polka are prime examples. African American swing, jazz, the Charleston, the Twist, and Latin dances, such as the salsa, tango, and rumba, greatly influenced Western social dance during the twentieth century. Social dance was often criticized as a promiscuous, vulgar activity performed by working-class citizens, such as the references to ballroom dancers as "dance hall evils" who generated "moral panics" in the twentieth century US due to their close physical contact and the public display of (female) bodies (Thiel-Stern 13, 24).

From the concert stage to popular screen, ethnic roots have been obscured when commodified and disseminated by and for the mainstream white audience (George-Graves; Kowal, "Review"; Manning). The representational visibility of whiteness continues on social media. African American Jalaiah Harmon originally created one of the most popular TikTok dance challenges, "Renegade," but it was popularized by white dancer Charli D'Amelio, who gets the credit as the dance's "C.E.O." (Lorenz).

Along with its recreational functions, social dance has carried ritualistic, religious, and national identities since colonialism. The Māori's haka and Polynesian's hula exemplify war dances that trained warriors in the past and were later used to celebrate national cultural identities against Christianity and Western colonialism. Plantation dances, such as the cakewalk and Afro-Brazilian martial art Capoeira, demonstrate the political nature of dance as a defense mechanism that was "outwardly entertaining while secretly satirical and deeply revolutionary" (Zenenga 68). Korean shamanic folk dance *kut* (*gut*), where shamans dance on a sharp knife, integrates ritual and entertainment and is a longstanding vernacular dance that survived Japanese colonialism. In globalization, world-renowned Irish step-dancing shows like *Riverdance* and *Lord of the Dance* have represented an Irish identity and sentiment during its globalization process (Farrell-Wortman). K-pop dance serves as a source of national pride on the local scale and promotes a Pan-Asian ethnicity in the US for Asian Americans (C. Oh, "Identity Passing").

Popular Dance on Screen

While social dance has primarily occurred at a physical venue, such as a dance hall, it has also been disseminated through various media since the late-nineteenth century. From vaudeville stars to modern dancers like Loie Fuller, dancers have appeared in print media, newsreels, films, and television shows. The Twist and the Charleston were transmitted via silent film and television in the early twentieth century "through *affective viewing* engaged through a feeling of recognition, desire, or belonging while watching, and *active viewing*" where some viewers connected to mediated images of dancing and others watched and danced (Harlig, "Communities of Practice" 58, original emphasis). Analyzing the popularity of ballroom dance in dance magazines in the 1920s, Julie Malnig explained that American teen girls copied the popular images of dancing women as "malleable artifact[s]" of performing liberatory "new women" (Malnig, "Athena Meets Venus" 36).

When social dance is mediated through legacy media and generates a large venue of socializing, it can turn into popular dance. Popular dance emerges from social dance in specific regions but differentiates itself as a "worldwide dance phenomenon" (Malnig, *Ballroom* 5), like hip-hop and Bollywood. While concert dance highlights the theatre as the core venue, popular dance relies on the screen. Sherril Dodds articulated how mainstream film and television alter the aesthetic features of dance. *Dancer-actors*, or what she called "the popular-screen dance bod [ies]," are idealized, sanitized, and technically competent, re-choreographed for the camera and for broadcasting companies' profits (Dodds "Values in Motion" 445). *Tiny Pretty Things* on Netflix is a great example of dancer-actors. While their upper bodies and facial expressions are as dramatic and polished as those of celebrity actors, their lower bodies showcase a highly satisfying level of dance foundation and skillful acrobatic performances. *Screendance* is another term that describes various dances on screens from internet videos, film, to dance on the internet (Bench; Rosenberg). On the internet, dance is shared and copied by the public beyond professional dancers ("Screendance 2.0" 184). Social media dance is the next generations after film and television with the rising social media apps and smartphone. It is a social-popular dance of the global youth on social media, a front stage to perform, a backstage to socialize, and the smallest but most transnational stage. The next section explains the five distinctive features of social media dance.

Social Media Dance

Social-Popular Dance of the Global Youth

Today, the increasing digitalization of dance on the internet challenges the previous distinctions across concert dance, social dance, and popular dance as categorized based on venue and accessibility. Social media dance is a social-popular dance of the global youth on social media on the smallest, most portable (smartphone) stage, located in our pockets. The internet space is not necessarily restricted by geography, accessibility, or popularity. As physical venues migrate from dance halls to the internet, the binary between social and popular dance is blurred. A (social) dance can go viral and quickly become a transnational phenomenon, a popular dance, like K-pop singer PSY's "Gangnam Style" (2012) horse dance. Albeit with a shorter lifespan, social dance on the internet can turn into a popular dance at any time and thus, become social-popular dance.

The change of the space – the stage – from a theatre to a smartphone screen alters the fundamental reception and display of dance. Social media alters the "conditions and rules of social interaction" (Dijck and Poell 2). Social media dance targets popularity as an indicator of social presence, and being social is connected to being popular. As people socialized in dance halls in the past, the global youth socialize on social media, using the front stage (the screen) to perform and the backstage (tags, hashtags, (un)follows, replies, and messages) to socialize.

As an example of social media dance, dance challenges prioritize participation over executing the dance correctly. As exemplified by a teenage British TikTokker dancing to "Savage Love" with his 77-year-old grandmother, a dance challenge is an inclusive site of sharing a social-popular dance. Dance challenges serve community building, socializing, entertaining, and creating new aesthetic trends focused on a visual-centric youth culture. By disseminating dance, participants socialize and identify with one another and with the mediated images of dancers on social media.

The Public's Participation Over Critics' Judgement

On social media, the number of "follows," "shares," or "likes" matter more than a critic's newspaper review. Unlike concert dance, social media dance does not need credentials or approvals from gatekeepers: choreographers, professors, teachers, directors, critics, or sponsors. Instead, social media dancers are entrepreneurs. As they can perform anytime, anywhere, the exclusive privilege of the theater stage is disrupted. Instead of expecting the renowned criticism of newspaper reviews, social media dancers instead check new followers, read the public's comments on threads, and communicate with the audience via direct messages. Rather than sensing the heat, smell, and sound of the audience or peeking at them from behind the curtain, social media dancers count the number of views. The quantity of views often matters more than elite critics' opinions about the quality of the dance.

With the number of "likes," a dance influencer's fifteen-second TikTok video can get more visibility than a two-hour-long masterpiece in the theatre.

Given the drastic changes in dance reception, it is hardly surprising that there were only two full-time dance critics in the US in 2015, which the *Atlantic* hesitantly called "the death of dance critics" (Mainwaring). Whether the decline of dance critics signifies the oversimplification of dance or a new chapter against elitism, social media dance has become more dependent on the audience, not their spectatorship but their participation. The performer and the audience binary is further blurred even without live audiences. The sacred liveness in theatre is replaced by the playful and unpredictable but measurable participation of the audience.

The "censorship algorithm" of social media often privileges certain racialized, gendered, and classed bodies for profitability (Kennedy 1073). Yet, the increasing role of audience participation still deserves attention, as it shifts copyright issues focused on the ownership of a physical form. On social media, people want to be copied. The original is trackable with a hashtag or a directly copied link. The public is no longer fully anonymous compared to television viewers, as the internet can track users' information, from their location to personal accounts.

TikTokkable Dance: Homogenized Simplicity and Transformability

The social media stage blurs geographical, ethnic, racial, and cultural boundaries. Popular makeup styles on Instagram, for instance, are imitable regardless of gender, ethnicity, or race. Influencers' faces often look alike and are racially or ethnically ambiguous. The desire of Instagrammers and their followers are not necessarily to be authentic to oneself but to experience being other, like the desire to be (like) Kylie Jenner; looking familiar or looking alike is important because it satisfies the desire to belong in society (Brucculieri). This homogeneity reveals that the myth of authenticity in social media, of "just being me" (Duffy and Wissinger 4652), is not an individual choice but a prescripted, choreographed desire.

Like those of social media dancers, makeup Instagrammers' faces are decontextualized, exhibited, and eventually sold through sponsorships and advertising, like a singular product. People do not care where they take their makeup photos, how their rooms are disorganized, where they live, or who they are. Their racial ambiguity appeals to a bigger audience group, opening up a wider transformability. When the style is imitable, it can be transnational. For example, Pony is a beauty guru with over 5.93 million subscribers on YouTube and a global cosmetic brand. She transforms herself into K-pop idols, Taylor Swift, Kylie Jenner, and Elsa from Disney's *Frozen* through makeup. Here, homogeneity co-exists with versatility. Precisely because of the imitable characteristics of popular content on social media, anyone can try it, be other, albeit temporarily, and experience a moment of transformable, performative identity passing.

The replicability of social media dance mirrors this homogenized (conventional) but at the same time versatile (adaptable) logics of social media. In dance challenges, dancers do not need to speak or sing and instead add embedded lip-syncs, text, existing pop songs, and an AI-generated voice that largely sounds like a young white woman. While English still operates as the hegemonic norm, there are less linguistic barriers or racial and ethnic stigmas associated with accents. Users can easily adapt the homogenous template of dance challenges regardless of geography, linguistic ties, dance training, and cultural background.

Historically, unlike concert dance that often privileges originality presented by professionals, popular and social dance relied on simplicity. A clear, simple, and homogenized basic structure of social dance allows improvisation, which contributes to its popularity (Harlig, "Communities of Practice" 63). For social media dance, too, simplicity allows the audience to enjoy and imitate dance. Social media dance has a clear template in movement, intention, and platform. Compared to in-studio classes, online dance classes likely offer simple, front-driven, and easy-to-follow movements. There are no instructors who can give personalized feedback in real time. Users might want to click other videos and "leave" the class on the screen if the dance is hard to learn, which is much easier than leaving a class in a dance studio. When dance is easy to learn, it is imitable and can be copied. Anyone can try and expect to be like the dancer by copying the dance with the motivation of "I can do better." This will increase participatory spreadability and eventually, the number of views of the new dancer's own content. Since the pre-historic era, people have never stopped dancing, even during war times. High-tech-infused social media brings dance's democratic functions to us. As long as dance is being copied, it receives the audience's attention, which keeps it alive on social media. Social media dance is homogenous and versatilely adaptable. It is entertaining, playable, clickable, and trendy. It is Tiktokkable.

Condensed Space and Time

Social media's specificity alters the choreographic mechanisms of social media dance: space and time. On TikTok, the performing space is different from previous mediums. In film, for example, the camera follows dancers, using various angles, multiple cameras, wide shots that include other dancers, and extreme close-ups of dancers' subtle facial expressions to the sophisticated execution of their feet across the spacious stage, all edited together by film professionals. The *dancer-actors* and their *superbodies* in a Hollywood dance film like *Step Up* exceed the physical capabilities of the human body, transgressing time and space, as they literally appear to fly while jumping with the help of editing technology and camera effects (Dodds, "Values" 447, 448).

Contrarily, the TikTok stage highlights *super ordinary bodies* within a limited space and time. They are ordinary but super, meaning they exude superfluous charm, because they want others to be like them. TikTok dance is usually created by a single sequence shot without multiple cuts or camera angles. The TikTok app equipped with editing software may be the only camera. The editing software that allows the modification of sounds and images replaces the traditional jobs done by professional lighting designers, set designers, musicians, film editors, and makeup artists. The camera primarily focuses on eye-level shots and close-ups that emphasize the dancer's face and upper body. Often, the audience can see the dancer's face closely, not because the camera zooms in but because the dancer walks towards the camera and abruptly stops recording. The rectangular, narrower width of the TikTok video frame that removes the rest of the horizontal area further reduces a possible spectrum of horizontal movement. Accordingly, the movement is front-driven, and dancers constantly gaze at the camera, taking up a narrow space.

The performing space's size is limited, like a small area in a bedroom, kitchen, backyard, parking lot, or hallway. However, those spaces are accessible to everyone, unlike the theatre, which is reserved for a few. Further, once a video is uploaded to the stage, it can be transnational with infinite dissemination and accessibility. Thus, social media dance has a much bigger stage than concert dance, which is restricted by a fixed space, time, and availability of the theatre.

Time is also condensed in social media dance in response to the limited space. Since dance achieved the status of "serious art" in the 1930s (Manning), the audience has willingly gone to see a show in the theatre, trying to decipher the hidden meaning of incomprehensible subtlety or pedestrian movements. Unlike theatregoers, social media audiences are less likely to stay and watch a dance for two hours. Most dance challenges are 15 seconds, but the social media audience is not even tolerant of that, as exemplified by the widely used "wait till the end" text banner on TikTok. The view count does not count a "view" until the audience watches it till the end. And then, the video automatically replays until a viewer swipes up. To make the audience engaged, performers must show the most enchanting, highlighted scene only. Like a movie trailer or preview music in iTunes, dance challenges aim to sell a snippet of dance. The goal, however, is not to bring the audience to see the original but to let them copy the dance as their own. A fifteen-second dance challenge may not need the same stamina required for a two-hour-long performance in the theatre. When time and space are condensed, and when everyone is doing the same short dance challenge movements, what matters is how to individualize the dance and catch the audience's attention in a few seconds – the face.

The Upper Body and Face Dance

In social media dance, participants individualize their dance via their faces. In the roundtable discussion "TikTok and Short-Form Screendance Before and After Covid" published by *The International Journal of Screendance*, I defined *face dance* in TikTok dance challenges (Harlig et al.). The face is a central part of human expression and individual identity (Dodds and Hooper 93). When people do the same dance routine in dance challenges, it is the face that distinguishes one from another. In dance challenges, the face itself dances: flirtatious winks, happy smiles, whimsical winks, biting lips, rolling eyes, grimaces, smirks, naïve eyes, sharp sidelong glances, unpredictable scowls, and seductive gazes at the camera. The face dance exhibits emotional intensity and variety within a few seconds – boredom, disinterest, distraction, lightheartedness, hesitancy, shyness, meanness, jealousy, silliness, joy, sexual ecstasy, and excitement. Face dance exists in daily life but is hard to capture, like a father dancing with his daughter at her wedding whose smile indicates more than happiness. Face dance imitates a fleeting, precious moment in life as choreographed authenticity.

Often, social media dance highlights a face so much that it even features nothing but the dancer's face, a face dance. A rising TikTok star, Bella Poarch is known for her zoomed-in lip-sync video "M to the B," where she exhibits her cartoonish,

TABLE 1.1 Dance from Theatre, to TV, and to Social Media

Stage	Live Theatre	Television & Film	Social Media
Main Genres	Western concert dance	Commercial Western popular dance	Global dance in all genres
Performers	Professional dancers as artists	Professional *dancer-actors* as commodities	Pro- and amateur dancers as entrepreneurs
Bodies	Disciplined bodies valued for artistic originality and convention	Edited *superbodies* for profitable familiarity	*Super ordinary bodies* for playable imitation
Techniques	Strong foundation of the legs and mastery of traditions	Acrobatic lower body and dramatic upper body	Gestural, charming upper body and face dance
Time & Space	Three-dimensional stage viewed for a few hours	Two-dimensional TV and film screen viewed for a few minutes to hours	Condensed, narrower portable smartphone screen viewed for a few seconds to minutes
Sponsors	The gatekeepers	Broadcasting companies and movie studios	Viewers
Audience	Niche theatregoers paying up to hundreds of dollars for tickets	Anonymous public with around $50 monthly subscriptions or $12 movie tickets	Global internet users accessing for free or free with ads and/or paid sponsorships
Spectatorship	Admiring artists via distanced, admiring viewing	Idealizing celebrities via affective viewing with "tear-jerker," "gasping" moments[1]	Idolizing and fandoming themselves via participatory viewing with an "I can do better" feeling
Values	Qualified by critics	Quantified by commercial success	Quantified by the number of views and followers

Source: Created by the author.

hypnotic facial expressions that suddenly shift to exaggerated rolling eyes and duck lips with chill bouncing. It is her face that whimsically dances with emotional variety. This eleven-second-long video shows her face only but has over 500 million views, approximately 41.5 million likes, and the most views and likes on TikTok as of November 2020. *BuzzFeed News* (2020) reported that her success relies on people's interests in "looking at 'attractive faces'" (Strapagiel).

Table 1.1 summarizes the differences from dance in the theatre, to television and film, and to social media. These characteristics are not definite and rather keep changing and overlapping across platforms. Instead of generalizing, this preliminary study aims to categorize some of the main characteristics of the different stages.

K-pop as Social Media Dance

Point choreography is not new in popular dance and music. The choreography to Los Del Río's "Macarena" and Michael Jackson's moonwalk, and Beyoncé's "Single Ladies" are some iconic examples. Mostly situated in a chorus line, it consists of a repetitive, eye-catching, memorable, and relatively simple dance to follow. What separates K-pop point choreography from other genres is its *gestural point choreography*. As Chapter 2 further explains, K-pop's gestural point choreography is short, graphic, accentuated, pictorial, front-driven, and densely synchronized in a precise coordination of upper-body movements: dramatic faces, delicate fingers, alluring hands, circling wrists, sharp elbows, undulating, popping chests, sexually suggestive shoulders, and flying hair. It showcases the clear body "line" with angular gestures and the dancers' most beautiful facial angles for short durations, like a sequence of model-like poses for a photoshoot. Dancers compensate for the two-dimensionality of the screen and a limited time and space with the emotional intensity and richness of movements from their faces to upper bodies, which add personalization, vibration, volume, and the semblance of three-dimensionality. Gestural point choreography provides a perfect source to play and perform on social media, which highlights one's upper body, face, and individual charm and has facilitated the global K-pop dance fandom from YouTube tutorials to TikTok dance challenges.

K-pop girl group BLACKPINK's "Kill This Love" dance challenge is a great example of social media dance. It was one of the five most influential TikTok dance challenges in 2019, according to *Dance Spirit* magazine (DeSantis). Los Angeles-based choreographer Kyle Hanagami choreographed the piece. Its gestural point choreography lasts approximately 20 seconds. In the original MV, BLACKPINK is clad in sensual warrior-like outfits, such as black leather and garter belts. With the chorus "[l]et's kill this love," the members of BLACKPINK fearlessly gaze at the camera, audaciously kick their elbows side to side, as if removing all barriers, reach out one arm toward the viewers as if firing a gun, and undulate their chests backward, pulling down their arms, constantly gazing at the front, and maximizing the impact of the gunshot movement. Then they playfully twist their hips, cheerfully sway and twirl their arms above their heads, smirking in a confident manner, and imitate the hand movements of police saluting. Their charming representation and charismatic upper body resonate with the "girl crush" concept of the group. Then they put their fists in front of their chests and dramatically pull them out, lifting their chins confidently, defiantly gazing at the camera, as if tearing out a heart. Like a musical, the choreography matches the lyrics "[k]ill this love."

The choreography is literal, gestural, and lasts approximately twenty seconds. The dancers change their facial expressions from dramatic smirks, to grimaces, to mischievous smiles, to side eying and, finally, to a defiant gaze. They switch formations back and forth, but they keep facing front and never show their backs. They take up a limited space so that they can maximize the front-driven impact of their dance. The dance consists of a visually simple and memorable routine that amateur fans can easily copy. The global popularity of Filipino dance influencers Ranz and Niana's "Kill This Love" dance challenge videos, performed with their younger sibling, denotes how accessible the gestural point choreography of the original "Kill This Love" is. Blackpink's bodies are conventionally attractive (light, flawless skin, and slim bodies) but differ along racial, ethnic, and cultural lines due to the members coming from Thailand, New Zealand, the US, and South Korea.

#Handwashing Dance Challenge

The song used in the handwashing dance is "Ghen Cô Vy" (meaning jealous of Coronavirus) based on a Vietnamese pop hit called "Ghen" by Min and Erik. During our interview, Đăng told me that he had choreographed for the song (English: "Jealous [of] Coronavirus") is a song by Vietnamese singers Min and Erik.based on three years ago, so he already had inspiration for the song. "It took only fifteen minutes [to make]," he added. They shot the video outside of his dance studio, Life Dance, with his dancers. He made the video "informative" so that it went along with the catchy song to draw the audience's attention. The dance starts with Đăng and another male dancer on a local market street. They wear casual pants, running shoes, and yellow tops. Once the chorus line begins with "let's wash your hands," Đăng brushes his hands, placing his hands on his left and then right cheek, moving back and forth, rhythmically stamping his feet, and lightly swaying his hips side to side. He wears a bright smile on his face, which emanates a joyful and uplifting mood. He shows a series of cheerful gestural movements by putting a V-sign with his hands around his eyes and mouth with his teeth showing, as he joyfully smiles and tilts his head.

When the lyrics talk about the virus, contrarily, his face turns into a serious expression, grimacing and intensely gazing at the camera without a smile. He lifts up his hands, leaning back, showing his palms to the front to the lyrics "[k]eep [the hands] away from eyes, noses, mouths." He steps side to side while his elbows are bent and he covers his face as his hands and fingers wave and curl in the other direction, like a "go away" gesture. To the lyrics "[t]ogether we shall beat the Coronavirus," he pushes his arms forward, gazing at the camera, and shifting his weight back and forth. His eyebrows pull down, furrowing, as if he is warning about the danger of the virus. To the lyrics "[c]onstantly improve your health," his face rapidly turns into a bright, hopeful smile and he winks. He spreads his arms widely to the side with bent elbows as he clenches his fists, which suggests healthy energy. In the next six handwashing gestures, he rubs his hands, lathers them, lifts them, and interlocks his fingers, rubbing them, and then rubbing under his nails. Each movement sequence is repetitive and takes up to four beats, while he regularly twists, grooves, bounces, and sways his upper body with a lighthearted vibe.

Đăng's dance has a strong presence accompanied by precise angles and clear body lines synchronized to each sharp movement and by animated facial expressions that change nearly every second. He restricts his space to a limited spot in front of the camera and constantly gazes at it. Even when looking to the side, he soon turns his head to the front as if he is aware of the audience, meaning the camera, in the front. Like Instagram microcelebrities who know the best angle for their selfies, Đăng appears to be fully aware of how his dance is visually perceived to the imaginary audience through the camera's gaze.

Invasion of Asia

On March 1, 2020, on an episode of HBO's news satire television show *Last Week Tonight,* John Oliver praised the handwashing dance, saying it "absolutely slaps" and is a "genuine club-banger." In my interview with him, Đăng expressed his gratitude to *Last Week Tonight,* which triggered the dance's popularity in the West. "He is kind of old, but he can still dance my choreography really easy, cool and swag. I think the audience sees that and feels that they can do that dance, too," Đăng said. In the talk show, Oliver talks about countries have handled COVID-19 with varying degrees of success, including Vietnam who "produced this incredible public information video about ... hygiene," Oliver says. Then the camera shows Đăng's handwashing video, and Oliver responds, "Yes, yes, yes, yes, yes," with an affirmative smile, nodding his head.

It is worth noting that Oliver compares Đăng's dance and song with the "Rubber Duckie" song by the iconic Muppet character Ernie from the children's TV show *Sesame Street.* Oliver says:

> The [handwashing] song ... makes all other songs about washing yourself look like trash. I am talking to you here, Ernie. Look, you've been on [top] for a long time, but you got complacent, didn't you? While other artists were out there, out there innovating, you kept singing the same old duckie song. You lost the hunger, son! You fell asleep [at] the wheel, and music moved on without you [*laughs*].

Based on Oliver's commentary, Ernie had been "singing the same old duckie song," while other artists, like Đăng, keep innovating new things. On March 30, 2020, *Sesame Street* released Ernie's handwashing video.

On the one hand, Oliver compliments Đăng's work as innovative and timely compared to Ernie's outdated song. Đăng, as an emerging dance influencer, signifies the transnational flow of global popular culture and "world dance" that extends Western conventions (Foster; Savigliano). On the other hand, Oliver compares a middle-aged, professional dancer's work with a humorous, troublemaking Muppet character from a children's television show. This juxtaposition could be purposeful to relieve anxiety surrounding COVID-19. Simultaneously, this comparison could negate Đăng's work as frivolous and mere entertainment and could reproduce social media dance's stereotype as the mere hobby of amateurs. Social media highlights the fun, free, and glamorous parts of life, which hides the emotional labor, self-branding effort, and "always-on mode of entrepreneurial labor" behind the scenes (Duffy and Wissinger 4652). In an interview with *Báo điện tử VTC News* (2020), Đăng said, "[B]efore composing the handwashing dance for fifteen minutes, I had ten years of hard training, pouring sweat, tears, even blood on the dance floor" (Sao). Oliver's commentary likely conflates simplicity as an aesthetic convention of social media dance with a lack of dancers' physical skills.

Moreover, by calling the Muppet a "son," Oliver guides the audience to identify with the Muppet, signifying cultural and emotional proximity. Such rhetoric potentially reinforces Đăng as a foreigner, reminiscent of the Orientalism that frames the West at the center of civilization and Asia as the Other, an invader (Said). It implies the colonial logic of racial, ethnic, and national hierarchies that require a white man's approval to give the video more credential.

The rhetoric of an "invasion of Asia" should be familiar to Asian artists and K-pop fans. When K-pop idols break a world record, the Western media often uses provocative words and phrases, such as "invasion" or "conquer" ("How Did K-Pop"; "How K-Pop Conquered the West"). Music and dance do not conquer the world, although they have been often used as a tool for propaganda. Dance is rather a conversation across cultures and people. Albeit utopianistic, it can bring people together, not by invading, but by inviting each other to hold hands.

Racialization is an implicit barrier for K-pop dancers and fans. K-pop dancers' sharp choreography and training systems are often negated as a "machine," which reproduces the West as a genius creator versus the East/Asia as a copycat as explained in the Introduction. Yet, if technical virtuosity is the opposite of creativity, Juilliard School graduates should lack creativity. Skill is a tool in the arts. It does not guarantee creativity, but it is a basic building block toward creativity, which can distinguish people-made arts (artificial beauty) from nature (natural beauty).

As other chapters will further elaborate, K-pop fans are not immune from racialized hierarchies and authenticity. Collegiate K-pop cover dancers have to justify their skills and fight against the prejudice that K-pop is not "an actual dance" compared to other dance teams and clubs. Racial discrimination often functions by questioning minorities' credibility, one of the ways through which racial hierarchy is maintained. As most of school dance teams consist of non-dance majors, questioning whether K-pop dance, comprised mostly of Asian Americans, is signaled out as not really dance seems inseparable from racial prejudice.

The Half-Body Dance and Face

During my interview with Đăng, I learned that what I thought I knew about him was a staged version of the dancer. Like a ballet dancer who plays a particular role in a repertoire, social media dancers exhibit facial choreography that matches their stage personae. I was first exposed to Đăng's work through YouTube and Instagram. His bright facial expressions in his dance videos were so noticeable that it nearly looked like his signature style. We met on July 31, 2020, at 5:50 pm Vietnam time via Zoom. When I first actually met and spoke to him, albeit online, I immediately noticed that he was quite different from his social media persona. He was around ten minutes late for the interview. He told me that he had rushed home from work and that people were anxious these days as COVID-19 had seemed to resurge recently. Unlike most of his dance videos, he barely smiled during the interview. He looked rather calm, serious, and slightly tired.

I asked him whether his smile was a part of his choreography or if it comes out of dancing naturally. He replied:

> That's just my style of dance. Because I find that when I smile, I have a good smile, so I want to use it more often. And about the choreography, I like to watch manga, you know? Japanese and Korean comics. I read a lot of manga and cartoons and a lot of similar stuff for children and for kids. When I choreograph, I want to put the smile cues in the dance.

In the handwashing dance, because of his constant cheerful smile, he often looks cartoonish, like a happy comic book character. Đăng's animated face supports that facial choreography works best in social media when it prioritizes lighthearted, carefree, playful, and "clickable" trendy content (Van Dijck and Poell 6–7). His experience as a movie actor may help him to better choreograph his facial expressions while dancing.

In dance challenges, dance is further facialized. A dance video is often conflated with a face. Facial expressions change frequently in unpredictable manners to prevent the audience from swiping up. They should not be too subtle but instead explicit and impressive, responding to gestural upper-body movements. Like sharp, delicately fabricated angular arms and hand movements around dancers' faces in voguing, dance challenges' upper-body movements draw the audience's attention to the facial area as a decorative backdrop of the face.

Đăng referred to social media dance as "the half-body dance": "It is *the half-body dance* [emphasis by the author]. I don't do the full-body dance. A lot of people on TikTok, they want to show off their personality so they can always do the dance with hands and with their facial expression like that." The half-body dance does not simply refer to the technical body parts dancers are using. Dancers need their whole bodies to dance, but the upper body in social media dance is the center of attention for a dancer's intention and the audience's gaze. From ballet, to tap, to tango, and to Flamenco, intricate footwork often demonstrates dancers' foundational training and virtuosity. But in social media dance, footwork is often invisible. The upper body and facial expressions overshadow the lower-body technique, which makes the dance more accessible to amateurs.

Đăng's understanding that the half-body dance reveals personality deserves closer attention. Since the face represents an individual's unique, personal identity, when the audience focuses on the dancers' upper bodies and faces, this potentially turns the audience's attention to the dancers as individuals. As social media dancers' videos are directly linked to their personal profiles and accounts, their dances become part of their personal brands. The fact that their half-body dance videos look appealing means that they – the dancers – look attractive. Thus, they can directly gain followers who not only follow the dancers' works but also might be interested in knowing them personally, sending a direct message to them on Instagram.

As "vlogging has replaced blogging" (Shtern et al. 1949), in social media dance, the body is often the dance itself. The attractive body and face often exceed the text. Upper-body movements certainly exceed lower-body movements that require years of training. The body is what Pierre Bourdieu would refer to as "cultural" and "social" capital that create aesthetic and commercial values in popularity, networking, monetization, and partnership deals. It is the dancer's body that evokes admiration and envy and provides the desire to be liked. The face becomes more than an individual identity but the center of the capital that directly sells the dance video and the creator's business. Đăng's body has as an attractive, conventional appearance with racial ambiguity. While his black eyes and hair read as Asian, his ethnic specificity seems rather vague in his video. His visual appearance can fit into the generic category of attractiveness regardless of his race, ethnicity, or cultural background. He is tall, fit, athletic, and light-skinned, wears trendy, casual clothing, and has a handsome smile.

Simplicity: A Copy is the Original

During an interview with *Business Insider* (2020), Đăng said that the handwashing song's "catchiness" and the "simplicity" of the dance contributed to its popularity. He further explained it to me:

> Unlike [the] theatre stage, when I choreograph for social media, I focus on simplicity. Because you have to imagine with this choreography, even your mom, your grandfather can do this like a piece of cake. My dance is very simple and cute. You can stand up, sit down or even dance on a toilet too. I did some hard, difficult dance, too, but nobody wants to copy it [*laughs*]. Because if it's too hard, they cannot feel it. So, if you have to put a simple, informative move with good quality so they can see, feel, and think they can do better.

The handwashing dance fits the dual expectations of social media dance: homogeneity and transformability. The video is simple and imitable and thus, can be versatile and transformative based on users' individual preferences.

Imitations have been devalued in Western history since Plato's Cave allegory, as an original invention has been given more value than a copy of a masterpiece (Wright). The imagery of a genius artist in an ivory tower has been challenged since postmodernism in the early and mid-1900s in pieces such as Andy Warhol's *Campbell's Soup Cans* paintings and Marcel Duchamp's readymade sculpture *Fountain*. From Walter Benjamin's groundbreaking work *The Work of Art in the Age of Mechanical Reproduction* (1935) to Jean Baudrillard's canonical work *Simulacra and Simulation* (1981), the issues of origin and aura have been redefined by the mechanical reproduction of arts in a mass-culture society. Yet, still, there is an implicit fear against imitation, as it conjures inauthenticity. Nevertheless, like a toddler learning a language by imitating her parents' words, learning dance can start with imitating the dance of others.

On social media, the authentic original matters less. Despite celebrities explaining their "fake" body photos on Instagram with behind-the-scenes photos, the public still predominantly follows the photoshopped, manufactured images of the stars. The rise of virtual (CGI) influencers like Lil Miquela (@lilmiquela) and Rozy (@rozy.gram) also signify that the singular, unchanged material presence of originality is changing.

When Philip Auslander wrote in 2008 that there is liveness in mediated performances circulated via digital spaces, he could not have predicted how social media explicitly demands copying dances, wherein imitations are as crucial as originality. TikTok is designed to encourage imitation and replication among users (Zulli and Zulli). Often, content does not achieve visibility unless it is imitable or sharable. In the early twentieth century, people imitated the Charleston and the Twist through mediated television and silent film screens to perform desirable, "charming" dancing bodies (Harlig, "Communities of Practice" 63). Dance challenges continue the desire of copying and being copied through the mediated consumption and exploring of alternative identities through dance; the global youth imitate dance challenges while dreaming of being the next TikTok star.

The Cosmopolitan Variety of Global Pop Dance

Competitive youth culture haunts social media, where everyone wants to be a celebrity yet also has a precarious, insecure sense of self (Boxman-Shabtai; Salvato; Saul). Like Apple and Samsung, which continually release new smartphones with only slightly different features, neoliberal capitalism demands constant purchases, which become a symbol of social status. Social media dancers feel pressure in the ever-updating environment where constant updates are the only way to maintain their visibility. A social media dance can rapidly arise with a hashtag event and so can its disappearance, like fast-fashion clothing, replaced with another quickly emerging star or dance challenge.

Nevertheless, social media opens new opportunities for marginalized dancers. Đăng started his career as a self-taught street dancer, but now seeks to open a gate for the next generation in Vietnam with his success on social media. His dance studio Life Dance offers various dance classes, such as jazz, K-pop, modern, and contemporary dance, for children to adults. His K-pop cover dances, dance challenges, and appearance on *Dancing 9*, a South Korean dance competition show, resonate with K-pop as a source of pan-Asian identity against the mainstream Western culture. "I want to bring the value, the quality of Vietnamese dance – how we dance, how we live, how we execute the dance – into the world," Đăng said.

> Some dancers only like one or two styles. But I just like to dance. Any style is okay, like jazz, hip-hop, house, popping, urban, contemporary, and traditional dance. I went to a lot of dance camps. I believe my strength is that I can try anything about dance. I just don't take high heel class because I don't feel like that's very good for me [*laughs*].

As an Asian dancer, he might have begun his career as an attempt to "be like," as Homi K. Bhabha said, Western colonizers. Yet, he eventually grew as a versatile dancer with his unique choreography that blends Western and Asian popular and traditional dance traditions. His choreography for *Vũ Nông Dân* ("Dancing Farmers") emblematizes his distinctive vision. Initially performed for a television show and shared on YouTube, he wants to develop the piece into a full-length choreography for theatre. *Vũ Nông Dân* uniquely blends urban, hip-hop, and breakdance with traditional Vietnamese sounds and vernacular agricultural cultural symbols symbolized by a conical hat, a *nón lá*.

Conclusion

In a traditional setting, the audience would pay upwards of several hundred dollars to see a two-hour-long live show and an expert they admire in the theatre. After long weekdays, they would probably go to the theatre on a Saturday night wearing a fancy suit. Audiences are ready to stand up and clap after Odile's 32 fouettés in Act Three of *Swan Lake*. In the theatre, there is only one star who can shine on stage. The audience often carefully reads a program note to learn about dancers' training and background information and the master choreographer's intention.

In social media, however, a relatable, copyable, and broad spectrum of dance styles is often more valued than an esoteric dance technique held in an ivory tower, as the former welcomes participation. There is a lesser predetermined context in social media, although the audience can search for more details online later under the potential manipulation of algorithms. Dance has become more fluid than ever. It has become increasingly challenging to pin down which genre or convention a dancer is rooted in and belongs to. On social media, the audience can watch a 15-second video for free (with advertising), while sitting on a coach any time to be entertained. They watch to participate, and they copy because they want to perform – to be heard and seen through comment threads, reply to messages, and ideally, their own dances. Social media opens an era where everyone can be a fan of themselves.

A few years ago, a dance major left the degree program I teach in during his second year. As a dance theory faculty member I do not know the full story, but it appeared that the institutional hierarchy between dancers (students) and choreographers (teachers) and commercial dance and "canonical" concert dance were the reasons. Above all, as a dance influencer, he already has the stage – social media – to share his works without any master's approval, jurisdiction, or network. Such accessibility without formal training could partially explain the decreasing number of dance majors in college (Laos). This openness could make traditional gatekeepers, who have often taken privileged positions regarding race, gender, ethnicity, citizenship, language, and education since the colonial era, feel less "happy" (Schechner 8). Nevertheless, as theatre becomes "anarchic" (8), social media will be the nostalgic theatre of the youth who will soon be the next generation of dance and performance studies.

When I was a teenage ballet dancer, I dreamed of playing the main role of Clara in *The Nutcracker*. Later, in *Swan Lake,* I was in the corps de ballet, standing under the dimmed lights, admiring the prima ballet dancer on center stage. Whenever the audition results were announced, I blamed myself, thinking that I was not the director's favorite. Today, dancers can shine on the social media stage. Whenever I encounter emerging dance influencers through their behind-the-stories or viral videos, they make me smile. I am happy for them because now they, or anyone, can at least get slightly more opportunities to shine, albeit in a fleeting moment. We are living in an era when anyone can dance anywhere, as if no one is watching, even if they know and even expect that everyone can watch. The next chapter will further expand social media dance by drawing examples from K-pop. It traces K-pop dance's evolution from the 1980s backup dance troupes at broadcasting companies to the 2020s global entrepreneurship on social media.

Note

1 See Dodds ("Values in Motion"), Dodds and Hooper, Elswit and Weisbrod for more discussions on dance on television, such as the reality TV show *So You Think You Can Dance* and the Hollywood film *Step Up*.

References

Anderson, Jon D. "Dance, Technology, and the Web Culture of Students." *Journal of Dance Education*, vol. 12, no. 1, 2012, pp. 21–24. *Taylor & Francis Online*, https://doi.org/10.1080/15290824.2011.621375.

Auslander, Philip. *Liveness: Performance In A Mediatized Culture.* Routledge, 2008.

Baudrillard, Jean. *Simulacra and Simulation.* U of Michigan P, 1994.

Bench, Harmony. "Screendance 2.0: Social Dance-Media." *Participations: International Journal of Audience Research*, vol. 7, no. 2, Nov. 2010, pp. 183–214.

Benjamin, Walter. *The Work of Art in the Age of Mechanical Reproduction*. Translated by J. A. Underwood, Penguin, 2008.

Bhabha, Homi K. *The Location of Culture*. Routledge, 2004.

Borelli, Melissa Blanco. "Introduction: Dance on Screen." In *The Oxford Handbook of Dance and the Popular Screen*, edited by Melissa Blanco Borelli, Oxford UP, 2014, pp. 1–17.

Boxman-Shabtai, Lillian. "The Practice of Parodying: YouTube as a Hybrid Field of Cultural Production." *Media, Culture & Society*, vol. 41, no. 1, 2019, pp. 3–20. *SAGE Journals*, https://doi.org/10.1177/0163443718772180.

Brucculieri, Julia. "Instagram Influencers Are All Starting To Look The Same. Here's Why." *HuffPost*, 9 March 2018, https://www.huffpost.com/entry/instagram-influencers beauty_n_5aa13616e4b002df2c6163bc.

Chakravorty, Pallabi. *This Is How We Dance Now!: Performance in the Age of Bollywood and Reality Shows*. Oxford UP, 2017.

"Coronavirus: Last Week Tonight with John Oliver (HBO)." *YouTube*, uploaded by LASTWEEKTONIGHT, 1 Mar. 2020, https://www.youtube.com/watch?v=c09m5f7Gnic.

Đăng, Quang [@im.quangdang]. "Cùng nâng cao và bảo vệ sức khỏe bằng cách lan tỏa." *TikTok*, 19 Feb. 2020, https://www.tiktok.com/@im.quangdang/video/6795172608770870529.

Đăng, Quang. Zoom interview with the author. 31 July 2020.

DeSantis, Marissa. "5 of the Best TikTok Dance Challenges—and How the App Is Changing the Dance World." *Dance Spirit*, 20 Sep. 2019, https://www.dancespirit.com/best-tiktok-dance-challenges-2640397990.html?rebelltitem=17#rebelltitem17.

Dodds, Sherril. *Dance on Screen: Genres and Media from Hollywood to Experimental Art*. Palgrave Macmillan, 2001.

Dodds, Sherril. "On Watching Screendance." *The International Journal of Screendance*, vol. 10, 2019. http://dx.doi.org/10.18061/ijsd.v10i0.6726.

Dodds, Sherril. "Values in Motion: Reflections on Popular Screen Dance." In *The Oxford Handbook of Dance and the Popular Screen*, edited by Melissa Blanco Borelli, Oxford UP, 2014, 445–454.

Dodds, Sherril, and Colleen Hooper. "Faces, Close-ups and Choreography: A Deleuzian Critique of *So You Think You Can Dance*." *The International Journal of Screendance*, vol. 4, 2014, http://dx.doi.org/10.18061/ijsd.v4i0.4524.

Duffy, Brooke Erin, and Elizabeth Wissinger. "Mythologies of Creative Work in the Social Media Age: Fun, Free, and 'Just Being Me.'" *International Journal of Communication*, vol. 11, 2017, pp. 4652–4671.

Easter, Makeda. "Rise of Dancefluencer: These L.A. Dancers Show How the Internet Is Helping Nontraditional Talent Break into the Industry." *Los Angeles Times*, 16 January 2020, https://www.latimes.com/projects/la-social-media-dance-influencer/.

Elswit, Kate. "*So You Think You Can Dance* Does Dance Studies." *TDR/The Drama Review*, vol. 56, no. 1, 2012, pp. 133–142. *MIT Press Direct*, https://doi.org/10.1162/DRAM_a_00148.

Farrell-Wortman, Laura. "The *Riverdance* Phenomenon and the Development of Irish Identity in The Global Era." *Studies in Musical Theatre*, vol. 4, no. 3, 2010, pp. 311–319.

Foster, Susan Leigh. "Worlding Dance—Introduction." In *Worlding Dance*, edited by Susan Leigh Foster, Palgrave Macmillian, 2009, pp. 1–13.

Franko, Mark. "Editor's Note: Taking (A)part: Investigations into Participation." *Dance Research Journal*, vol. 45, no. 3, 2013, pp. 1–2. *Cambridge Core*, https://doi.org/10.1017/S0149767713000247.

Gaunt, Kyra D. "YouTube, Twerking and You: Context Collapse and the Handheld Co-Presence of Black Girls and Miley Cyrus." *Journal of Popular Music Studies*, vol. 27, no. 3, 2015, pp. 244–273. *Wiley Online Library*, https://doi.org/10.1111/jpms.12130.

George-Graves, Nadine. "'Just Like Being at the Zoo': Primitivity and Ragtime Dance." In *Ballroom, Boogie, Shimmy Sham, Shake: A Social and Popular Dance Reader*, edited by Julie Malnig, U of Illinois P, 2009, pp. 55–71.

Greep, Monica. "Could K-pop Dancing Eclipse Ballet and Tap?" *The Daily Mail*, 19 January 2020, https://www.dailymail.co.uk/femail/article-7904463/K-pop-mania-Industry-experts-claim-Korean-boyband-bigger-tap.html.

Guo, Lei, and Lorin Lee. "The Critique of YouTube-based Vernacular Discourse: A Case Study of YouTube's Asian Community." *Critical Studies in Media Communication*, vol. 30, no. 5, 2013, pp.391–406. *Taylor and Francis Online*, https://doi.org/10.1080/15295036.2012.755048.

Haasch, Palmer. "How Mysterious Influencer Bella Poarch Shot to Fame with TikTok's Most-liked Video in Just a Few Months." *Insider*, 14 May 2021, https://www.insider.com/bella-poarch-tiktok-tyga-tattoo-navy-age-military-how-old-2020-10#a-conspiracy-theory-spread-on-tiktok-in-october-that-poarch-sold-her-soul-to-the-illuminati-for-tiktok-clout-8.

Hammami, Amri, et al. "Physical Activity and Coronavirus Disease 2019 (COVID-19): Specific Recommendations for Home-based Physical Training." *Managing Sport and Leisure*, 2020, pp. 1–6. *Taylor and Francis Online*, https://doi.org/10.1080/23750472.2020.1757494.

Harlig, Alexandra. "Communities of Practice: Active and Affective Viewing of Early Social Dance on the Popular Screen." In *The Oxford Handbook of Dance and the Popular Screen*, edited by Melissa Blanco Borelli, Oxford UP, 2014, pp. 57–67.

Harlig, Alexandra. "'Fresher Than You': Commercial Use of YouTube-Native Dance and Videographic Techniques." *The International Journal of Screendance*, vol. 9, 2018, pp. 50–71.

Harlig, Alexandra, et al. "TikTok and Short-form Screendance before and after Covid." *The International Journal of Screendance*, 12, 2021, pp. 190–209, http://dx.doi.org/10.18061/ijsd.v12i0.8348.

Heyang, Tuomeiciren, and Rose Martin. "A Reimagined World: International Tertiary Dance Education in Light of COVID-19." *Research in Dance Education*, vol. 22, no. 3, 2020, pp. 306–320. *Taylor and Francis Online*, https://doi.org/10.1080/14647893.2020.1780206.

"How Did K-Pop Conquer the World?" *BBC*, https://www.bbc.com/culture/article/20190529-how-did-k-pop-conquer-the-world.

Jean-Philippe, McKenzie. "What Is TikTok's 'Renegade' Challenge? All About the Viral Dance." *The Oprah Magazine*, 20 February 2020, https://www.oprahmag.com/entertainment/a30626080/what-is-the-renegade-challenge-tiktok/#:~:text=After%20learning%20the%20quick%20routine,traced%20back%20to%20fall%202019.

Kennedy, Melanie. "'If the Rise of the TikTok Dance and E-girl Aesthetic Has Taught Us Anything, It's That Teenage Girls Rule the Internet Right Now': TikTok Celebrity, Girls and the Coronavirus Crisis." *European Journal of Cultural Studies*, vol. 23, no. 6, 2020, pp. 1069–1076. *SAGE Journals*, https://doi.org/10.1177/1367549420945341.

"Kill This Love." Directed by Seo Hyun-seung, *YouTube*, uploaded by BLACKPINK, 4 April 2019, https://www.youtube.com/watch?v=2S24-y0Ij3Y.

Kim, Suk-Young. *K-pop Live: Fans, Idols, and Multimedia Performance*. Stanford UP, 2018.

Klug, Daniel. "'It Took Me Almost 30 Minutes to Practice This.' Performance and Production Practices in Dance Challenge Videos on TikTok." *arXiv*, 2020. https://arxiv.org/abs/2008.13040. PDF download, presentation from NCA 106th Annual Convention: Communication at the Crossroads.

Kowal, Rebekah J. *Dancing the World Smaller: Staging Globalism in Mid-century America*. Oxford UP, 2020.

Kowal, Rebekah J. "Review of *Choreographing the Folk: The Dance Stagings of Zora Neale Hurston*, by Anthea Kraut." *Dance Research Journal*, vol. 43, no. 1, summer 2011, pp. 103–105.

Kwan, SanSan. "Performing a Geography of Asian America: The Chop Suey Circuit." *TDR/The Drama Review*, vol. 55, no. 1, 2011, pp. 120–136.

Laos, Robert Rene. *Social Media and Its Effects in the Commercial Dance World.* 2019. University of California, Irvine, PhD Dissertation. eScholarship, https://escholarship.org/uc/item/6dj8x3wp.

Li, Zihao, et al. "Mobile Technology in Dance Education: A Case Study of Three Canadian High School Dance Programs." *Research in Dance Education* vol. 19, no. 2, 2018, pp. 183–196. *Taylor and Francis Online*, https://doi.org/10.1080/14647893.2017.1370449.

Lorenz, Taylor. "The Original Renegade. A 14-Year-Old in Atlanta Created One of the Biggest Dances on the Internet. But Nobody Really Knows That." *The New York Times*, 13 February 2020, https://www.nytimes.com/2020/02/13/style/the-original-renegade.html.

Mainwaring, Madison. "The Death of the American Dance Critic. Why Are There So Few Mainstream Outlets Covering the Art Form?" *The Atlantic*, 6 August 2015, https://www.theatlantic.com/entertainment/archive/2015/08/american-dance-critic/399908/.

Malnig, Julie. "Athena Meets Venus: Visions of Women in Social Dance in the Teens and Early 1920s." *Dance Research Journal*, vol. 31, no. 2, 1999, pp. 34–62.

Malnig, Julie. "Introduction." In *Ballroom, Boogie, Shimmy Sham, Shake: A Social and Popular Dance Reader*, edited by Julie Malnig, U of Illinois P, 2009, pp. 1–18.

Manning, Susan. *Modern Dance, Negro Dance: Race in Motion.* U of Minnesota P, 2004.

Marshall, Wayne. "Social Dance in the Age of (Anti-)Social Media: *Fortnite*, Online Video, and the Jook at a Virtual Crossroads." *Journal of Popular Music Studies*, vol. 31, no. 4, 2019, pp. 3–15. https://doi.org/10.1525/jpms.2019.31.4.3.

Martin, Carol. "Reclaiming the Real: Introduction." *TDR/The Drama Review*, vol. 61, no. 4, 2017, p. 8. *Project Muse*, https://muse.jhu.edu/article/677823.

McLuhan, Marshall. "The Medium is the Message." In *Media and Cultural Studies: Keyworks*, edited by Meenakshi Gigi Durham and Douglas M. Kellner, Wiley-Blackwell, 2006, pp. 107–116.

Miller, Kiri. *Playable Bodies: Dance Games and Intimate Media.* Oxford UP, 2017.

Murphy, Siobhan. "Screendance Portraiture: Truth, Transaction, and Seriality in *52 Portraits*." *Dance Research Journal*, vol. 52, no. 3, 2020, pp. 42–57. *Cambridge Core*, https://doi.org/10.1017/S0149767720000376.

Norman, Kyra, and Marisa Zanotti. "Editorial: Expanded Screendance." *The International Journal of Screendance*, vol. 11, 2020, pp. 1–3. http://dx.doi.org/10.18061/ijsd.v11i0.7967.

Oh, Chuyun. "From Seoul to Copenhagen: Migrating K-Pop Cover Dance and Performing Diasporic Youth in Social Media." *Dance Research Journal*, vol. 52, no. 1, 2020, pp. 20–32. *Cambridge Core*, https://doi.org/10.1017/S0149767720000030.

Oh, Chuyun. "Identity Passing in Intercultural Performance of K-pop Cover Dance." *Journal of Intercultural Communication Research*, vol. 49, no. 5, 2020, pp. 472–483. *Taylor and Francis Online*, https://doi.org/10.1080/17475759.2020.1803103.

Oh, Chuyun. "The Politics of the Dancing Body: Racialized and Gendered Femininity in K-pop." In *The Korean Wave: Korean Popular Culture in Global Context*, edited by Yasue Kuwahara, Palgrave Macmillan, 2014, pp.53–81.

"Quang Đăng x LIFEDANCE— Vũ Nông Dân (Official M/V)." *YouTube*, uploaded by QUANG ĐĂNG, 20 April 2018, https://www.youtube.com/watch?v=WUW-XUflShc.

"Quang Đăng x LIFEDANCE—Vũ Nông Dân 2 (Official M/V)." *YouTube*, uploaded by QUANG ĐĂNG, 17 Jan. 2019, https://www.youtube.com/watch?v=-iACJWDTq8k.

Reason, Matthew, and Dee Reynolds. "Special Issue Editorial: Screen Dance Audiences— Why Now?" *Participations: International Journal of Audience Research*, vol. 7, no. 2, 2010. https://www.participations.org/Volume%207/Issue%202/special/introduction.htm.

Rosenberg, Douglas, ed. *The Oxford Handbook of Screendance Studies*. Oxford UP, 2016.

Said, Edward W. *Orientalism*. Vintage P, 1979.

Salvato, Nick. "Out of Hand: YouTube Amateurs and Professionals." *TDR/The Drama Review*, vol. 53, no. 3, 2009, 67–83. *MIT Press Direct*, https://doi.org/10.1162/dram. 2009.53.3.67.

Sao Việt. "Quang Đăng: Before 'the Hand Wash Dance,' [I Had] 10 Years of Sweat and Blood on the Dance Floor." *VTC News*, 7 July 2020, https://vtc.vn/quang-dang-truoc-vu-dieu-rua-tay-la-10-nam-do-mo-hoi-va-ca-mau-tren-san-nhay-ar556303.html.

Saul, Roger. "KevJumba and the Adolescence of YouTube." *Educational Studies*, vol. 46, no. 5, 2010, pp. 457–477. *Taylor and Francis Online*, https://doi.org/10.1080/00131946. 2010.510404.

Savigliano, Marta Elena. "Worlding Dance and Dancing Out There in the World." In *Worlding Dance*, edited by Susan Leigh Foster, Palgrave Macmillan, 2009, pp. 163–190.

Schechner, Richard. "The Big Issues and the Happy Few." *TDR/The Drama Review*, vol. 48, no. 2, 2004, pp. 6–8. *JSTOR*, https://www.jstor.org/stable/4488545.

Scolieri, Paul. "Global/Mobile: Re-Orienting Dance and Migration Studies." *Dance Research Journal*, vol. 40, no. 2, winter 2008, pp. v–xx. *Cambridge Core*, https://doi.org/ 10.1017/S0149767700000346.

Shtern, Jeremy, et al. "Social Media Influence: Performative Authenticity and the Relational Work of Audience Commodification in the Philippines." *International Journal of Communication*, vol. 13, 2019, pp. 1939–1958.

Strapagiel, Lauren. "Here's Why People Can't Stop Watching Those Bella Poarch TikTok's." *BuzzFeed*, 1 Oct. 2020, https://www.buzzfeednews.com/article/laurenstrapa giel/heres-why-those-bella-poarch-tiktoks-are-so-damn-addictive.

Thiel-Stern, Shayla. *From the Dance Hall to Facebook: Teen Girls, Mass Media, and Moral Panic in the United States, 1905–2010*. U of Massachusetts P, 2014.

Thompson, James and Richard Schechner. "Why 'Social Theatre'?" *TDR/The Drama Review*, vol. 48, no. 3, autumn 2004, pp. 11–16. *JSTOR*, https://www.jstor.org/stable/ 4488567.

Van Dijck, José and Thomas Poell. "Understanding Social Media Logic." *Media and Communication*, vol. 1, no. 1, 2013, pp. 2–14. *COGITATIO*, https://doi.org/10.17645/mac. v1i1.70.

Wang, Amy X. "How K-Pop Conquered the West." *Rolling Stone*, 21 Aug. 2018, https://www. rollingstone.com/music/music-features/bts-kpop-albums-bands-global-takeover-707139/.

Wang, Kaitlyn. "How a Coronavirus Safety-themed Dance Took the World by Storm, According to the TikTok Star Who Created It." *Business Insider*, 26 March 2020, http s://www.businessinsider.com/coronavirus-song-dance-wash-hands-quang-dang-2020-3.

Weisbrod, Alexis A. "Defining Dance, Creating Commodity: The Rhetoric of *So You Think You Can Dance*." In *The Oxford Handbook of Dance and the Popular Screen*, edited by Melissa Blanco Borelli, Oxford UP, 2014, pp. 320–334.

Wong, Yutian. *Choreographing Asian America*. Wesleyan UP, 2010.

Wright, John Henry. "The Origin of Plato's Cave." *Harvard Studies in Classical Philology*, vol. 17, 1906, pp. 131–142. *JSTOR*, https://doi.org/10.2307/310313.

Zenenga, Praise. "Power and the Body: Revisiting Dance and Theatre Aesthetic of Resistance in the Academy." *Congress on Research in Dance Conference Proceedings*, vol. 2011, spring 2011, 65–69. *Cambridge Core*, https://doi.org/10.1017/S0149767711000313.

Zulli, Diana, and David James Zulli. "Extending the Internet Meme: Conceptualizing Technological Mimesis and Imitation Publics on the TikTok Platform." *New Media and Society*, December 2020. *SAGE Journals*, https://doi.org/10.1177/1461444820983603.

2

THE EVOLUTION OF K-POP DANCE FROM THE 1980S TO THE 2020S

This chapter provides a conceptual framework on the evolution of K-pop dance from the 1980s to 2020s based on preliminary case studies. In 2021, SM Entertainment released a "Remastering Project" in collaboration with YouTube to digitalize and restore old K-pop MVs from the 1990s. Thanks to generational accumulation, K-pop has been established as a distinctive dance genre taught and performed worldwide in the 2020s. Tracing the evolution of K-pop dance, this chapter sheds light on the hidden efforts of dancers over decades.

K-pop dance history is a history of people – performance directors who failed in their idol careers, trainees who survived harsh competitions, backup and street dancers who learned dance from nightclubs to stage choruses, and finally, K-pop fan dancers whose audacious dream and talented engagements shape the versatile, transnational K-pop dance today. Describing stylistic, aesthetical, and structural progresses of K-pop dance over four decades, the chapter clarifies its defining characteristics and contextualizes how it has been established an independent, distinctive dance genre in the 2020s.

K-pop dance continues evolving, along with idols' careers, stretching over decades. The distinctions across decades can overlap. K-pop is a part of the long tradition of Korean music, and not all K-pop is dance music. This chapter focuses on dance music only and does not address other genres, such as Korean ballads, indie, rock, and metal. Naming K-pop singers as dancers does not aim to negate the musical aspects of K-pop. Instead, it seeks to illuminate K-pop dance as an independent genre of music, such as salsa, tango, and hip-hop.

This book is not an encyclopedia, so only select cases are addressed that mark notable choreographic progress. I analyse approximately two artists/groups in each decade and their point choreographies in their hit songs. In addition to news media coverage published in Korean and English, I gather visual data from official music videos and live performances aired at major music programs: MBC's *Saturday Night Music Show, Inkigayo Best 50, Music Core*, KBS' *Night Music Show, Top 10*, and SBS' *Inkigayo*, all available online. I translate Korean to English. The book

DOI: 10.4324/9781003212188-4

uses Western name order, except K-pop idols whose names are often used as proper nouns. For K-pop idols, I use Korean name order (last name and first name) and their stage names.

The 1980s: Broadcasting Dance Troupes

Before the 1980s, Western social dance and music shaped early Korean popular culture. Since Korea's independence from Japan in 1945 and the Korean War from 1950 to 1953, a neo-colonial relationship was built between Korea and the US, and Westernization became a symbol of modernity (Kim and Choi). The South Korean film *Madame Freedom* (1956) represents the turbulent era where Western social dances became popular among "modern girls" who were stigmatized as promiscuous and dangerous. Western social dances that became popular included the waltz, foxtrot, cha-cha-cha, tango, mambo, swing, boogie-woogie, and samba in the 1950s and later the Twist, disco, and pop songs, mainly imported by the US military from the 1960s to the 1970s. Although these dances are often categorized under the umbrella term of "Western" dances, many of them have African, Cuban, Brazilian, and Latin American roots. The Kim Sisters were one of the first Korean-born female dancer-singer groups with a successful career in the 1950s and 1960s US. Choi Seung-hee (1911–1969) was another "modern girl," globally renowned dancer, and feminist activist who presented a combination of Western and Korean dances on her world tour.

In the 1980s, locally renowned dancer-singers paved the way of dance music. American and African American pop music inspired the initial formation of K-pop dance. Kim Wan-sun and Park Nam Jung were called "Korea's Madonna" and "Korea's Michael Jackson," respectively. The popularity of idol cultures across France, Canada, Latin America, and Japan, such as Menudo and New Kids On The Block, also influenced K-pop. The boy group So Bang Cha (meaning "fire truck" in Korean) was modeled on the huge idol culture in the 1980s, and their dances resonate with the athletic university dance team culture in Korea. Their hit song "Story of Last Night" (1987) presents a butt-kick jump, tumbling, and side-split jump and was inspired by athletic, acrobatic, and gymnastic routines.

These pioneers in the 1980s departed from *trot*. *Trot* is traditional Korean pop music developed since the 1920s. It integrates *gugak, pansori* (both are traditional Korean music), and Western folk-pop (Son). It is known for its catchy rhythms and sentimental lyrics and is beloved by working-class citizens. Despite the rising popularity of dance music, *ttan-tta-la* was a derogatory term to describe dancer-singers as frivolous entertainers, reflecting their low status in the 1980s.

The 1980s were the heyday of performing arts troupes at broadcasting companies such as KBS (Korean Broadcasting System), MBC (Munhwa Broadcasting Corporation), and SBS (Seoul Broadcasting System). The troupes consisted of dancers, an orchestra, and choir teams. Many K-pop singers began their careers as chorus backup dancers. Park Nam Jung was first a choir member at MBC where he honed his vocal and performance skills. Dancers in the troupes were professional but also quite general. They performed jazz, aerobics, ballet, modern dance, gymnastics, traditional Korean dance, and more. Backup dancing at the companies was a full-time, competitive, and professional career, and they were paid as much as business workers at conglomerates. Only one out of two hundred were accepted ("Broadcasting Arts Troupe"). Audition participants were expected to have dance training either from college or private institutions, and once accepted, they learned traditional Korean music, drum, modern dance, and ballet.

Although they performed nearly five shows per day on televised music programs and concerts in the mid-1980s ("Broadcasting Arts Troupe"), the popularity of backup dancing declined with the rise of dancer-singers lip-syncing and having their own backup dance teams. For example, the MBC troupe had nearly two-hundred-fifty members in the 1980s but was reduced to around forty in the early 2000s, many of whom are now part-time ("Broadcasting Arts Troupe"). KBS closed its troupe in 2016. Today, some broadcasting troupes remain but mostly perform at live *trot* music shows, concerts, or amateur music festivals for the elderly, unlike K-pop which targets a young global audience. Yet, the genealogy of *broadcasting dance* continues in the 2020s in conservatory arts schools and community colleges.

In the early 2000s, as a freshman (and a proud dance major), I liked to dance in a nightclub in Gangnam and Hongdae in Seoul. My friends and I often entered the club as early as 6 p.m., when it was free, danced until dawn and headed to our morning class right away, wearing sweaty and perhaps smelly outfits and smudged makeup that did not fit a college classroom. I enjoyed the liberation in dance clubs. Compared to the strict discipline in a dance studio, I felt free and better enjoyed the movements of my body without the feeling of censorship. People often asked us in the clubs if they could see us on television, assuming that we worked for broadcasting companies. The broadcasting performing arts troupes were the primary image of dancers in Korea until the 2000s, except for ballet or traditional Korean folk dance.

Despite its high visibility, backup dancing choreography was not an integral part of performance. It was often made independently from singers' dance routines. Backup dancers often needed to prepare for and perform on multiple stages for different singers in one day. A KBS backup dancer said that program directors wanted to have as many backup dancers as possible for a song, and dancers struggled to memorize different dance routines for a couple of different songs within a short amount of time. A KBS choreographer said that "other dance companies practice for about six months to complete a choreography for a song, but we have to practice ten or more songs and choreographies a week" (Shin, "The KBS"). Most of the backup dancing routines were relatively simple. They largely faced front, stood in two rows, and barely changed their formations throughout the songs. There was hardly any direct contact or between the dancers and singers. This separated structure implied that the backup dance could be easily replaceable as a generic stage prop that could match with and be recycled for other stages. Indeed, performances of Kim Wan-sun's "The Dance in Rhythm" (1987–88) present different choreographic variations, although some main scenes remain similar. Her backup dance choreographies dramatically differ in formation, movement style, and the number of dancers based on the music program.

Choreographies in the 1980s were loose and improvisational, but they were also the precursors of *point choreography*, the main feature of K-pop dance. Like PSY's "horse dance" in "Gangnam Style" (2012), point choreography is usually situated in the chorus line with a repetitive, addictive, and simple movement. It is front-driven, picturesque, clear-cut, sharp, and speedy and emphasizes vertical lines and clear formations for a two-dimensional screen. In the 1980s, singers blended Western and Korean cultures, often teaching themselves. Park Nam Jung said that "because there was no training system or place to learn dance, I practiced dance in nightclubs and learned by watching Western movies" (E. Lee). This mediated dance education resonates with Vietnamese dance influencer Quang Đăng in Chapter 1, who taught himself with limited educational resources when growing up by watching Western movies. Singers in the 1980s developed iconic dance scenes, such as Park Nam Jung's "L dance crazy" from "Missing You" (1989), which he improvisationally choreographed during a rehearsal (E. Lee). It consists of his neck repetitively moving side to side, while his flattened hand moves horizontally underneath his chin and then vertically next to his ear, drawing the shapes of Korean characters ㄱ and ㄴ. Kim Wan-sun often performed Michael Jackson's "moonwalk" and the "rabbit dance" popularized by Bobby Brown and MC Hammer in the 1990s ("From the Legendary Moonwalk Dance"). In a live show at MBC's *Saturday Night Music Show* in 1988, Kim and Park presented a "robot dance," like a breakdance that imitates a robot's mechanical movement, set to *Samul nori*, traditional Korean percussion music.

Kim Wan-sun was in the first generation of the idol training system. She came from a dance family, received relatively systematic training from an early age, and performed internationally. Han Baek-hee, arguably Korea's first female manager and producer, is Kim's aunt. Han was a singer performing Latin and American pop songs for the US military in Korea in the 1970s. Kim is also the great-grand-daughter of Han Sung-Joon, the father of modern Korean dance and a master of *pansori*, traditional Korean opera, and who also taught Koran dance to Choi Seung-hee. Kim spent three years learning dancing, singing, composition, musical instruments, and foreign languages until she debuted at 18 years old. Kim's career inspired the SM agency's initial training model for BoA and the global idol business discussed in the next section (J. Park).

The 1990s: The First Generation of K-pop Idols

In the 1990s, idol dance music became popularized with Seo Taiji and Boys, a male trio that debuted in 1992, consisting of Seo Taiji, Yang Hyun-suk, and Lee Juno. Before their debut, Seo was a member of a heavy metal rock band. Yang, who became the founder of YG Entertainment, was a member of Park Nam Jung's dance team called "Park Nam Jung and Friends." Lee Juno was a member of Kim Wan-sun's backup dance group called "Kim Wan-sun and Shadow." Yang and Lee were both well-known street dancers at the Moon Night Club in Itaewon, Seoul, a district previously known for attracting tourists, immigrants, and US soldiers. The club was the hub of street and hip-hop dancing in the early 1990s.

As skilled dancers, Yang and Lee choreographed for the group, and their presence replaced backup dancers, while Seo composed the songs. They elevated the status of *ttan-tta-la* to "idols" who created their own music and dance. Seo was known for his androgynous look, trendy fashion, and musicality. The group as the "President of Culture," advocated political aptness for teens around issues such as government censorship, the education system, school violence, and the North and South Korea division. The imagery of resistive teens talking about social issues has continued since then, as seen in groups such as H.O.T., EXO, and BTS, whose role models include Seo Taiji and Boys. The group integrated the sentimental melody from Korean ballads, *trot*, traditional sounds, contemporary R&B, rap, metal, hip-hop, rock, techno, and more (Shim; Jin).

Seo Taiji and Boys established the K-pop dance formula for music videos. With the increasing popularity of music videos, dance became visualized, and music moved from radio to television. When legendary *trot* and folk-pop singer Cho Yong-pil's first music video "The Empty Sky" (1985) premiered, the music video was not yet an independent genre. Choreography for music videos barely existed. Kim Wan-sun presented her song "The Dance in Rhythm" as a "dance video music" or "video music" (*yeongsang-eum-ag*) at a 1988 live *Saturday Night Music Show*, which was nearly unprecedented. Surrounded by theatrical installations, such as mirrors, walls, and mannequins, she dances across the space, interacting with backup dancers and using stage props, showcasing modern dance routines integrating dance and lyrics like in musical theatre.

Seo Taiji and Boys' debut song "I Know" (1992) was presented in a dance-centric music video with point choreography, like the "tornado dance" made by Yang and Lee where they nimbly switch their stomping feet in one spot. Yang and Lee's breakdancing during the chorus appears improvisational and changes depending on the music programs they performed on. Yet, the "tornado dance" was always fixed with a clear formation of the three. The song structure consists of a rap intro, vocal melody, and catchy chorus. The "I Know" music video set the formula for the K-pop music video: plain backgrounds that highlight singers' dancing, cinematic settings that match with lyrics, camera work that makes the choreography stand out, and camera angles and editing that make the singer's face appear more attractive (Ki-yoon Kim).

In the 1980s, lip-syncing was common due to imperfect sound technology. However, it was not until the 1990s that lip-syncing became criticized with the rise of dancer-singers. In an interview, Seo Taiji responded to the criticism:

> Unlike the prevalent belief, lip-syncing is quite common in Western dance music. Michael Jackson often performs even without a mic. This means that the focus of the stage is a dance over music. Our dance routines are so

challenging that we need oxygen masks during our concert when we come backstage to change our clothes before the next song. Singing a song is not our only responsibility.

(Kang)

The next generations further expanded his vision as a performer.

In the mid-1990s, the three major agencies, SM Entertainment, YG Entertainment, and JYP Entertainment (SM, YG, JYP, hereafter) were established. The first generation of K-pop idols continued the music video convention Seo Taiji and Boys established. SM's boy group H.O.T.'s "Candy" (1996) and girl group S.E.S.' "I Am Your Girl" (1997) popularized the idol culture that inspired the local youth from fashion to lifestyle. SM director Lee Soo-man systematically formed H.O.T. based on surveys on teen girls' preferences for idols. Kim Wan-sun said that although her training was arduous in the 1980s, actual dance practices mainly consisted of improvisation where her aunt turned on the music and asked her to dance to it (Jisoo Kim). In the 1990s, SM provided more systematic training but still did not have a proper studio yet. The dance studio was in a residential house without a mirror, so H.O.T had to practice at night so that they could use the window as a mirror ("'Singerella' Moon Hee-joon").

S.E.S. received years of training like H.O.T., and they were fluent in Korean, Japanese, and English to target all of Asia. Their debut song "I Am Your Girl" (1997) was choreographed by H.O.T.'s Moon Hee-joon. The point choreography consists of swinging their arms up, down, and to the side, drawing a big circle with their arms, and lightly stamping four times to the left and right. Their hips initiate each jump by tilting their hips and heads in the same direction. Their heads bend to the side and their tilted hips create an arch on their waists, highlighting a feminine line of their bodies. Their bright, innocent, and animated images and light movements created a "fairy syndrome" among teens.

S.E.S. and H.O.T. opened the era of K-pop dance that makes imitation desirable and is imitable in its form and style. They set the prototypes of gender, such as the innocent "schoolgirls" and "schoolboys" images that continued into the 2020s. They showcased a fixed formation, clear characters, iconic movements, and advanced camera work that moves along with the dancers. Backup dancing was fixed too. The backup dancing to S.E.S.' "I Am Your Girl" consists of the same dancers, movements, and outfits that match those of the singers throughout the different music programs.

The 2000s: Cultural Technology and Training Systems for Singing Entertainers

In the 2000s, the three agencies, SM, YM, and JYP, established their unique styles. *Gayo* was used to refer to Korean popular music and songs. The term *K-pop* became popularized in the mid-2000s with idol groups (Shin, "Reconsidering" 106). SM founder Lee Soo-man was a former singer. He majored in computer science at prestigious universities in Korea and the US. Typically, SM is known for neat, organized, and eye-catching performances by perfectly polished, doll-like idols; they are often cited as creating "the textbook" of K-pop. Examples are Girls' Generation, SHINee, Super Junior, BoA, EXO, NCT, Red Velvet, and Aespa.

Yang Hyun-suk from Seo Taiji and Boys established YG, which is known for its virtuosic adaptations of hip-hop and the artists' strong, rebellious, and individualized styles. Artists include Jinusean, 1TYM, and BIGBANG, 2EN1, Winner, PSY, iKON, and Blackpink. Compared to SM's synchronous group dances, YG emphasizes "play." YG choreographer Lee Jae Wook said that they make dance as if it is "play," like they are having a dance party for fun. To do so, the actual performance is thoroughly and systematically calculated, he added ("Interviews with K-POP's Hidden Protagonists: Choreographer Lee Jae-Wook & PD Ahn Joon-Young"). Founded by dancer-singer and songwriter Park J. Y., JYP generally presents R&B, EDM, ballads, and dance pop music and often emphasizes bold individuality and sensuality. They represent Wonder Girls, Miss A, and 2AM, 2PM, ITZY, and Stray Kids represent JYP. As a renowned dancer-singer in the 1980s, J. Y. Park still performs onstage, often collaborating with his former idols such as Rain in "Switch To Me" (2020) and Sunmi in "When We Disco" (2020).

The major agencies more firmly established their training systems and expanded their market across Asia. Idols were advertised with their MV teasers played on billboards, like blockbuster movies, from Tokyo to New York. SM director Lee presented the innovative idea of *singing entertainers* who embraced lip-syncing as a performance technique. In an interview with *The Korea Herald* in 2005, he highlighted *cultural technology* (CT), a market-driven business model for rising stars. He said dancer-singers could blur language barriers, and "the biggest stars come from the biggest markets," which meant Asia (Seo). His vision was fully actualized in the 2020s with the rising global K-pop cover dancers who lip-sync songs as a part of the choreography, as explored from Chapters 4 to 6. K-pop idols have become the idols of the global youth culture, as Asia has become the rising force of the global economy.

SM created the prototype of SM Music Performance (SMP), a genre of professionally trained artists who can sing live *while* dancing effortlessly. BoA epitomizes the prodigy training system. She started her training when she was twelve years old and debuted in 2000 when she was fifteen with unquestionable skills in dancing, singing, and speaking in English and Japanese. SM spent $3 billion to raise BoA, nearly all of its income made from H.O.T. (Seo). She became "the Star of Asia" with massive success in Japan. Some Japanese audiences did not know that she was actually Korean. Indeed, BoA said she went to Japan as a J-pop singer to compete with Japanese singers (Shin, "Reconsidering" 107).

The K-pop training system is often criticized and referred to as a "factory" system. Its discussion in this chapter is not to diminish the human rights issues but to illuminate specificities of its physical education. A strict, systematic bodily discipline from childhood is essential to raise professionals in a field that requires the development of physical strength, versatility, endurance, and flexibility from an early age. Sometimes, no pain, no gain. For example, the youngest Olympic medalist is 13 years old. In the US, children start playing football between the ages of three and five years old in preparation for professional careers. Albeit not entirely free from the pressure of parents or society, as long as idols choose to be idols, infrastructural support, such as employment after retirement and mental and physical health care, might help those young dancers whose dreams are bigger than the physical pain. The rhetoric of "protecting" K-pop idols can be dangerous because it can neglect the dignity and agency of individuals and even of cultural values, even if those values do not match with the Western idea of democracy. Women do not always need men to protect and open the door for them. Muslim women wearing hijab do not always need Western feminists for their liberation.

After several years of prodigy training, BoA's "No. 1" (2002) presents artistically and athletically expressive, powerful, and energetic routines with a fixed formation of the same eight backup dancers. Some of her dance is literal and gestural but also barely flirtatious, which continues the tradition from the dances of her labelmates S.E.S. Her sporty legs and firm core provide a strong foundation for her dancing. Her voice is strong even when she is dancing energetically. She belongs to a genealogy of female soloists, such as Uhm Jung Hwa and Park Jee Yun in the 1990s, Lee Hyori in the 2000s, and Sunmi and HyunA in the 2010s.

If BoA represents the development of female soloists, Rain represents that for male soloists. Starting his training at JYP, he is known for his duality. He has a fit, tall body that exhibits masculine movements, such as swaggering punches, hip-hop, and vigorous jumping and breathing. He also presents an undulating torso, body rolls, and caressing hands with delicate arms. His facial choreography, such as his sweet smile and winking, along with his androgynous, youthful face and elongated eyes, further creates a juxtaposition. His "Rainism" (2008) embodies evocative sounds such as breathing and exclamations of "ha" while dancing. Based on hip-hop, martial arts, and boxing-inspired movements, the choreography is sophisticated in terms of levels (from kneeling down to jumping), speed (from the slow gestural salute to fast, nimble jumping feet), and formations (from narrow rows to a big circle). With his backup dancing experience, Rain no longer used backup dancers as a mere backdrop but placed them as a major part of the choreography. His backup dancers are Rain's dance crew, "Wild Rabbit," who collaborated with and even taught Rain for his performances and who have their own fandom ("Rain's"). Each member has a distinctive fashion and movement style, and they often perform in duets and even in front of Rain, which is unusual for backup dancers. The point choreography in "Rainism" is called *stick dance*. He brings a fluorescent light stick, called a *magic stick*. He taps the stick, jumps around, adroitly rotates the stick in the air, and twirls it detached from his hands like a magic show. The backup dancers surround him, impelling their arms downward towards Rain. He places the stick between his legs, shoves his shoulders left to right, as if evading a bullet in *The Matrix,* undulates his body, thrusts his pelvis toward the stick, and gradually and rhythmically bends his back backward, shortening himself, like in a limbo dance. Due to the sexual connotations, his performance evoked controversy over censorship (Jung-ju Kim).

Rain elevated flirtation into a formally fixed movement with virtuosity. He choreographed sexuality and represented the idea of sexiness via sexually suggestive but systematically practiced, demanding movements. Through "Rainism," dancers can learn and practice various uses of personae, sexuality, facial choreography, spaces, levels, speeds, and breath. "Rainism" is in the classical repertoire for boy idols, like the example of BTS' cover dance of it at the 2016 MBC *Gayo Daejejeon*.

Interestingly, BoA tended to avoid explicit sex appeal, while Rain was the opposite. Female dancers can face a stronger stigma of promiscuity and presenting a less sexual choreography can be a safer strategy for promoting them as respected artists. Female sexuality is marketable, but it can also negate their serious dance and vocal skills. Contrarily, Rain's sexuality does not necessarily contradict his artistry, although the performance of "Rainism" received criticism.

BoA is not the only outcome of K-pop prodigy education. BIGBANG debuted in 2006 is known for their musicality and popularity and as charismatic artists who make their own music. BIGBANG's G-Dragon spent nearly eleven years as a trainee. His career started at the age of six as a group member of Little Roo'Ra, like today's cover dance group. Roo'Ra was a famous dance group in the 1990s. Inspired by the Wu-Tang Clan, he became the youngest rapper in Korea at thirteen years old, participating in the Korean hip-hop album *Flex* in 2001. Another member Taeyang trained for approximately six years, starting his career as child rapper Little Jinusean in 2001 and performing for Jinusean's "A-Yo" (2002) on stage. BANGBANG's "Bang Bang Bang" (2015) has a point choreography, but the entire performance is filled with emotionally intense facial expressions, improvisational-looking, stylistic gestures made along with the singing, and expressive body language that communicates with the camera.

From the Mid to the Late 2000s: The K-pop Body, Synchronized Group Dance, and Gestural Point Choreography

From the mid to late 2000s, backup dancers gradually disappeared as the large size of idol group members came to fully occupy the stage. Idols set gender prototypes: either innocent schoolgirls or boys, the seductive, sassy "girl crush," or the rebellious, powerful boy groups. Boy groups more freely explored from effeminate features called "flower boys," to typical masculinity called "beast idols" and cross-dressing without much criticism, which denotes the representational privilege of men in a patriarchy (C. Oh and D. Oh; C. Oh, "Types"). Contrarily, this gendered dichotomy restricts the spectrum of girl groups' dances more so than boy groups. K-pop boy groups' dance routines are often called "the most dangerous" and "hardest," but those of girl groups are usually limited to being "cute."

My previous research (C. Oh, "Politics" and *K-popscape*) examined the gender representations of SM's Girls' Generation and YG's 2NE1. Girls' Generation epitomized "good girls": balletic, white, heterosexual, and "hypergirlish" femininity. 2NE1 member CL presented an image of a strong "bad girl" inspired by third-world womanhood, sisterhood, and hip-hop. Albeit with variations, this "good" (bright, innocent, chaste, and submissive) versus "bad" (dark, fearless, defiant, and sexually expressive) dichotomy continues in the 2020s. TWICE, GFriend, and Oh My Girl for the former, and BLACKPINK for the latter are examples.

The K-pop Body

In the 2000s, the ideal "K-pop body" was established. Each dance genre tends to have a preferred body, from functionality (muscle type, body size, weight, and height) to visuality (age, skin, race, and gender), reflecting cultural stereotypes and roots. Different ideal bodies are commonly imagined in hip-hop, ballet, tango, and ballroom dance. Typically, the K-pop body is juvenile and thin with a pale East Asian skin tone. These characteristics highlight the clear line of dance on the two-dimensional screen, along with dancers' racial and ethnic ambiguity, flawlessly polished faces, and transnational, ageless, and cosmopolitan looks. The sleek, artificial K-pop body, from their faces to legs, is so strong that it even affects the increasing plastic surgery tourism to Korea and "K-beauty" products across the globe. The lead dancers of Girls' Generation's Yoon-ah, and SHINee's Taemin, emblematized the establishment of the classical K-pop body.

As the K-pop body has become standardized in its visual aesthetics, K-pop dance has become less about movement and more about the "right look." Girls' Generation's bodies *are* the dance. Like the *corps de ballet* in the classical ballet *Swan Lake*, which is celebrated and criticized for its monolithic bodies, the power of Girls' Generation's dance came from their homogenized collective bodies as one visual identity – slender, light-skinned, and youthful bodies, elongated legs, and mostly long, straight hair, albeit each with distinctive faces.

A male collegiate cover dancer in California told me that some K-pop dance looks simple and is relatively easy to learn, but it is nearly impossible to "look as good as" K-pop idols. As Chapter 1 theorizes, the body is the capital on social media. Social media seems to promote the "free" and "authentic me" under the name of the *meconomy*, me plus economy, for the MZ generation. Yet, competitive, neoliberal capitalism often haunts self-love and identifies selfhood through material consumption or production, including the creation of the perfect body, selfie photos, and dance videos. K-pop fans, too, are not free from the pressure of being noticed on social media with sleek, "Instagrammable" bodies.

The Synchronous Group Dance and Point Choreography

Since the mid-2000s, idols standardized the formula of K-pop dance: synchronized group dance called *knife-like*, meaning as clear and precise as a knife cut. Girls' Generation, the "textbook" of K-pop girl groups, exemplified synchronized dance. They each received an average of five years of training, starting around twelve or thirteen years old, in vocals, singing, acting, and speaking foreign languages until they debuted at sixteen to eighteen years old. They practiced "Into the New World" (2007) for a year so that they could match "every 'angle,' from the fingertips to the stride length" (Moon).

The synchronized group dance can maximize the effect of point choreography. Initially debuting with nine members, Girls' Generation's merit lies in its harmony rather than individuality. Performance director Shim Jae Won said, "It is rare to see a team made up of several people who move perfectly as one" (Hyun Woo Lee). When they move as a unit, their size can create a holistic effect, and their charm reaches the maximum. As a unit, they advanced intricate floor patterns and formations such as V, reverse V, X, A, heart, and diamond shapes through which all members got a chance to dance at the center, seamlessly switching their spots back and forth, not even turning their backs on stage.

Point choreography has existed since the 1980s, but it clearly became the symbol of K-pop dance in the late 2000s. Son Sung Deuk, BTS' performance director at entertainment company HYBE, mentioned that K-pop is a perfect combination of music, visuals, and (dance) performance. YG's performance director Lee Jae Wook said that Japanese pop songs have cute point choreographies but lack a trendy style, while European pop songs have trendy vibes, but the dance is not clear enough to remember. K-pop combines the strengths of the two: clear point choreography and trendy style ("Interviews with K-POP's Hidden Protagonists: Choreographer Lee Jae-Wook & PD Ahn Joon-Young").

Girls' Generation's "crab dance" in "Gee" (2009) and the "*Jegi chagi* dance," a traditional Korean game similar to hacky sack, in "Tell Me Your Wish (Genie)" (2009) exemplify K-pop point choreography. In the "crab dance," putting their arms akimbo, they pop out their chests four times from the front, diagonally, and to the side; rhythmically bounce and tilt their pelvis to the side, twisting one foot outward; and step to the side, crossing their knees in and out precisely four times and moving their heads side to side like a crab. As all the members move precisely in identical speeds, directions, and spaces, they look like dolls. In the "*Jegi chagi* dance," they draw a semi-circle with their lower legs precisely four times, like a *rond de jambe* in ballet, while their standing legs remain the same. Their upper bodies are also limited to a minimum wave of their shoulders, responding to each circle of the legs and tossing their arms above their heads so that the audience can entirely focus on their lean, mannequin-like legs clad in uniforms.

Gestural Point Choreography

Point choreography gradually evolved into *gestural point choreography*. As K-pop became more dance-centric, dancers needed to attach their feet to the floor in case they needed to sing live, so that their dance would barely affect their singing. Otherwise, gravity would impact their breathing when their feet landed. It is still front-driven and two-dimensional, like point choreography, but has evolved into denser movements, highlighting decorative, sophisticated movements of the waist, arms, chests, fingers, face, necks, shoulders, and hair. It is so detailed that singers use each finger to make different angles and shapes every second. In addition to the emotional intensity delivered via the upper bodies, multiple camera tricks compensate for the flatness with rapid, rhythmical zooms in and out and other various techniques. Point choreography commonly consists of musical–theatre-like storytelling and the use of facial expressions to literally express lyrics. Advanced gestural point choreography focuses on the face, what I call *face dance* in Chapter 1. The face is emotionally intensive, expressive, and vulnerable. Its movements are choreographed, but it can variously appear naïve and sexually suggestive, and it can whimsically change every second. The face is the area that best signals the individuality of dancers. Idols need to stand out when dancing with multiple other idols doing the same dance. They constantly look at the camera with an intense gaze while maintaining their front-portrait at eye level. The emphasis on the upper body generates a limited use of space. All of these traits are a precursor to social media dance, exemplified by the viral dance challenges in the 2020s explored in Chapter 1.

The Innocent Face, Seductive Hips

Gestural point choreography highlights the upper body and thus, divides it from the lower body. François Delsarte argued that the upper body, like the head and torso, expresses mental and emotional spirituality, and the lower body highlights visceral physical feelings (Stebbins). Girls' Generation's upper and lower bodies exemplify such a binary – spirituality versus sensuality – and the "virgin-whore" dichotomy in patriarchy: chaste but sexually available.

In "Gee" (2009), their upper bodies showcase girlish, restricted, and docile gestures and faces that express their intimidation and *aegyo* (cute, affectionate facial and gestural expressions), such as innocent eye contact, winking, and naïve, shy smiles, with plain makeup and long straight hair. They narrowly place their forearms together in front of their mouths with clenched fists, shrinking their chests, as if they feel shy, to cover their faces. Singing "[i]t's so bright, my eyes are blinded," they cheerfully flip their palms back and forth next to their chins, like a child describing the shiny light of a star. Singing "I'm so surprised oh oh oh oh oh," they bend their knees, tilting their heads to the side like a cute, animated character, clenching their fists, bending their wrists upward, and clumsily and quickly twitching and moving their stretched arms up and down to the side as if surprised they do not know what to do. They appear writhing like helpless, intimidated babies or physically incompetent juveniles moving awkwardly. Along with the limited movement, their plain white and gray t-shirts covering their wrists and palms make their bodies appear smaller, covered, and protected and thus, vulnerable and fragile.

However, their lower bodies signal otherwise. Saying "[s]weet scent oh yeah yeah yeah," covering their mouths as if they are shy, they hold their upper bodies immobile. Simultaneously, they push out their hips backward and shake their hips up and down, like a slower version of twerking. Their legs are displayed and extended to the side, nimbly drawing circles on the floor in a seductive way as they undulate their chests and caress their hands on their hips. Their tight, short fluorescent pink, yellow, and green-colored pants and white high-heel, strap ankle boots further contradict their plain long-sleeve shirts. The rubric of the lower-versus upper-body division continues in the 2020. Brave Girls' "Rollin'" (2020), for example, is composed with sensual hip circle moves squatting down on a chair, while their upper bodies remain immobile. They rest their chins on their hands, tilting their heads to the side with innocent, girlish facial expressions.

If Girls' Generation set the standard for K-pop girl groups, SHINee did so for boy groups. Their "Reply" (2008) escalated the "flower boy" sensation, which refers to polished, androgynous, and beautiful young men with bright, soft, and romantic personae. Contrarily, their "Ring Ding Dong" (2009) and "Lucifer" (2010) present intense, dark, vigorous, and sharp movements in futuristic settings. In "Everybody" (2013), SHINee wear military-inspired uniforms that enhance the artificial clarity of their dance as child toy robots. The video is so dance-centric that its climax is not a high-pitched voice but a "windmill spinning" dance scene. Everyone moves seamlessly and harmoniously in a domino sequence of a windmill wing. Instead of all members doing the same movement in a knife group dance, they move as one but execute different movements, like Lego pieces being fit together, by creating meticulous and ubiquitous angles and fluctuations, like the thousand-armed Buddha.

The 2010s: Performance Directors and Globalizing the Formula

In the 2010s, former idols returned as "performance directors." They design the entire performance, including choreography, facial expressions, styling, music video concepts, and stage performances. They correct dancers' movements back-stage until the last minutes before the show. Korean American Teddy Park, a former member of 1TYM, which popularized "gangster" US hip-hop in the 1990s, is YG's main producer and performance director.

Shim Jae Won is a performance director at SM, who taught BoA, Girls' Generation, Super Junior, SHINee, and more. He debuted as a member of the boy group Black Beat in 2002, but the group was not successful. He helps the audience "see music":

> I highly appreciate artists who can show music. Some artists make a difference between just listening to their music and listening to them while watching the stage. Through the expression of the body, the taste of the music is also added. The phrase "seeing music" may sound like a contradiction, but we really feel it. It's not necessarily the dance that makes the difference. Maybe it's the intense eyes.
>
> ("Behind the Stage")

In addition to his intuitive insight on visualizing music, he tailors foreign choreographers' works into K-pop based on his hands-on experience as an idol. "Foreign choreographers usually present dances with a strong sense of the dancer. They often do not fit the Korean sentiment. The process of reinterpreting dance is essential," he said. Another former Black Beat member, SM performance director Hwang Sang Hoon also added that he tries to make each character appear more charming in front of the camera ("Behind the Stage").

Performance directors translate a three-dimensional movement made by one dancer in a studio to a two-dimensional gestural point choreography that show-cases multiple dancers' faces and characters for the camera. Shim modifies detailed body angles so that each member shows the most charming individual character-istics during their short solo for the camera, which will help their future career as models or actors after their retirement ("Behind the Stage"). "I am with you as the 10th member of Girls' Generation, the 6th member of TVXQ, and the 14th member of Super Junior," he said (H. Lee). Seeing himself as a part of the idols he teaches, he emphasizes sympathizing offstage as a team, which can lead to a better performance onstage.

While retired idols return as directors, more backup dancers achieve their dream to become idols. Backup dancers shed light on the compositional development as well as the genealogy of K-pop dance. TVXQ's Yunho, Rain, and IZ★ONE's Lee Chae-yeon, Chungha, After School's Kahi, and 9Muses' Kyungri, to name a few, started their careers as backup dancers, learning from previous K-pop singers. BTS' Jungkook and J-Hope danced for 2AM member Jo Kwon's "I'm Da One" (2012). Stray Kids' Lee Know danced in BTS' "Fire" (2016) and "Spring Day" (2017). Currently, BTS has nearly ninety backup dancers (W. Lee), and the size is as big as any professional dance company.

The bigger size of groups does not mean that K-pop dance lost its synchronous group dance. BTS choreographer Sienna Lalau mentioned a "crispy and delicious" clarity of group dance:

> The process of completing the choreography is called "Cleaning." We rehearse for at least 8 hours each day before the performance. If you practice until the details, movements, and lines all match, your body gets tired, and you get injured frequently. But the result is a clean, "crispy and delicious" choreography.
>
> *(K. Kim)*

With the rise of competition dance styles, backup dancing returned to K-pop with multiethnic and multiracial dancers. The size of the backup dance crew can increase the emotional and physical intensity of the choreography.

With the increasing size of groups, the *ending pose* became popular. At the end of the performance, dancers wait until the camera zooms in on each member's face. Their heavy breathing, sweaty faces, and intense eye contact with the camera enthusiastically draws fans in due to the pose's potentially sensual appeal, intimacy, and allusion to the sexual imagination. Dancers' technical skills are advanced and often appear impossible to imitate not only because of their athleticism but also artistry. In "Move" (2017), Taemin does not make large movements but rather writhes in a hyper subtle, nuanced way. Yet, his rich presence itself is dance.

K-pop girl and boy groups in the 2010s replicated the previously successful models, expanding K-pop fandom globally. K-pop became a strategically assembled product, like a gift package, that showcased various charms and ethnic, racial, national, and linguistic identities, as well as talent from acting to fashion, while cultivating composition, choreography, and dance skills. Official English subtitles became widely available on YouTube music videos after once being offered by fans. English in song titles and group names became more common to target global and Western audiences.

SM's EXO continue these conventions at an advanced level. Their debut in 2011 was impressive in terms of the size of the group, initially twelve members, the various ethnic and cultural backgrounds, and an ambitious plan targeting the global stage and Asia. EXO's "Teaser 4_KAI (2) One Take ver" (2011) features the lead dancer, Kai, and his androgynously fluid but sharp and powerful dance solo without singing. The group's perfectly synchronous, articulated, and smooth but strong movements appear like a futuristic machine. SuperM debuted in 2019 consisting of seven members from SM's existing groups SHINee, EXO, NCT 127, and WayV. They also debuted in the US via *The Ellen Show*, where they spoke in English. Despite the groups' unquestionable virtuosic dance and singing skills, because they follow the SM formula too well and too perfectly, some of their performances are slightly predictable. The rigid formula of K-pop dance emblematized by SM is of merit but, simultaneously, could be a drawback that stymies a groundbreaking innovation and artists' creativity.

From the Mid to the Late 2010s: The Expansion of Choreography as Capital

It was not until the mid-2010s that K-pop choreographers began to receive the credit they deserved. Rain's backup dancer said that choreographers used to be paid from $3,000 to $5,000 per piece, which is barely minimum wage. But PSY's "Gangnam Style" "horse dance" syndrome in 2012 promoted awareness on copyright issues ("Rain's"). With the increasing number of foreign choreographers, choreographers' names became officially available around the mid-2010s. Agencies and artists began sharing their works and crediting each other on Twitter with hashtags that blur geographical boundaries.

Choreography quickly became a global investment. SM invested more than $100 million for SHINee's "Sherlock" (2013) performance ("Fans"). Japanese Rino Nakasone who began her career in K-pop with SHINee's "Replay" in 2008, and American Tony Testa for SHINee's "Sherlock" (2012) were precursors of the exponential influx of foreign choreographers since the 2010s. From New Zealand to France, choreographers have come to the K-pop industry, including Parris Goebel, Keone Madrid, Brian Puspos, Kiel Tutin, Kyle Hanagami, Rie Hata, Yanis Marshall, Nicholas Bass, Ian Anthony Eastwood, Carlo Darang, Napoleon and Tabitha D'umo (known together as Nappytabs), Jonte' Moaning, to name a few. Asian American and ethnic minority dancers' contributions are also visible, reaffirming K-pop as a pan-Asian identity.

From the late 2010s to the 2020s, local choreographers have also thrived. Bae Yoon Jung and Choi Youngjoon have made signature K-pop choreographies and become well known as dance trainers and choreographers on survival shows, such as *Produce 101* (2016) and *Produce X 101* (2019). After *Street Woman Fighter* (2021), Mnet's female dance crew competition show, Honey J also became popular. In the commercial "#ygx and honey J # Nike" (2021), she dances with members from *Street Woman Fighter* and showcases powerful, defiant, and liberatory urban and hip-hop dance on the street. The ad ends with the line "everywhere is a stage, as long as you have confidence" (originally in Korean). A competition needs an established criteria and distinctive conventions to judge. The rise of global K-pop dance competitions and TV shows in the 2020s demonstrates K-pop dance as an independent genre with educatable formula along with expected bodies, aesthetics, and mastery of techniques beyond a certain ethnicity.

Former idols have come back as a "return of legends" from music videos to TV shows. Kim Wan-sun's stunning tango, cha-cha-cha, and rumba on MBC's *Dancing with the Stars* Season 3 in 2013 truly amazed her loyal fans. Jinusean was a judge on the fourth season of *Show Me the Money* (2015), a rap competition TV show. BoA served as a judge on *Street Woman Fighter* in 2021. Many of them are no longer "idols" as they are past their thirties. The 1990s icon Uhm Jung Hwa's "Ending Credit" (2017) is a retro-style pop song with its vogue-inspired, stunning performance with her signature male backup dancers, which nostalgically recalls the beautiful old days of a pop diva. The 1980s and 1990s idols and their trajectories reflect a history of K-pop – lifetime growth, aging, success, and failure. Some have transformed from idols to artists or executive directors, and others are remembered or forgotten with various life events like marriage, retirement, scandal, suicide, and military service.

Underground hip-hop dance crews, b-boys/girls, and street dancers, who have paved the way for K-pop dance since the 1980s, have won international dance battles such as *Red Bull BC One, Battle Of The Year,* and *Keep on Dancing (KOD) Street Dance World Cup.* They also work as dance teachers from community arts colleges to K-pop management companies and as judges at international dance competitions and TV shows. J-Black (or J-pink, his onstage feminine persona) became popular in the mainstream as the founder of Korean street dance and "Korean Zombie dance" after his performance on *Dancing 9* in 2015, a dance survival reality TV show on Mnet. He also appeared as a judge on *Dancing High* (2018), a dance battle audition program on KBS. Other judges at *Dancing High* (2018) included Nam Hyun-joon (Poppin' Hyun Joon), a pioneer of Korean breakdancing, and B-boy Snake, a founding member of Gorilla Crew. Gorilla Crew is known as one of the first freestyle dance teams and part of the first generation of Korean hip-hop and b-boying, along with Expression Crew and People Crew, which were both formed in 1997. Gorilla Crew can be traced back to Lee

Juno's (a member of Seo Taiji and Boys) "Dance Factory" video in 1998 ("Do You Know 'Gorilla Crew'").

The 2020s: K-pop Dance as Global Entrepreneurship

Dance Videos, YouTube Choreographies, and Education

Turning to the 2020s, K-pop choreography itself has become the capital. More idols are "self-produced." Artists such as Seventeen, Winner, and Pentagon actively produce, compose, and choreograph their performances, such as Seventeen, Winner, Pentagon, Mamamoo, (G)I-DLE, and Stray Kids. Their individualized artistry could exceed the mass-produced K-pop formula in the future (Yoon). K-pop dance is perceived as an independent and entrepreneurial career. It builds upon international collaboration, business, monetization, advertising, sponsorship, and fame. There is barely any boundary between K-pop singers and dancers. The famous YouTube dance channel 1MILLION Dance Studio collaborated with B.I, a former member of boy group iKON, in 2021 to perform choreography by Youngbeen Joo to Drake's single "What's Next." This collaboration reflects the tendency of dance influencers to choreograph to a trendy pop song, videotape it in a studio with other dancers and a cheering audience and share it on social media. Dance influencer Matt Steffanina's choreography videos on YouTube, recorded in the Millennium Dance Complex studio in Los Angeles, exemplify the trend. B.I appears solely as a dancer whose movements seamlessly combine urban, contemporary, hip-hop, and K-pop. Former Sistar19 member Hyolyn's dance practice video of "Dally" (2018), made by her production company Brid3, is an earlier example of the combination of YouTube choreography and K-pop. She showcases the popular high-heel dance with her choreographer Aliya Janell.

With the rise of K-pop dance as an independent genre, dance practice videos have also evolved. Dance practice videos used to be made with a relatively fixed angle, minimum theatrical setting, and a shaky camera and simply showed dancers practicing in a studio. Due to their exposed vulnerability, relatable amateur aesthetics, intimacy, and the practical functions of learning dance (C. Oh, "'Cinderella'"), dance practice videos have become popular since the 2010s. Girls' Generation's debut song "Into the New World" (2007) has only an unofficial dance practice video available. SHINee's "Lucifer" (2010) and "Sherlock" (2012) are also some of the earliest examples of dance practice videos. Dance practice videos provide "solid base material for choreography enthusiasts," which strengthens fans' "embodied sense of connection" with idols (H. Park).

Dance version videos, or *choreography videos*, are more formal than *dance practice videos* but more minimal than original music videos. Dance version videos share full choreographies without the interruption of story, setting, or backdrop, and the stage settings and costumes resemble the original themes of the music videos. The dance version video for BLACKPINK's "How You Like That" (2020) surpassed 100 million views on YouTube within fifteen days of its release, twice as fast as the dance practice video of their previous hit song "Kill This Love" (2019) (Kyung-wook Kim). The video is set to a minimal but impressive pink backdrop. They are clad in slightly casual outfits compared to the more extravagant stage costumes of the original music video. The camera moderately varies the angles to maximize the impact of dance routines. The popularity of dance videos demonstrates that K-pop is consumed both as music and dance, and the latter often exceeds the former.

Various variations of K-pop dance videos have risen exponentially on social media: dance version videos, original choreography videos, remakes, parodies, random play dance, part switch, rehearsal, relay dance, dance break version, reverse dance, cover dance, dance challenge, dance tutorial and more. Such dance fandom demonstrates how K-pop dance provides a source to play with as social media dance. It is both a top-down, bottom-up voluntary engagement by global fans, amateur and professional dancers, and idols. Such dance fandom on social media extends to the growing tourism and physical mobility of fans in reality, as explained in Chapter 5. The increasing number of international students, along with tourists, who join K-pop dance is included in the government's official travel guide to Seoul. 1MILLION Dance Studio said that approximately seventy percent of class attendees are tourists and K-pop fans from across the globe, including Asia, the Americas, Europe, and Africa (D. Lee).

Some choreographers extend the geographical, stylistic, and educational boundaries of K-pop dance even further. Lia Kim, the co-founder of 1MILLION Dance Studio, is known for iconic choreographies, such as TWICE's "TT" (2016) and Sunmi's "Gashina" (2017). She has trained idols at SM, YG, and JYP, including Girls' Generation, BoA, 2NE1, TWICE, and 2PM. She is a faculty member at the Broadway Dance Center in New York. Her classes are categorized as "hip hop/street styles." She is also a lecturer at community arts colleges and universities in Korea. Her 1MILLION Dance Studio YouTube channel shares choreographies to pop songs as well as contemporary, modern, and traditional Korean dance, often addressing social issues.

Studio Choom is a YouTube channel launched by Mnet Digital Studio in 2019. *Choom* (춤) means "dance" in Korean. *Muyong* (무용) also means "dance," but it implies conventional artistic concert dance. Contrarily, *choom* can refer to a broader range of dance, from ancient rituals to children's improvisation. Studio Choom converges all K-pop idols' dance, from high-quality close-up gestural dances to experimental choreographies that transgress specific genres. The choreography in Hoody's MV "When The Rain Stops" (2021) resonates with experimental choreography in postmodern dance like that of Pina Bausch, who highlighted the fragile, graceful vulnerability of female dancers via fluid, self-reflective movements. In addition to the stylistic expansion of dance on social media, social media also allows for the rise of micro-celebrity dancers. SM's choreographer Kasper and YG's Kwon Twins, twin choreographers, have become famous on social media with an increasing number of followers. The popularity of *trot*, indie, and shamanic Korean folk music and dance further diversifies K-pop dance, along with idols who debut as soloists showcasing their unique talents.

Virtual Collaboration and Copyright

Increasing virtual collaborations change the definition of copyright that once belonged to a single master choreographer. An LA-based K-pop dance teacher and studio owner told me that the hidden labor of K-pop choreography includes anonymous dance crews. They are recruited via social media. Whether or not agencies include some portions of their dance in a final choreography, they get paid by sending their choreography video files to the agencies. Their names are unlikely to appear in the credits, but they advertise their contributions on their social media accounts, extending their business as choreographers.

In 2017, Keone Madrid shared photos on his Twitter after attending BTS' concert in California. He wrote: "Finally! A few years choreographing for these guys, and I haven't seen them perform it in person. Thanks for having us @BTS_twt!" It is uncommon in concert dance for a piece to have more than one choreographer because a choreographer (often the gatekeeper) mostly devises all the movements, themes, and concepts based on her/his embodied training and aesthetic preferences, which cannot be easily shared or even agreed upon with others. However, as dance is now sold like a digital file, copyright is no longer limited to a dancer's physical body. The origin of a movement is clearly trackable to the original file as evidence, but when many files exist as the movement drafts of a choreography, the discussion of *the* origin becomes less important. This is why many choreographers rather say that they "assist" K-pop idols' choreographies.

Virtual collaboration also changes the aesthetics of dance. Like the cases of BTS and Coldplay's "My Universe" (2021), Lady Gaga and BLACKPINK's "Sour Candy" (2020), and PSY's "Hangover" (2014) with Snoop Dogg, whether for music or dance, a collaboration no longer requires a months-long physical residency together. In "My Universe," BTS and Coldplay's dance is far away from a live physical duet or group dance where dancers can literally feel the heat, mood, and even weight of each other. Instead, like Marvel superheroes whose bodies are edited, copied, pasted, and juxtaposed with one another, their dance exists in a harmonious virtual world with animated characters. Like TikTok's duet function, it is a virtual duet without a physical presence.

Choreography is no longer the genius invention of a lonely solo artist but a global, collective, and open creation. Announcing EXO's "Love Shot" (2018) teaser, SM said that the performance was "attended" by Phillip Chbeeb, Sienna Lalau, and Back Mihawk ("COMBACK D-1 EXO, New Song 'Love Shot' Attached to the Charm!"). Sunmi's "24 Hours" (2014) choreography was a collaboration with local choreographers, modern dancers, Jonte' Moaning, J. Y. Park, and Wonder Girls (Jeong). Like Apple's smartphone that has aesthetic features and technical functions made by the top brains across the world, the final outcome of K-pop dance is the collective labor of an uncountable number of artists across the globe. While global capitalism escalates collaborations, it also means the end of an independent (genius) solo artist, albeit social media still provides solo artists a small hope for recognition.

In addition to multiple inputs, unpredictability in the choreographic process could be a reason why agencies barely list chorographers in their credits. Just as a song sounds different based on a singer's voice, a movement may appear different based on a dancer's characteristics. Movements can keep changing, evolving, and transforming into a sequence as dancers practice. A choreographer can take instant inspiration from a dancer, and vice versa, through which a move can be gradually modified, polished, and included in the final choreography. In this case, no one knows the origin of the movement.

K-pop Agencies as IT Tech-Infused Performing Arts Conglomerates

As of the 2020s, K-pop agencies have transformed from record labels to IT tech-infused, multidisciplinary global conglomerate performing arts companies. Like Cirque du Soleil hiring globally talented artists and often outsourcing its inspiration, K-pop agencies use global audiences to recruit talented artists and prodigies from across the world. Weverse, an app created by BTS' management company HYBE, merges previous platforms, such as V app, online fan communities, and YouTube content, into one platform where BTS can directly reply to a fan's comment and vice versa. In 2021, it bought Ithaca, the US management company of Justin Bieber, Ariana Grande, and Demi Lovato. Just as Amazon is not a mere shipping company, HYBE is more than a music label.

The virtual presence of K-pop further escalated after COVID blurs the boundaries across the live stage, animation, 3-D films, and computer games, such as SM's foray into virtual and reality girl group Aespa. Visual aesthetics converge to match the highest level of budgets spent. Idols are as artificial and flawless as computer-generated blockbuster movie characters. Still, their social media presence compensates for this distance by sharing approachable and even silly "boys/girls next door" aspects of daily life. Idols directly communicate with fans on social media apps, like "lysn" and "V Live". Idols' performances on variety TV shows, entertainment programs, documentaries, soap dramas, and films further open up a multi-directional, participatory fandom.

The Idol Economy

With global capitalism, the idol economy has begun. In 2011, Girl's Generation earned approximately $50 million (Kim and Jo). Debuting in 2013, BTS became even more successful than their role model BIGBANG as the biggest boy band in the world. In 2018, BTS made up 0.3% of South Korea's GDP with their annual revenue of $4.65 billion that year, and their scale was as big as Samsung, KIA, and LG (Abramovitch).

K-pop idols extend their stage presence to daily life as philanthropists and fashionistas. In 2020, BTS and HYBE donated $1 million to Black Lives Matter and so did their fan group ARMY. Their humanitarian speeches, performances, and donations for UNICEF and the "Love Myself" campaign are noticeable.

BIGBANG's G-Dragon, often called the "King of K-pop," paved the way for K-pop idols to be luxury brand ambassadors as the first Asian muse and later global ambassador of Chanel in 2016, followed by EXO's Kai for Gucci, BLACKPINK's Jennie for Chanel, and BTS for Louis Vuitton in the 2020s. K-pop fans have further extended the humanitarian vision. TikTok teens whose fake reservations left hundreds of seats empty at the former President Trump's rally in Tulsa, Oklahoma, on June 20, 2020, were in the news headlines from *The New York Times* to *Billboard*.

De-Ethnicizing and Globalizing K-pop Dance Competitions

A competition is impossible without clear, tested evaluation criteria—the formula. The rise of the global K-pop dance competition, reality, and survival audition TV shows demonstrates the establishment of K-pop dance as an independent genre that is possible to teach and thus, possible to compete in. TV shows such as *Kingdom: Legendary War* (2021), *Girls Planet 999* (2021), and *Idol School* (2017) *Hit the Stage* (2016), *Dancing 9* (2013), *Produce 101* (2016), and *WIN: Who is Next* (2013) showcase the clear expectation of judges, from face dance to body type, to formation, and to a mastery of previous K-pop dance repertoires. Notably, *My Teenage Girl* (2021) stages trainees just above ten years old. Despite their young age, they already look like professional K-pop idols because they are the beneficiaries, or victims, of the accumulative prodigy education system in Korea present since the 1990s.

The ideal K-pop body has also been extended. As shown by Jessi and Mamamoo's Hwasa in *Street Woman Fighter* (2021) female singers' bodies appear more tanned, bigger, more glamorous, more athletic, and stronger with their fearless personae compared to those of the submissive, fragile, and thin bodies of Girls' Generation. These new body types reflect the changing gender dynamics in Korea with the increasing awareness of women's rights and feminism. It also suggests the changing global beauty standards, which have become more inclusive and more racially and ethnically diverse and even ambiguous beyond the Caucasian body.

Interestingly, once a formula is established, the next star often comes from those who break that very formula. As Chapter 3 will fully explain, BTS is built on the K-pop dance formula but personalizes, innovates, and challenges that very system. They seamlessly integrate classical, popular, Western, and Asian dances. They extend the two-dimensional, flat, and front-driven gestural point choreography in a narrow space to a full version of extensive dance films and dance breaks with a three-dimensional, voluminal effect, expanding the different spectrums of space, level (lifted legs and feet and head drops), body size, costume, backup dancers, and the gaze.

Ballet, hip-hop, and Broadway musicals can be examples of "ethnic dance" rooted in "common genetic, linguistic, and cultural ties" (Kealiinohomoku 39), which have turned into global phenomena. Likewise, K-pop has been de-ethnicized and globalized with a clear formula, iconic repertoires, expected body types, and a mastery of techniques. As a dance teacher in London forecasts, K-pop "could be as big as tap or ballet" (Greep). BLACKPINK's Lisa, born in Thailand, and her solo "LALISA" (2021) demonstrate that K-pop dance has been established as a technical style and genre beyond a certain race, ethnicity, or nationality. The breathtaking skills and talent of winners on *The Mexico K-pop Stars 2021* at the Teatro Metropólitan in Mexico also represent the de-ethnicization of K-pop as a social media dance of the global youth.

BoA aimed to compete with Japanese singers by being a J-pop singer in the 2000s, but in the 2020s, K-pop idols perform as K-pop singers whose identities are expanded to multiple races, ethnicities, and nationalities. K-pop's racial, ethnic, and national identities have been diversified with non-Koreans, although many of them have been Asian. In the 2020s, there are entirely non-Korean K-pop groups formed outside of Korea, like Mandarin pop group Boy Story, Japanese girl group NiziU by YG, and multiethnic and multiracial boy group EXP EDITION. Those non-Korean K-pop groups appear as K-pop idols and perform based on the original formula and body types developed since the 1990s.

K-pop Education: From Technique to Repertoire

A repertoire is a complete package of music, dance, costume, choreography, character, storyline, and lyrics, like *Swan Lake* and *The Nutcracker* in ballet, and *The Lion King* in Broadway musicals. Repertoires help the audience remember and consume a dance at ease with stories, characters, and other accustomed habits. While a repertoire contributes to dissemination, a signature technique marks a dance genre as it is, like ballet's toe work, turn out, and fouettes. "32 fouettes" can be a "point choreographies" of *Swan Lake* repertoire that displays the ultimate toe and turnout technique along with its symbolic airy arm gestures. Repertoires used to be hourlong in theatre but now up to 3 minutes (music video) to 15 seconds (dance challenge) on social media.

The evolution from a technique to a repertoire means a dancer's transition to a choreographer. Examples include modern dancer Martha Graham's "contraction and release" technique in Lamentation, Jose Limon's "fall and recovery" technique in The Moor's Pavane, postmodern dancer Yvonne Rainer's pedestrian movement technique in Tro A, John Cage's 4'33' that exhibits his idea, or technique, on silence as music, and Ohad Naharin's "Gaga" technique in Deca Dance. Each genre's techniques are training methods that dancers hone their skills by practicing a role in a repertoire. Through repertoires, dancers not only master iconic techniques but also develop familiarity with music, rhythm, characters, and the preferred body type based on the repetitive training.

Likewise, K-pop dance has evolved from a signature dance to repertoire. Talented individuals' iconic "dance craze" in the 1980s paved the way for the 1990s "point choreography" that established its signature technique – gestural point choreography – since the 2000s. The point choreographies became the "repertoires" of K-pop repeated, practiced, and presented by global cover dancer fans. Being globally institutionalized like hip hop and ballet, K-pop dance classes are offered at entertainment agencies, universities, and online studios worldwide for professional career and leisure activities. There are emerging global K-pop dance influencers and education and entertainment channels: 1Million Dance Studio, YG's X Academy on YouTube, Ellen and Brian's K-pop dance on STEEZY dance app, Just Dance video game, K-pop lip-sync dance battle app Amazer, and emerging K-pop dance fitness videos, to name a few. An established education system can make a synergy. Prodigies are discovered across the globe, start their training early, better shape physical and psychological conditions for K-pop, and perform longer before retirement. Along with accumulated education, advanced medical care, nutrition, and quality of life, K-pop dancers' bodies appear taller, athletic, visually polished, and more premature than those of previous generations.

Conclusion

K-pop dance has become an embodied culture accumulated over generations. BLACKPINK's Jennie said in the Netflix documentary *Blackpink: Light Up the Sky* (2020), "I think what makes K-pop K-pop is the time that we spend as a trainee." Anyone can imitate K-pop dance, but no one really knows what the K-pop dancers have experienced to shine on the sparkling stage. Trainees living together is not uncommon in a field that requires a high level of teamwork, like ballet or sports. By living together from an early age, they understand each other as people and develop chemistry that will be delivered through synchronous, harmonious group dance. Idols' backstage moments, tears, bullying, injuries, dramas, frustrations, competitions, hatred, and love – the ways they *feel* about the dance, about each other, and their fans – are all part of K-pop dance. Chapter 3 focuses on BTS as modern dancers and how they return to theatre, challenging the conventions of social media dance.

References

Abramovitch, Seth. "BTS Is Back: Music's Billion-Dollar Boy Band Takes the Next Step." *The Hollywood Reporter*, 2 October 2019, https://www.hollywoodreporter.com/movies/movie-features/bts-is-back-musics-billion-dollar-boy-band-takes-next-step-1244580/.

"(Bang Bang Bang) M/V." YouTube, uploaded by BIGBANG, 1 June 2015, https://www.youtube.com/watch?v=2ips2mM7Zqw.

"Behind the Stage." *W Korea*, 2 October 2013, https://www.wkorea.com/2013/10/04/%EB%AC%B4%EC%8C%80%EC%9D%98-%EB%B0%B0%ED%9B%84/..

"BLACKPINK—'How You Like That' DANCE PERFORMANCE VIDEO." YouTube, uploaded by BLACKPINK, 5 July 2020, https://www.youtube.com/watch?v=32si5cfrCNc.

Blackpink: Light Up the Sky. RadicalMedia, 2020. Netflix app.

"BoA 보아' No. 1' MV." YouTube, uploaded by SMTOWN, 24 September 2009, https://www.youtube.com/watch?v=ceZc-5p3g1w.

"Broadcasting Arts Troupe 'Oh, Old Times." *JoongAng Ilbo*, 1 December 2003, https://news.joins.com/article/264142.

"Coldplay X BTS My Universe (Official Video)." YouTube, 29 September 2021, uploaded by Coldplay, https://www.youtube.com/watch?v=3YqPKLZF_WU.

"COMBACK D-1 EXO, New Song 'Love Shot' Attached to the Charm!" *SM Entertainment*, 12 December 2018, https://smentertainment.com/PressCenter/Details/2436.

"Do You Know 'Gorilla Crew,' Where the Best Dancers from Various Genres Gather?" *ETNEWS*, 29 March 2017, https://m.etnews.com/20170329000257#cb.

"EXO Teaser 4_KAI (2) One Take ver." YouTube, uploaded by SMTOWN, 29 December 2011, https://www.youtube.com/watch?v=_dsmteGxiq8.

"Fans Were Surprised to Find Out How Much SM Entertainment Really Invested in SHINee's 'Sherlock' Choreography." *KStarLive*, 22 November 2019, https://www.kstarlive.com/news/2019/11/22/fans-were-surprised-to-find-out-that-sm-entertainment-invested-money-for-shinee-s-sherlock-choreography-301777.

"From the Legendary Moonwalk Dance to the Rabbit Dance!" *YouTube*, 3 March 2019, https://www.youtube.com/watch?v=UjDmsLSR4YA.

"Girls' Generation 소녀시대 'Gee' MV." YouTube, uploaded by SMTOWN, 8 June 2009, https://www.youtube.com/watch?v=U7mPqycQ0tQ.

"Girls' Generation 소녀시대 '소원을 말해봐 (Genie)' MV." YouTube, uploaded by SMTOWN. 25 February 2010, https://www.youtube.com/watch?v=6SwiSpudKWI.

Greep, Monica. "Could K-pop Dancing Eclipse Ballet and Tap?" *The Daily Mail*. 19 January 2020, https://www.dailymail.co.uk/femail/article-7904463/K-pop-mania-Industry-experts-claim-Korean-boyband-bigger-tap.html.

"Interviews with K-POP's Hidden Protagonists: Choreographer Lee Jae-Wook & PD Ahn Joon-Young." *Paradise*, 21 January 2017, https://blog.paradise.co.kr/671.

Jeong, Byeong-geun. "Why Did Sunmi Dance Barefoot?" *CBS Nocut News*, 22 Aug. 2013, https://www.nocutnews.co.kr/news/1087725.

Jin, Dal Yong, and Woongjae Ryoo. "Critical Interpretation of Hybrid K-Pop: The Global-Local Paradigm of English Mixing in Lyrics." *Popular Music and Society*, vol. 37, no. 2, 2012, pp. 113–131. *Taylor & Francis Online*, https://doi.org/10.1080/03007766.2012.731721.

J. K. "BTS's Longtime Choreographer Keone Madrid Finally Gets to See Them Perform, Shares Backstage Photos and Videos." *Soompi*, 3 April 2017, https://www.soompi.com/article/968951wpp/btss-longtime-choreographer-keone-madrid-finally-gets-to-see-them-perform-shares-backstage-photos-and-video.

Jun, Gianna. "H.O.T. Member Kangta Who Struck the Heart of a Girl in the Late 1990s." *Maekyung Media*, 28 April 2017. https://www.mk.co.kr/premium/behind-story/view/2017/04/18564/.

Kang, Heon. "The First Issue of *Review* – Kang Heon vs Seo Taiji" [리뷰창간호 인터뷰 강헌 vs 서태지]. *SEOTAIJI Archive*, 19 October 1994. https://www.seotaiji-archive.com/xe/taijimania_memorial/358659.

Kealiinohomoku, Joann. "An Anthropologist Looks at Ballet as a Form of Ethnic Dance." In *Moving History/Dancing Cultures: A Dance History Reader*, edited by Ann Dils and Ann Cooper Albright, Wesleyan UP, 2001, pp. 33–43.

Kim, Chang Nam. *K-POP: Roots and Blossoming of Korean Popular Music*. Hollym International Corporation, 2012.

Kim, Chinson. 현대성의 형성: 서울에 딴스홀을 허하라 [The Formation of Modernity: Allow Dance Halls in Seoul]. Hyŏnsil Munhwa Yŏn'gu, 1999.

Kim, Elaine H. and Chungmoo Choi. *Dangerous Women: Gender and Korean Nationalism*. Routledge, 1997.

Kim, Jisoo. "[김지수의 인터스텔라] '즐거움 좇아 계속 하며 산다' 김완선의 인생 그 루브" [[Kim Ji-soo's Interstellar] "I Continue to Live after the Joy." Kim Wan-sun's Life Grove]. *Chosunbiz*, 13 June 2020, https://biz.chosun.com/site/data/html_dir/2020/06/11/2020061104847.html.

Kim, Jung-ju. "Rain 'Rainism' Lyrics—Choreography, It's Too lewd." *Money Today*, 26 October 2008. https://news.mt.co.kr/mtview.php?no=2008102209565149369.

Kim, Ki-yoon. "BTS Choreographer 'Sienna Lalau,' Praised as 'A Musical, Not an Idol Choreography.'" *Dong-A Ilbo*, 9 July 2019, https://www.donga.com/news/Culture/article/all/20190709/96393549/1.

Kim, Kyung-wook. "Evolving K-pop Choreography Video … There's a Reason It's Surpassed 500 Million Views." *Hankyoreh Newspaper*, 19 January 2021, https://www.hani.co.kr/arti/culture/music/979348.html#csidx2078842690edf43b9485169449d09d4.

Kim, Pil-gyu and Ik-shin Jo. "소녀시대 지난해만 500억 수익 '걸어다니는 중견기업 '" [Girls' Generation alone Earned 50 Million Last Year as a 'Walking Medium-sized Company']. JTBC, 21 May 2012, https://news.jtbc.joins.com/article/ArticlePrint.aspx?news_id=NB10111481.

Lee, Danbee. "Star Choreographer Inspires in Four-minute Offerings." *The Korea Economic Daily*, 21 October 2020, https://www.kedglobal.com/newsView/ked202010200011.

Lee, Hyun Woo. "Girls' Generation's 10th Member Shim Jae-won, 'Girls' Generation, Every Time You Fall … .'" *The Star News*, 20 April 2012. https://www.mk.co.kr/star/musics/view/2012/04/242429/.

Lee, Eunjung. "박남정 'ㄱㄴ춤'은 즉흥 안무...은퇴 안했으니 노래해야죠 [Park Nam-jung, 'The "ㄱㄴDance" Is improvised Choreography...I Haven't Retired, So I have to Sing]. *Yonhap News*, 30 April 2017. https://www.yna.co.kr/view/AKR20170430029200005.

Lee, Wonseon. "A Star Who Was a 'Backup Dancer' before Debut and Became an 'Idol' with a Unique Talent." *Insight*, 24 February 2021, https://www.insight.co.kr/news/326034.

Lim, Hee-yoon. "Seo Taiji's Return and K-Pop." *Dong-A Ilbo*, 25 October 2014, https://www.donga.com/news/View?gid=67427496&date=20141024.

Madrid, Keone [@keonemadrid]. "Finally! A few years choreographing for these guys and I haven't seen them perform it in person." *Twitter*, 3 April 2017, https://twitter.com/KeoneMadrid/status/848925240587567104.

Moon, Ji-yeon. "You Quiz on the Block 'Girls' Generation is My Country' 14th Anniversary of Debut, Full Comeback Possibility." *Chosun Ilbo*, 2 September 2021, https://www.chosun.com/entertainments/entertain_photo/2021/09/02/LKMANQJP6CYF4GB737AC7DE4CU/.

"[MV] 브레이브걸스 (Brave Girls) - 롤린 (Rollin') (Clean ver.)." YouTube, uploaded by Brave Entertainment, 4 February 2020, https://www.youtube.com/watch?v=3cZrxpK2EAQ.

Oh, Chuyun. "'Cinderella' in Reverse: Eroticizing Bodily Labor of Sympathetic Men in K-pop Dance Practice Video." In *East Asian Men: Masculinity, Sexuality and Desire*, edited by Xiaodong Lin et al., Palgrave Macmillan, 2016. pp. 123–142.

Oh, Chuyun. *K-popscape: Gender Fluidity and Racial Hybridity in Transnational Korean Pop Dance*. 2015. The University of Texas at Austin, PhD Dissertation. Texas ScholarWorks, http://hdl.handle.net/2152/31700.

Oh, Chuyun. "Queering Spectatorship in K-pop: The Androgynous Male Dancing Body and Western Female Fandom." *The Journal of Fandom Studies*, vol. 3, no. 1, 2015, pp. 59–78.

Oh, Chuyun. "The Politics of the Dancing Body: Racialized and Gendered Femininity in K-pop." In *The Korean Wave: Korean Popular Culture in Global Context*, edited by Yasue Kuwahara, Palgrave Macmillan, 2014, pp. 53–81.

Oh, Chuyun. "Types of K-pop Music Video Choreography." In *Cambridge Companion to K-pop*, edited by Suk-Young Kim, Cambridge UP, 2022, forthcoming.

Oh, Chuyun, and David C.Oh. "Unmasking Queerness: Blurring and Solidifying Queer Lines through K-pop Cross-dressing." *The Journal of Popular Culture*, vol. 50, no. 1, 2017, pp. 9–29. *Wiley Online Library*, https://doi.org/10.1111/jpcu.12506.

Park, Han-sol. "Why Have K-pop Dance Practice Videos Become So Popular?" *The Korea Times*, 21 January 2021, https://www.koreatimes.co.kr/www/art/2021/06/732_302847. html.

Park, Ji-ryun. "Kim Wan-sun 'Before BoA's Debut, I Often Saw SM Lee Soo Man in the Office.'" *Newsen*, 30 August 2014, https://newsen.com/news_view.php?uid= 201408300816303110..

"Rain's 10-year Choreography Team 'Wild Rabbit.'" *Gyeongsang Ilbo*, 16 Jan. 2014, http:// www.ksilbo.co.kr/news/articleView.html?idxno=439907.

"[RAIN/비] 5th—Rainism M/V Full Version (2008.10.15) [Official MV]." YouTube, uploaded by RAIN's Official Channel, 19 June 2012, https://www.youtube.com/wa tch?v=IVBW7sI8IhY.

Seo, Byung-ki. "Why Did Lee Soo-Man and BoA Not Have 'Anti'?" *The Korea Herald*, 20 October 2005, https://entertain.naver.com/read?oid=112&aid=0000019096.

"S.E.S.—I'm Your Girl (Official Music Video)." YouTube, uploaded by S.E.S., 24 September 2016, https://www.youtube.com/watch?v=QdTkdfRur-c.

Shim, Doobo. "Hybridity and the Rise of Korean Popular Culture in Asia." *Media, Culture & Society*, vol. 28, no. 1, 2006, pp. 25–44. *SAGE Journals*, https://doi.org/10.1177/ 0163443706059278.

"SHINee 샤이니'Everybody' MV." YouTube, uploaded by SMTOWN, 10 October 2013, https://www.youtube.com/watch?v=hKbNV-4b_g8.

Shin, Hyunjoon. "Reconsidering Transnational Cultural Flows of Popular Music in East Asia: Transbordering Musicians in Japan and Korea Searching for 'Asia.'" *Korean Studies*, vol. 33, no. 1, 2009, pp. 101–123. *JSTOR*, https://www.jstor.org/stable/23719262.

Shin, Hyun-kyung. "The KBS People Hidden behind the Splendor: KBS Dance Troupe and Choir that Shines Singers." *Labor Today*, 20 April 2008, https://www.labortoday.co. kr/news/articleView.html?idxno=79346..

"'Singerella' Moon Hee-joon, 'When I Think of the Practice Environment before the H. O.T. Debut, Tears Fall.'" *Hankyun News*, 13 Jan. 2017, https://www.hankyung.com/ news/article/201701132427k.

Son, Min Jung. *The Politics of the Traditional Korean Popular Song Style T'ŭrot'ŭ*. 2004. The University of Texas at Austin. PhD dissertation. Texas Scholar Works, http://hdl.handle. net/2152/1699.

Stebbins, Genevieve. *Delsarte System of Expression*. Edgar S. Werner Publishing & Supply Co., 1902.

"TAEMIN 태민'Move' #1 MV." YouTube, uploaded by SMTOWN, 16 October 2017, https://www.youtube.com/watch?v=rcEyUNeZqmY.

"Without Lee Soo Man, There Would Be No BTS." *Hankyoreh*, 22 December 2020, http s://www.hani.co.kr/arti/culture/music/975298.html#csidx3b47bbb045ae3cf8dcf2e8db2 fcb5f1.

Yoon, Jun-ho. "Stray Kids – (G)I-DLE, Self-produced Idols Are Trending." *Money Today*, 13 April 2020, https://news.mt.co.kr/mtview.php?no=2020041309147250849.

"김완선 - 리듬 속의 그 춤을 1988.01.30 (토요일 토요일은 즐거워)" [Kim Wan-Sun – The Dance in Rhythm 1988.01.30 (*Saturday Night Music Show*)] *YouTube*, uploaded by 예전노래, 9 November 2014, https://www.youtube.com/watch?v=lg-p GruRAjM.

"김완선 박남정 로봇춤" [Kim Wan-Sun Park Nam-jung Robot Dance" (*Saturday Night Music Show* 1988 MBC Archive)]. YouTube, uploaded by 달마홍이, 11 April 2021, https://www.youtube.com/watch?v=fl0vDvXXKlA.

"[고화질] 김완선 KIMWANSUN 팩스뮤지카 - 리듬속의 그 춤을" [[High Quality] Kim Wan-Sun KIMWANSUN Pax Musica - The Dance in Rhythm"]. YouTube, uploaded by 김완선TV, 16 June 2019, https://www.youtube.com/watch?v=Nyd_6G3EGIY.

"리듬속의 그춤을 - 김완선(1987)" [The Dance in Rhythm - Kim Wan-Sun (1987)]. YouTube, uploaded by 김완선TV, 29 October 2020, https://www.youtube.com/watch?v=Mj3lnUIG3bM.

"박남정 – '널 그리며' [가요톱10, 1989] | Park Nam Jung – 'Missing you'" [Park Nam-jung – "Missing You"]. YouTube, uploaded by Again 가요톱10: KBS KPOP Classic, 1 October 2018, https://www.youtube.com/watch?v=g21lBGfnzfs.

"서태지와 아이들(Seotaiji and Boys) - 난 알아요 (I Know) M/V]" [Seotaiji and Boys – I Know M/V"]. YouTube, uploaded by seotaiji, 27 November 2012, https://www.youtube.com/watch?v=OEDHEzs5kyk.

"엄정화 (Uhm Jung Hwa) - Ending Credit MV." YouTube, uploaded by Stone Music Entertainment, 13 December 2017, https://www.youtube.com/watch?v=v-5jAM0Zt4w.

"#ygx and honey J # Nike." YouTube, uploaded by Hazel D., 4 November 2021, https://www.youtube.com/watch?v=mfMt2b4p53c.

"[1988] 소방차 - 어젯밤 이야기 (응답하라 1988 삽입곡)" [[1988] Fire Truck - Story of Last Night (Reply 1988 OST)]. YouTube, uploaded by 옛송TV, 23 April 2015, https://www.youtube.com/watch?v=3xwe4tXnajo.

3

BTS

The Modern Dancers

While K-pop dance appears all over social media, some dancers return to theatre physically and symbolically. As an extended case study, this chapter offers a descriptive analysis of BTS. BTS shifts the binary between classical dance in theatre and popular dance on social media. BTS' "Black Swan" (2020) and "On" (2020) both released in two versions on YouTube – an MV and a dance film – denote the status of YouTube that partially replaces the traditional role of theatre.

YouTube has become a symbolic theatre on social media. In the past, holistic viewing was reserved for the dark theatre auditorium, what Sherril Dodds called "cinema spectatorship" (Dodds 144). A contemporary viewing, however, shifts to "online spectatorship" that values "novelty, brevity, [and] spectacle" (Dodds, "On Watching Screendance" 144). In the 2020s, YouTube offers relatively "holistic" viewing focused more on performance than text. Entertainment companies release their official teasers on YouTube. More extended, even full-length, official choreographies from professional dance companies to amateurs appear on YouTube. Unlike TikTok or Instagram, it moves away from synchronous commenting or liking *while* viewing. The audience has to scroll down from the video to see and post comments, which can be less distracting, limiting synchronous participation while viewing.

This chapter first explains the symbolic meanings of black and white swans in Western cultures and their representations from films to the ballet *Swan Lake*. It also contextualizes modern dance, focusing on Martha Graham. This chapter categorizes BTS as modern dancers, male dancers as warriors, and Korean folk dancers. Employing descriptive analysis, it provides a close reading of their songs "Black Swan," "On," and their performance of "Idol" (2018) and other live performances at the Melon Music Awards (MMA).

I argue that BTS exhibits the expansion of K-pop dance in the 2020s by seamlessly integrating classical, popular, Western, and Asian dances. In addition, they

DOI: 10.4324/9781003212188-5

extend two-dimensional, front-driven gestural point choreography to three-dimensional voluminal dance films by expanding the spectrums of space, size, level (lifted legs and feet and head drops), and the gaze. In "Black Swan," BTS symbolically and physically embodies modern dance philosophy via self-exploration, abstract themes, bare feet, and breath technique. It exemplifies the de-ethnicization of K-pop dance as a global dance genre. Their transformation to black swans signifies rebirth and the exposure of their true egos, departing from convention and conquering the symbolic death of an artist. In "On," they represent the long legacy of male dancers as warriors in a war dance that bridges shamanic rituals with festivals and resistance with peace. Their 2018 and 2019 MMA performances represent BTS as Korean folk dancers who integrate ballet and modern with traditional Korean dance. They extend the definition of "world dance" (Foster, *Worlding Dance*) that has been often essentialized as traditional and indigenous.

This chapter highlights BTS members Jimin and Jungkook. This is not to neglect other BTS members but instead to illuminate their dance-centric natures and focus on the visible roles they played in the two videos. *Contemporary dance* refers to a dance that is "happening now," including concert dance, world dance, and popular dance (Kwan 39), so BTS' works belong to contemporary dance. Yet, by highlighting ballet and modern dance aspects, this chapter sheds light on the boundary-crossing aspects of BTS instead of generalizing Western dance as universal. Indeed, research on ballet and modern dance's influences on K-pop are scarce, compared to that of hip-hop and African American dance culture (Anderson; Song). By situating BTS in a larger genealogy of concert dance history, this chapter aims to challenge the binary between pop versus classical dances and Asian versus Western dances and to address self-exploration as a fundamental theme in art creation.

As BTS mentions elsewhere, their works are open to various interpretations for their fans and "ARMY theorists." This chapter contributes to the revolutionary and participatory "aca-fan" culture by providing an in-depth dance analysis. I believe that readers of this book will be able to further enrich K-pop dance studies, drawing theories from theatre, music, communication, media studies, cultural studies, and more.

Adaptations of Ballet Swans

In Western fauna, folklore, and fairy tale, white swans are the archetype of beauty and grace. Contrarily, black swans, which in ancient times were not believed to exist, are deemed as unexpected, rare discoveries and encounters and symbolized as liberatory. Their massive symbolic impact challenges the status quo and "carr[ies] an extraordinary cumulative effect" (Taleb xxix). BTS' "Black Swan" is inspired by the American thriller film *Black Swan* (2010), directed by Darren Aronofsky. It is the story of prima ballerina Nina (played by Natalie Portman) and her perfectionism and struggles in performing and transforming into the dual roles, the white and black swan, in a ballet production of *Swan Lake*. Nina, whose personality is docile and submissive, is good at performing the fragile, delicate femininity presented by the white swan. She, however, struggles with performing the black swan that emblematizes a femme fatale, seductive femininity.

Contrarily, Lily (played by Mila Kunis) better personifies the black swan with her rebellious and charismatic persona. With their rivalry, Nina wants to be Lily and hopes to perform the black swan like Lily and assimilate into Lily's life, following her drinking and sexual life, including her homoerotic desires. Like K-pop cover dancers addressed from Chapter 4 to 6, the notion of *identity passing* is found in Nina's desire to be someone else. In the end, Nina successfully transforms into the black swan and performs the poisonously seductive role onstage. Her tragic death at the end of the film signifies the patriarchal punishment of women whose sexualities, gender roles, and ambitions do not fit into disciplinary, docile femininity. The dual femininity of black and white swans is also racialized. In the movie, Nina, who represents the "ideal" (white) femininity, has a lighter, brighter hair and skin tone, and Lily has a darker skin tone, hair, and makeup, with tattoos on her back.

The original theme of the film *Black Swan* derives from the ballet *Swan Lake*. Premiering in 1877 by the Bolshoi Ballet at the Bolshoi Theatre in Moscow, Russia, *Swan Lake* is one of the most iconic repertoires in dance history. Based on Russian composer Pyotr Ilyich Tchaikovsky's music, it tells a story from Russian and German folk tales. Princess Odette (the white swan) turns into a swan because of an evil magician's curse. However, an oath of everlasting love and marriage can break the curse. The story reaches its climax when Prince Siegfried swears an oath to Odile (the black swan), the sorcerer's daughter, who has deceived him, and Odette and Siegfried decide to die together. Czech choreographer Julius Wentsel Reisinger created the original choreography. Among the many revivals afterward, French choreographer Marius Petipa's and Russian choreographer Lev Ivanov's staging in 1895 by the Imperial Ballet at the Mariinsky Theatre in St. Petersburg, Russia, is one of the most widely circulated versions, with a happy ending where the two defy the sorcerer.

Technique-wise, *Swan Lake* is a rite of passage for prima ballerinas. The same prima dancer performs the black and white swans, and thus, she should demonstrate a transformation across the white and black swans with two different stage personae, almost like acting, embodied in the movement technique. For example, the white swan's movements are more fluid, airy, and regulated in tempo. Her facial expression is somber and naïve, albeit graceful, with indirect eye contact with the audience and the prince. Contrarily, the black swan directly gazes at the audience and the prince, with more sharp, angular, quick, and brisk movements and a somehow unpredictable and whimsical facial expression with a manipulative, devilish smile. Unlike the white swan who evades the prince at first, the black swan is sexually suggestive, explicit, and seductive.

Another significant aspect of *Swan Lake* is that it emblematizes conventional femininity in Western culture. The white swan has been referred to as "the classic of all classical ballets" and as a symbol of passive, gentle, and fragile white femininity (Juhasz 54; Banes). When ballet privileges a light-skinned, slim, and heterosexual-looking European (female) body, the white swan is at the center of such racialized and gendered beauty.

The Dying Swan is another notable part of the repertoire that adapts white femininity. Compared to the full-length *Swan Lake* production that lasts more than two hours, *The Dying Swan* is a four-minute-long solo choreographed for the legendary Russian ballerina Anna Pavlova, who performed the piece nearly four thousand times. Choreographed by Mikhail Fokin, it premiered in St. Petersburg, Russia, in 1905. The solo encapsulates the delicate, unearthly, and tragic imagery of a white swan who later in the show kneels and imitates a moment of death with her airy, fragile, and instinctive arm movements.

Artists from figure skating to pop music have adapted the image of swans. Examples include Taylor Swift's music video "Shake It Off" (2014); Les Ballets Trockadero de Monte Carlo's humorous adaptation of *The Dying Swan*; Matthew Bourne's *Swan Lake*, which became sensational with its animalistic, vigorous, and homoerotic representation of all-male swans with the male prince; and street dancer Lil Buck's "The Dying Swan" at the Vail International Dance Festival (2011) where he encapsulated the airy, elegant, and fluid movement of the white swan while wearing casual jeans and sneakers.

BTS' "Black Swan" continues the contemporary adaptation of *Swan Lake* with alternative interpretations. "Black Swan" has two versions. One is the "BTS 'Black Swan' Art Film" directed by Yong Seok Choi and choreographed and performed by Slovenian-based MN Dance Company. The other one is the "BTS 'Black Swan' Official MV" performed by BTS and videotaped in the Los Angeles Theatre. The art film takes inspiration from modern dance. It starts with a quotation by Martha Graham: "A dancer dies twice, once when they stop dancing and this first death is more painful."

Martha Graham and Modern Dance

Graham was a Jewish dancer who was deemed as the first generation of American modern dance. *Modern dance* refers to a theatrical concert dance that advocated "freedom" and primarily emerged from the US and Europe in the late nineteenth century. Notably, the first generation of modern dance was unprecedently pioneered by female choreographers, such as Isadora Duncan, Doris Humphrey, and Loie Fuller, followed by a second generation of male choreographers, including Merce Cunningham, José Limón, and Alvin Ailey. Pioneering black female artists, such as Josephine Baker, Pearl Primus, and Katherine Dunham, made outstanding contributions by bringing African aesthetics to the predominantly white dance field.

In the early twentieth century, social movements swept across the US, including the civil rights movement and the women's suffrage movement. Onstage, vaudeville, a combination of comedic skits, music, dance, theatre, variety acts, and burlesque, replaced the popularity of minstrelsy. Minstrelsy was one of the first performing arts developed in the US, created in the nineteenth century, where white actors in blackface mocked enslaved Africans with racial stereotypes. Ruth St. Denis started her career as a vaudeville dancer known for her splits. Her late performances evoked sacred, mysterious goodness through her uncritical appropriation of "spectacle Otherness," such as her appropriation of Japanese geishas and the Hindu goddess Radha for whom she darkened her skin so that she appeared to be authentically Indian (Desmond 42). With her husband Ted Shawn, she co-founded the Denishawn School of Dancing and Related Arts, presenting Native American, "Negro," Asian, and Spanish folk dances. Despite explicit Orientalism, as racially unmarked white bodies, they were not criticized but celebrated as genius inventors, which speaks to a longer legacy of white dancers' artistic and representational "privilege" in Western dance history (Manning xv). As a former student of Denishawn in the 1910s, Graham later recalled that she left the school because she was tired of performing the Other. Although, her works still mirrored Orientalism, such as the dance *Three Gopi Maidens* (1926), which depicts the worship of a Hindu god. Modern dance is now fully institutionalized with rigid movement training. However, new conventions would not be possible without the pioneers who broke the previous conventions. This circle of challenging conventions, succeeding, creating a new canon and waiting to be challenged by the next generation is also repeated in K-pop dance.

Meanwhile, ballet was newly imported, considered "foreign" and "exotic" until the mid-twentieth century in the US, and often performed by working-class amateur young girls. "Ballet in the 1930s was not only exotic – that is, thought of as Russian – but it hadn't found its entertainment niche. Was it vaudeville? Broadway? Nightclub material?" wrote Erin K. Maher (409). George Balanchine (1904–1984), an immigrant from Russia and the father of American ballet, co-founded the New York City Ballet in 1948 and established the neoclassical ballet style. Yet, the social status of ballet was still being questioned because of its officially sanctioned display of young female dancers' bodies and legs for the pleasure of the male gaze (Daly).

Graham's works challenged the prevalent decorative ballet, vaudeville, and Orientalist Denishawn style of the era. She confronted the objectification of women and the perception of dance as frivolous entertainment. Scholars have warned against the danger of universalizing modern dance because it reflects dancers' experiences primarily in the US. Indeed, Graham's modern dance can be considered an American ethnic dance, which refers to any dance that reflects a "group which holds in common genetic, linguistic, and cultural ties, with special emphasis on cultural tradition" (Kealiinohomoku 39). The Graham technique uses English terminology, such as contractions, releases, jumps, and leaps, and American choreographic themes, such as freedom of assembly and Puritanism. *American Provincials* (1934), *Frontier* (1935), *American Lyric* (1937), and *American Document* (1938) echo with her work commonly known as an "uniquely American style" (Freedman 47).

Her iconic solo *Lamentation* (1930) exemplifies her unique style. In it, she is clad in a long, plain jersey dress. Her dress resembles New York skyscrapers and covers all her body except her face, hands, and feet. She twists and writhes her upper body and hands side to side in a controlled manner with a serious, contemplative facial expression and somber background music. She extends her body and movement by plunging her hands into the dress composed of stretchy fabric, creating an angular arch. Instead of pleasing the male gaze as a visual spectacle of the female body, the piece expresses the human condition, emotional intensity, and abstract feeling vis-à-vis expressionism.

As demonstrated in *Lamentation,* Graham invented unique movements called the *Graham technique* that consists of contraction and release. As a choreographer, she departed from the gendered hierarchy between (older) male choreographers/directors and (younger) female dancers. She also challenged bodily restrictions in ballet, such as the uplifted, stiff torso, restrictive toe shoes, and decorative, corset-like costumes. Graham's bare feet accompanied with contraction and release expressed emotional intensity, such as mourning, unbearable sorrow, and grief, and created a dramatic impact onstage. Many of her performances were created by and for herself as an autobiographical "self-investment" (Thoms 12). She performed the main protagonists she created for over 50 years until she could "barely walk" (Thoms 4).

Graham also introduced the notion of *female spectatorship* to modern dance. Feminists who became financially independent and activists were enthusiastic supporters of her works. Her Martha Graham Dance Company, founded in 1926, was an all-female troupe that presented strong, independent, and fierce images of heroic women. Erick Hawkins (1909–1994), Graham's student and 15 years her junior, later became her husband. He was the first male dancer to perform with her in a duet she created. In many of Graham's pieces, male dancers displayed their torsos and legs, while female dancers, including Graham, were in the leading roles clad in long dresses. Critics generally viewed her works as too serious about eye candy and "ugly" (Martin) without sparkly dancing shoes, except for a few like John Martin (1893–1985). Martin was the first dance critic of *The New York Times* and was known for his advocacy of Graham and her role in increasing the social status of dance to "high art" (Freedman; Franko).

"Black Swan": BTS as Modern Dancers

Symbolically and physically, BTS' performances and status resonate with ballet's black swan and modern dance. K-pop has faced a multilayered stigma as Asian and pop music, and dance has faced a stigma as frivolous entertainment. BTS challenges these high versus popular dance hierarchies and elevates K-pop dance to an art that integrates popular, classical, Western, and Asian dance. They destigmatize racial connotations of K-pop by de-ethnicizing and globalizing its repertoire. Like Graham freeing her body from corset-like tutus and toe shoes by re-interpreting previous traditions, BTS has adapted the previous conventions of ballet, hip-hop, and modern dance, and K-pop and has created a new convention with their liberating bare feet. BTS fans' activism in relation to Black Lives Matter and Stop Asian Hate also speaks to the activism inspired by and inspiring the artists they follow, like the activism of Graham's fans. As BTS extends their work to art, so too do the fans. Connect, BTS is an international art project by fans who support sculptures and experimental art installations in Berlin, Buenos Aires, London, New York, and Seoul. As BTS' dance skills increase, fans too have produced complete versions of experimental, artistic dance film inspired by their idols, not to mention the "hardest K-pop dance" videos requiring enormous athleticism.

The Art Film: Black Swan and the First Death

The "Black Swan" art film is set in a foggy, dusty grey industrial second-floor building that looks like it is under construction. Instead of the seven BTS members, seven light-skinned dancers clad in black suits and bare feet walk into the building. A topless male dancer is facing back and slowly waves and moves his arms side to side in a fluid way, slapping his back with one arm bent behind, like a bird fluttering its wings. The tapping sounds echo in the silent, empty building. His pale skin, bony back, and wiggling muscles create a primordial and slightly grotesque impression.

All the other dancers clad in black suits gather behind him, reaching their hands above the front dancer's back, undulating side to side with his waving arms. The male soloist appears to escape from the crowd. His movement is often initiated and controlled by others who move across and step on him, while the lyrics describe BTS' feelings of being lost, as if trapped in the deep dark bottom of the ocean. All the dancers are connected, holding hands, extending their limbs horizontally, and drawing a small circle. The male dancer is at the edge of the circle, wiggling and undulating his head and spine outwardly. This scene seems to physicalize the frustration symbolized in the lyrics of being lost amid being an artist who must keep producing even when losing creativity and inspiration, who has nowhere to go other than being an artist, and whom no one can hear or help in the fight with themselves. He is being lifted, dragged, and pulled up and down, constantly wriggling in the air but trapped.

The male soloist departs from the crowd. For the first time in the film, he pulls up his body like a rebirth or transformation, gradually and smoothly extending and straightening his writhing arms and legs as he begins to walk like a human, walking down a stopped escalator. In the second part of the film, he shakes off the others approaching him. The camera does a close-up of him with his arms elongated and enlarged in a distorted way. In the end, the others lift him up. He continually waves his arms like a swan, looking up as if he will keep flying. The rest, who have appeared as a hurdle, now support him so that he can reach higher. The camera angle slowly moves up from the male dancer in the air to where he is gazing, the roof where sunlight breaks through. The moment appears to symbolize the endless efforts and dreams of artists who will keep creating even if they are aware of their limitations.

Thanks to BTS' "Black Swan" art film and its quote from Martha Graham, K-pop fans have expressed their expanded knowledge of and experience in dance in general. Even the "Black Swan" official dance practice video is filmed in a highly conventional dance studio with black curtains and a black Marley floor. A male collegiate K-pop cover dancer in San Diego told me that he got into K-pop dance when he was in high school after seeing BTS at the American Music Awards in 2018. As a Vietnamese American, he felt proud to see Asians at the major music award show. During the interview, he said that he felt uncomfortable watching BTS' "Black Swan" art film partially due to the topless male dancer whose body is explicitly fragile and vulnerable, a trope quite common in modern dance. When I asked if he had ever watched concert dance (like modern dance), his answer was no. While he started his dance experience in college because of K-pop, he gradually expanded his interests to "urban dance," which integrates hip-hop, K-pop, contemporary, competition, and other genres. He became interested in dance in general and expressed his interest in taking some classes from the dance department at his university.

The song "Black Swan" encapsulates BTS' conflicted inner selves and struggles as artists. The lyrics echo with Graham's "first death quote, her lifetime dedication to dance, and her autobiographical self-exploration. The lyrics start with[1]:

> The heart no longer races
> When hearing the music play
> Tryna pull up
> Seems like time has stopped
> Oh that would be my first death
> I been always afraid of
> If this can longer resonate
> No longer make my heart vibrate
> Then like this may be how I die my first death
> But what if that moment's right now
> ....
> No song affects me anymore
> Crying out a silent cry

The lyrics delineate the fear and symbolic death of an artist whose heart no longer vibrates responding to an art piece or creation. Where does the fear come from? Artists have to keep creating artwork because when they stop producing, they may or may not be an artist anymore. Many artists are technically self-employed and work for a non-profit organization without proper health insurance or a secure income. The arts are often relatively feminized, and artists' labor is often treated free as a "gift economy" based on the prejudice that the arts are not measurable, and thus, not exchangeable in a capitalistic structure (Spiegel 123). This assumption seems to forget that artists also need to pay rent and do the grocery shopping. With the lack of sustainable infrastructure, to keep producing work is one of the few ways to maintain artists' self-esteem and identities against an insecure social status.

Nevertheless, productivity can be unpredictable, as creativity is neither mass-produced nor automatically delivered from a conveyor belt monthly. As artists grow older, they can have other priorities, such as family, marriage, parenting, health, or financial issues. Creativity can also run out over time, a process called *mannerism*. Ironically, establishing a distinctive style can have the pitfall of hindering progress or new experimentation. Simultaneously, artists can also be criticized for lacking a unique style if they produce completely incoherent pieces. Thus, artists' selves can be the biggest enemy they have to conquer, love, and reconcile with to remain as an artist.

Further, aging is an unavoidable barrier in dance, a potential death. Like Olympic athletes, younger dancers have an advantage, as dancing is bound to physical ability. Youth is even more relevant to dancers in the pop culture industry, where youthful appearances have a commercial value. South Korean male citizens are obligated to serve in the military for approximately eighteen to twenty months with a few exceptions, such as artists or athletes who win at international competitions like the Olympics. As some of the BTS members reach their late twenties, they will soon be expected to serve in the military.

Serving in the military means that they cannot practice like before. When I was a child, my teacher, who was a retired prima ballet dancer, told me that dancers should not take a break for more than three consecutive days. She said, "You know when you take a one-day break. Your teacher knows if you take two days of break. Your audience will know if you take three days of break." Since my childhood until I quit my professional dance career in my late twenties, I never took a break for more than three days. When my friends and I went on a trip for the first time in college, I did bar exercises in a hotel room while everyone was drinking. I admit that I was a workaholic, but I was afraid of the fact that the body never waits but keeps changing. Unlike tangible artifacts, such as painting, writing, and recorded music, dance is done by the dancer's body. Whenever her body stops dancing, her dance also stops. That is why dancers' rehearsals are exhaustingly repetitive. They are so repetitive that it often feels like a ritual that has an intrinsic value. Repetition has immense meaning for those who repeat the practice as a daily life ritual, even if the value of repetition is incomprehensible to outsiders.

When reaching the top of a mountain, descending is inevitable. It is only a matter of how long dances stay at the top. As BTS is one of the most successful pop groups of the era, their potential fear of "the first death" and the pressure of creating original works while younger and fresher K-pop idols debut almost weekly is understandable. Like the cases of BIGBANG and SHINee, whose careers imply multiple stages of potential deaths, fans can only hope that groups will return even after their first death. BTS might want to dance until their second death, like Graham, who danced until she could "barely walk." In this case, the audience has the privilege to meet not just sleek dancers on stage but rather human beings whose imperfections and precarious lives become an enduring performance that inspires all of us.

The Official Music Video: From Social Media to Theatre

Choreographed by Brazilian-born choreographer Sergio Reis, the "Black Swan" official music video starts with BTS clad in white suits barefoot on stage under the spotlight in a lavish Baroque-style theatre. There are scratches on the black wood floor that represent years of the sweat, practice, and labor of performers who have danced on the floor. To an ethereal string instrument sound, they gaze at their hands lifted above their heads with dreamy eyes, while they lightly circle, twitch, and flick their wrists in the air, like a bird shivering its feathers, and then slowly descend them, like a water drop. The camera zooms out and shows the grandiose theatre.

The scene overlaps with Jimin's brief solo. After an acrobatic jump, he drops his forearms and head in a jolting manner, quickly lifts his front elbow, and kicks his right leg backward in preparation, shifting his weight to the left foot. He swings his right leg to the front and side, like a *rond de jambe* in ballet, stretches, circles, and folds his arms, bending his knees and upper body inward with his head, and quickly recovers from the floor with an airy inhale, gracefully reaching his fluid arms high. When Suga and RM rap on the apron stage and in front of a staircase in the theatre hallway, shadows echoing the swans' flowing arm movements are projected on the gold brocade drapes and walls.

The point choreography is featured in front of the grand central staircase in the lobby. They are clad in black suits with black dress shoes. They twist their upper bodies side to side, in synchronization with their feet turning outwards and their shoulders waving. Their elbows are placed at chest level, flattened, and crossed, moving side to side in an angular manner. They keep swaying side to side, now crossing their wrists above their heads, showing their palms, and roughly popping their chests as if trying to escape. Echoing with the lyrics "My wandering feet held in a rut," the movement seems to suggest something is blocking their eyes and hindering them from moving forward. To the lyrics "Every noise and sound has been cut," all members glide on the floor, reach out one hand, and stand on the other hand on the floor. Jimin travels from the back to the front, sliding his arms and feet in a zigzag, reaching his arm forward, and dramatically grabbing his neck to the lyrics "Killin' me now."

The next scene starts with BTS clad in white dancing on a stage. Jimin kneels down in an empty, archaic auditorium, slowly rolling up his spine, standing as if he has been reborn. In black suits, Jimin and Jungkook have corset-like leather bands on their waists, which echoes the tight ballet tutu of female ballerinas. The tight waistlines of their bodies exposed via the corset belts emanate an androgynous appeal. In the transition to the second verse, they sing lyrics in a whispering, unearthly, and echoey voice, "Do your thang, Do your thang with me now … What's my thang, What's my thang tell me now." The members are gracefully sitting in the staircase, calmly and deeply gazing at the camera. The camera takes a low angle shot which enhances the authoritative image of the figures. Jimin stands on the stage apron, looking up at the light, and turns into a black swan with black wings dramatically scattering out from his back.

Suga and J-Hope's rap parts begin:

I think I'm goin' deeper
I keep losing focus
No, just let go of me
Let my own feet carry me
I'll go in myself.

Their feet rhythmically stagger, as if expressing exhaustion and the feeling of being lost, with expressive gestures and self-reflective facial expressions. To the lyrics "In the deepest depths / I saw myself," J-Hope sharply grabs Suga's wrist, makes him turn around, and gazes at him deeply, reaching his hands towards himself, as if J-Hope sees himself in Suga. In the lyrics, "Slowly I open my eyes / I'm in my workroom, it's my studio / The waves go darkly by in the throe / But I'll never get dragged away again," Suga raps on the apron stage facing the empty, dark auditorium as if reassuring himself that he will never give up, even if there is no audience.

The official music video for "Black Swan" advances the previous formula of K-pop dance. As Chapter 2 explains, point choreography is a visual identifier of K-pop dance. It is situated in catchy chorus lines that commonly consist of simple, easy (often English) words talking about romantic love or heartbreak. It is pre-sentational, bright, entertaining, and easy to remember, often literally embodying lyrics like in a musical. In TWICE's "TT" (2016), for example, the members flip their second fingers upside down and make "T" shapes with their first fingers extended inward horizontally, hiding the rest of the fingers, making direct eye contact, and smiling at the camera. The point choreography compensates for its front-driven flatness by adding popping, jolting, and accentuated upper-body movement. Compared to point choreography situated in the main chorus when dancers are singing, a *dance break* is composed of extensive dancing only. This phrase is more commonly used to describe K-pop dance in the 2020s, as more and more MVs focus on extensive "wow" dancing moments.

However, the point choreography in "Black Swan" official music video is not limited to literal, easy gestures. It is rather a sequence of continuously emerging, abstract movements. The lyrics to "Black Swan" are symbolic and so too is their dance. The song itself is less reliant on the chorus and instead creates a strong musical vibe with dreamy echoes and whispering, poetic lyrics. The movements embody abstract feelings in the continuum of modern dance, which has advocated for representations of abstract ideas, like Graham's *Lamentation*. The "Black Swan" dance is not necessarily literal but rather poetic. Their entire body movements, whether they dance or not, are fully filled with rich, symbolic meanings and nuances that are open to multiple interpretations. Their performance speaks to the essential functions of art that address basic human conditions like literature or poetry.

To the lyrics, "Nothing can devour me / I shout out with ferocity," Jin walks into a room filled with multiple mirrors. He turns around and looks at the camera

with a somehow conflicted but defiant gaze. But his figures reflected on the multiple mirrors do not move, as if they are frozen or anonymous personae outside himself. Then all the members appear on the stage wearing black suits. This time, the camera is on the stage featuring the dancers and the empty auditorium behind them.

The film ends with Jungkook offstage, as a black swan, sitting on the edge of the balcony of the theatre. He turns back, looking down at the stage. Onstage, the main curtain is closed; now the show is over. A shadow folds its arms and descends to the floor until it disappears. It is the same shadow, the inner persona, that appeared on the main curtain earlier when Suga talks on the apron about the "first death" in the beginning. When there is no more shadow on stage, Jungkook walks out of the theatre with a confident gaze toward the back of the auditorium.

Metaphorically, BTS can be racialized as the "black swan" whose unexpected emergence challenges the conventional "white swan," mainstream Western pop music. Further, a theatre indicates conventional discipline or the status quo, and thus, their presence as white swans onstage could mean the generalized performing arts or K-pop industry. In this case, white swans could imply the public personae of docile, conventional idols, and black swans could mean a subversion. The final scene thus implies the death of their "first death." The artists conquer their first death in theatre and are reborn as black swans who go to the world beyond theatre (convention) as multidisciplinary artists and global activists.

The Core and Breath

Jimin studied modern dance in conservatory arts high schools. Conservatory arts schools in Korea usually teach three genres – modern, ballet, and classical Korean dance – in addition to street and commercial dance. Although concert dance should not be prioritized over popular dance, Jimin's training experiences in academia expanded the spectrum of his movement, including using breath as a technique.

His solo in "Black Swan" epitomizes the effective use of breath as a technique. To the lyrics of "Ocean with all light silenced shut yeah yeah yeah / My wandering feet held in a rut yeah yeah yeah," Jimin sharply traverses across the stage in front of the other members standing in a diagonal. He quickly reaches his right arm high, spreading his right leg to the side, and shifting his weight from left to right, while his torso resists and twists to the left. The extension works as momentum that leads to a contraction. His left hand dramatically covers his face that turns to the opposite side with his torso. He then abruptly jolts, twists his upper body to the left, along with extended left elbow, as if he resists and shakes off his hand that covers his eyes. He twirls his arms, spinning, then throws his arms forward, like splashing water, facing the diagonal he is heading to. As his arm reaches out further, the more his center decreases. His throwing arm movement, as fluid as water, initiates from his core and extends to his fingertips. The movement is light and airy but dense and richly heavy at the same time. He soon turns with a self-centered, indirect gaze, fully absorbed in the movement.

A transition occurs when he extends his arm high, shifting his weight forward and dragging his feet. He drops his upper body forward, floundering his arms, and quickly rolls up and recovers, lifting his elbows sideways in an inhaling motion, undulating his spine and lightly tilting, thrusting his pelvis forward, and swinging and circling his leg from back to front. Maintaining this off-balance position, he keeps moving forward, hobbling, and purposefully staggering and dragging one foot on the floor while waving and rippling his elbow like a swan. The camera takes a low angle shot. As he comes closer to the camera, his arms and legs appear elongated.

It is possible that Jimin's solo described above could consist of one deep inhale and exhale, or at least, it appears so. He effortlessly traverses the stage without a pause, like a graceful swan gliding on the water with its unseen nimble feet underneath. Like a gymnast's high jump, a temporal holding of the breath can assist a speedy, quick, compact, and cohesive tension of the muscles in the air. Potentially, he could take a quick inhale when he first starts the solo, extending his legs and arms, and then exhale when he completely drops his torso after the short transition, and after a quick inhale, he would temporarily hold his breath until he finishes the solo at the end of the diagonal. In dance, *kinesthetic empathy* – "how one felt another's feeling" – occurs (Foster 11); the audience can feel how the dancer might feel physically and, possibly, emotionally, and even psychologically. Watching his solo, the audience might feel it is "breathtaking" not only because of his agile virtuosity but also because of contagious connectivity, as well as his natural, skillful maneuvering of breath during the approximately seven seconds of solo dance.

Typically, dancers' use of the breath is deeply interconnected with their use of the torso, which is often called the *brain* or *core*. The use of the breath is at the center of movement initiation and completion. The proper and precise landing of the feet in terms of the right timing, angle, location, and foot position all serve the proper momentum and transition into the next movement. Although the use of the core sounds esoteric, anyone who has tried home workout exercises in a standing pose could understand the significance of the core and the difficulty in landing or not landing the feet properly. Often, legs fall when they should not, and feet drop in a place and moment you do not want. Without the strength, stable balance, and manipulation of the core and breath, coordination can be lost. Limb movements might look messy, unstructured. The feet could shake and totter, and the arms move like soulless puppetry. Dance skills can be evaluated by the soundlessness of movements. With the successful control of the core, a dancer's movement should look weightless and land silently and delicately from a jump, using each toe as a cushion for a gradual, smooth landing.

In phenomenology, scholars have argued that dancers' bodies are also the mind and soul, not just physical flesh (Fraleigh; Sheets-Johnstone). A dancer's mind is in the body that is able to be aware of itself, its spatial location, fluidity, and rhythm of movement. Observing dancers' fingertips is a useful tool to evaluate dancers' skillfulness. The more trained the dancers, the more they are fully and precisely aware of how each body part, even their fingertips, are moving. When their bodies are full of embodied cognition, the movement no longer looks like that of someone else. When the breath is seamlessly integrated into movements, it further enriches the human, raw nature of dance, such as the primordial impulse, and thus, can enlighten the individual personality and even spirituality uniquely embodied in one's physical movement.

Barefoot

Going barefoot is common in concert dance but not necessarily in pop dance. K-pop female singer Sunmi in "24 hours" (2013), GAIN in "Paradise Lost" (2015), and HyunA are some of the few examples of performers who perform barefoot. The former two explicitly highlight female sexuality with song themes, lyrics, and costumes (mostly tight bodysuits) with sensual floor movements. In her comeback stage performance for "Bubble Pop!" (2011), HyunA took off her high heels while dancing due to the rain that made the outdoor stage slippery. It was not planned, and HyunA later recalled that she cried after the show (Shin). Yet, the video went viral in the media with catchy headlines, such as HyunA's "sexy barefoot dance." It is even more uncommon for K-pop male singers to dance barefoot.

What dancers wear or do not wear matters. In terms of gender, female dancers can liberate themselves from high heels that can restrict movements due to the danger of losing balance. For male dancers, high heels are an exciting tool to expand movement capabilities, often called *high-heel choreography* or *girlish choreography* and popularized by Yanis Marshall, Harper Watters, and James B Whiteside, just to name a few. They have shown how high-heel inspired movement can extend the expressive spectrum of movement due to the alignment of the spine, which may include the use of girlish hand gestures, the highlighting of curved lines and body shapes, a precariously balanced, animalistic, and fearless gait, and sensual floor movements pointing high heels in the air.

Dancing barefoot implies emotional vulnerability. Nudity became a costume and choreographic choice in experimental choreography in the twenty-first century to indicate the minimalist aesthetics of postmodern dance. Likewise, a bare foot is also a choreographic choice, the nudity of the feet. When dancers expose their bodies, they are emotionally affected. A sense of embarrassing, uncomfortable, or primordial feelings can arise. Dancing barefoot is almost like an actress acting in front of an HD camera without makeup. It is uncommon to see someone barefoot in a public space. One's bedroom can be one of the few places people can feel safe with bare feet.

In addition to emotional vulnerability and intimacy, being barefoot physically affects movements. Dance or running shoes are designed for protection and increasing performance, such as cushion, a slip resistance inside, or leather on the forefoot area that reduces friction while turning, reducing the danger of a sprained ankle. While dancing barefoot, however, dancers can feel the friction, temperature, and subtle texture of the floor with their raw bare feet. They absorb weight and gravity with their feet and knees and handle friction with their skin. The breath can help, like pulling up the spine with an inhale while turning so as to reduce gravity and thus, friction. A moment of losing balance or tottering cannot be hidden because the audience will see a dancer's toes wiggling. Because of the importance of feet, dancers tailor exercises to strengthen the instep and sole muscles of each toe. In this vein, dancing barefoot implies mental and physical strength. Dancers would not be able to dance barefoot unless they were fully ready. Moreover, dancing barefoot extends movement possibilities because the feet themselves are a medium to express, like the face, fingertips, chest, pelvis, and legs.

The final chorus in the "Black Swan" official music video illustrates a sophistication of barefoot movements. They turn out their toes, opening their knees outward like a *plié* in second position, and slowly sway side to side, while gently and firmly pressing the floor, delicately shifting weight from the heels to the toes. They rhythmically undulate their upper bodies, pushing away the air with the inside of their forearms and palms to the other direction, and release and wave their chests initiated by their heads, like a bird. Along with their faces, their exposed, bare toes peeking out of their black attire are highlighted with their jiggling, subtle, raw, and fragile presence. Simultaneously, they bend and contract their palms while extending their arms and contracting the core so that the contraction of the palm matches with the torso and enhances the dramatic expression and intensity of contraction, which speaks to the contraction and release of Graham's technique. The fluidity of the movement also echoes with a technique in modern and contemporary dance as well as in breakdance; dancers imagine that they have a rolling ball moving inside of their bodies, and as follows, their movement creates a wave or a break, like a spontaneous, freely moving ball in the water.

Level: Lifted Legs, Feet, and the Dropped Head

The "Black Swan" official music video choreography contains various level changes of their bodies. They lift their feet off the floor and circle their legs in the air. They fall, drop their entire bodies and heads, and recover. As the range of tone and deepness of a voice is essential in singing, such extended level and range of movement matter in dance. Fully dropping one's head is not as easy as it appears because dancers can lose balance, stumble, and miss the tempo. Standing on one leg and circling the other leg also needs properly controlled breath, flexibility, and coordination. Many people even struggle to stand on one leg in a quiet yoga class. Due to gravity, gymnasts can split up to 180 degrees in the air only if they can easily stretch over 180 degrees on the floor. In addition to flexibility, dancers need a sense of balance and responsiveness. Dancers can make a mistake on stage that they have never made in the studio because of distractions from the audience, body condition, or stage lights so bright that it blocks eyesight. Unless a dancer can easily lift a leg up even while closing his/her eyes, there is always a possibility of losing balance on one leg.

In gestural choreography, the feet are barely in the air. This is because once the feet and legs are off the floor, they can significantly affect singing, creating unwanted noise such as gasps while landing on the feet. The other reason pop music choreography tends to stick the feet to the floor is that the inhale and exhale timing for dancing may not be the same as it is for singing. Yet, the breath is necessary for effective movement, as commonly found in fitness or yoga exercises that consist of inhaling and exhaling in response to the release and contraction of the muscle. Unless a singer has strong vocals and trained throat muscles, it is nearly impossible to dance and sing perfectly simultaneously. This explains why professional dancers like ballet or modern dancers barely speak (or sing) while dancing and why singers have backup dancers instead.

"On": BTS as Male Dancers as Warriors

BTS' official MV for "On" (2020) further articulates the expansion of K-pop dance from gestural point choreography to a dance break. In the dance break of "On," the video shows various angles of the bodies from diagonal, front, back, and side along with extended horizontal widths, vertical depths, and the height of the movements. They use the full space with various movement patterns from floor gliding to jumping across the stage. Like "Black Swan," "On" has two versions, a cinematic music video and a five-minute-long dance film: "'ON' Official MV," performed by BTS, and "'ON' Kinetic Manifesto Film: Come Prima," performed by BTS and a group of multi-ethnic and multiracial backup dancers. The official MV was filmed in the Vasquez Rocks Natural Area Park in California. The kinetic manifesto film was recorded at Sepulveda Dam in California. Along with that of the "Black Swan" official music video featured in Los Angeles, the locations are rare for BTS whose works are mostly filmed in Korea. In the "'On' MV Shooting Sketch" (2020) video, BTS said that it was the first MV that took more than a week to film. V said in Korean that it shows "the pinnacle" of their dancing.

The "On" official MV features a thematic, dystopian universe and ends with a promising scene as they each climb to the top of a giant rock. The on-screen text "No More Dream," which comes from BTS' debut title track, fades into just "Dream." It appears to indicate the MV's major message, resilience, as HYBE announced. As fans noticed, the MV has references to TV shows and films, such as *Game of Thrones, The Lion King, The Maze Runner, The Hunger Games,* and *Alice in Wonderland,* as well as Biblical motifs, such as Noah's Ark and Adam and Eve, and it creates a BTS universe (Delgado). Visual signifiers include church-inspired settings, an imperial wall, an impaled white dove, a battlefield, a BTS member running from a prison wearing thorny handcuffs, and costumes that resemble those of pontiffs, civilians, and warriors. Fans playfully used their imaginations to interpret. A fan wrote on Twitter about RM's Noah moment: "Noah's Ark and Alpacas and Namjoon.? Wtf is Namjoon Noah the one who got on the boat with BTS and haters and rappers who used to mock him were left to get destroyed behind sksksksk" (Delgado).

Coming from Hawaii, the choreographer Sienna Lalau is known as a 19-year-old "K-pop-fan-turned-celebrity-choreographer" (Murray). She danced in the BTS' film with her crew, the Lab Studios based in Los Angeles, best known for winning season two of *World Of Dance*, an American reality dance competition TV series. Lalau started dancing to hip-hop when she was four years old. She grew up listening and dancing to K-pop groups like Girls' Generation, and her first K-pop choreography was for EXO's "Love Shot" (2018). Her dance is as boundary-crossing as K-pop, being inspired by and learning from "all genres," including modern dance, musicals, ballet, hip-hop, jazz, R&B, and popping (Russo).

In the official "On" MV, the dance break starts with a grandiose sound. BTS appears with a defiant, ritualistic, and sacred vibe. Like an ancient combat dance and ritual, they move furiously without any hesitation, almost up to the level of cathartic transformation: stomping their nimble feet, creating dust; hitting their chests aggressively, like krumping; quivering their palms primordially and expeditiously; rotating their arms as if in a trance; staggering their bodies precariously across the space; shifting and manipulating their weight in various directions; abruptly turning; and instinctively, impulsively, and vigorously jumping and thrusting their legs in the air as if they are lost in time and space before hunting or a battle. They fully extend their fluid arms to the side while descending with their knees opened widely to the side. Their bodies take up the maximum space vertically and horizontally, creating a movement, not a pose. Their bodies are liberated, filled with audacity – confrontational but inviting, aggressive but peaceful, raw but graceful. Meanwhile, the "On" kinetic manifesto film version is a pure dance film without characters or cinematic symbols. BTS staged the full dance version of the "'ON' Kinetic Manifesto Film" on *The Tonight Show Starring Jimmy Fallon* at New York City's Grand Central Station and on a Mnet comeback special stage in Korea with different variations.

The Gaze

Gestural choreography tends to divide the lower and upper body, highlighting the upper body and the face for the camera. The camera is fascinated with the face, and dancers almost never lose eye contact with the camera. Yet, BTS nearly removes their eye contact from the camera. During the dance break, they focus less on gazing at the camera. Compared to the intense, constant, and direct eye contact with the camera commonly found in point choreography, in "On," the camera moves along with their bodies in space, not necessarily with their faces. In fact, due to the highly energetic, speedy, and spacious movements constantly changing, there is not much time for the audience to figure out where the dancers are looking. BTS' gaze is rather self-centered, focusing on the sensation and execution of their movements. A less-trained dancer tends to rely more on a mirror to practice because they have not yet fully developed a clear sense between how they move and how they appear.

As exemplified in ballet, a mirror (a front portrait) implies self-discipline and the self-objectification of a dancer, which potentially detaches the body from the self

(Lindner). The more dancers are trained, however, the less they care about how they might look because the ways they move match the ways they imagine how they should move. Direct eye contact with the camera implies that the dancers are aware of the presence of the audience and that they are being watched. Indirect, aversive eye contact can imply that dancers are either willingly internalizing the objectification of dancers or simply ignoring the power dynamics between spectators (those who gaze) and dancers (the objects of the gaze).

While dancing in the "On" official MV, the members of BTS grimace. Their facial expressions differ from the choreographed, presentational grimacing commonly found in male dancers' hip thrusts, enhancing sexual tension. Instead, they possess a natural facial expression aroused from their laborious, extensive movement. When dancers are fully absorbed in the movement, they can remain vulnerable and selfless, exposing themselves to the audience. Such exposure invites the audience to comfortably watch and enjoy the dance because the dancers are dancing as if no one is watching. They are fully ready to dance while everyone watches.

In history, dance has never been limited to a certain gender, age, or body type. From a toddler dancing to a Christmas carol to a grandmother dancing Tango in a milonga club, dancing has belonged to all since the prehistoric era. In ancient times, dancing was a core part of shamanic rituals and theatrical spectacles, such as rites of passage, as exemplified by cave paintings that portray people dancing for making rain or hunting. "War dances" also trained warriors and hunters by enhancing physical strength, flexibility, stamina, and coordination. With collective chanting, drumming, and stomping feet, dance can boost morale and produce adrenaline for warriors before battles. Dancing has also been a tool used for community building and self-protection since the colonial era, often against colonizers, disguised as entertainment and passed down as cultural identities over generations. Hula, Capoeira, and haka are great examples of such diverse generational, physical, communal, and egalitarian functions of dance. The "On" official MV continues the long legacy of male dancers whose bodies bridge community and arts, ritual and spectacle, and arts and athleticism and who bring different cultures and spectators together.

Despite its equalitarian functions in rituals to festivals, dance has been feminized despite its physically demanding aspects. Cheerleading dance is a prime example (Grindstaff and West), not to mention ballet. The popular films *Billy Elliot* (2000) and *Magic Mike* (2012) portray such stereotypes. In the former, a young boy fights against negative stereotypes of male ballet dancers and becomes a prima dancer at the end. The ending scene features Matthew Bourne's *Swan Lake*. In the latter, male dancers are portrayed as working-class, heterosexual, hyper-masculine strippers, which compensates for the pervasive images of male dancers as effeminate (Tsai). Such stigmas can be traced back to Romantic ballet in the early to mid-nineteenth century, primarily in England and France, when ballet was a popular entertainment displaying female bodies, and male patrons were not pleased to see male dancers onstage (Burt). The stigma against male dancers still remains as exemplified by the common phrase "real men don't dance" (Craig).

As some of the most well-known male dancers in history, BTS revisits the stigma against male dancers by willingly displaying their bodies for female spectatorship. Fan-made dance compilation videos that highlight sensual and powerful movements, such as grimacing, hip-thrusting, sweating, closing the eyes, licking the lips, and re-creating homoeroticism, are examples of the female gaze and how fans "choreograph" their desire against the patriarchal restriction of female chasteness as well as negative stereotypes on male dancers as effeminate (C. Oh, "Queering Spectatorship"). The global BTS fandom also signifies the rising economic power of young women who have become the major consumers of global pop culture.

From Gestural Point Choreography to Dance Breaks

Compared to BTS' initial choreographies in videos such as "No More Dream" (2013) and "Boy in Luv" (2014), the official music videos for "Black Swan" (2020) and "On" (2020) denote their transition from two-dimensional, front-driven gestural point choreography to boundaryless dance breaks with an extended spectrum in volume, space, size, level, and gaze. Technically, not all BTS members are in charge of dance. As an idol group, each member has his specialty in composition, rap, vocals, or dance. Yet, as of 2020, any of their movements, even a gait, looks performative. Any of their facial expressions appear as deep as professional actors' because of their strong presence, charisma, and confidence as individuals. Like a top fashion model who still looks appealing wearing an idiosyncratic outfit, skillful performers can digest a wide spectrum of movement without awkwardness.

The official music videos for "On" (2020) and "Black Swan" (2020) have clear structures and formations, but the movements seem less rigid, less codified than their earlier work. The main focus is no longer synchronizing their external forms as in knife group dance or point choreography. Instead, they emphasize an enormous level of collective energy, flow, and harmony of movement. Like a virtuosic singer singing a difficult song, K-pop dance becomes more challenging to fully revive "how" they dance, although it is possible to imitate "what" they dance. The subtle, nuanced feeling, sophistication, and skills emanating through movements become so much of the dancers themselves and cannot be easily categorized due to the in-depth, densely self-centered, personalized, and reflective movements. Dance is not simply about what but how. If a dancer's movement is hard to imitate, that means it has individuality; it embodies the dancer's life. Then, the dance is no longer about what the movement is, but how they move and who they are. They are their dance.

Size and the Body

With the transition from gestural point choreography to dance breaks, it is not surprising that the ideal "K-pop body" has also changed. As Chapter 2 fully analyzes, K-pop dancers in the 2020s tend to have more muscle and sizable bodies with various skin tones, like Jessi and Mamamoo, compared to the artificially lean and pale bodies clad in skinny jeans of Girls' Generation and SHINee in the 2010s. Dancers' clothes also change. K-pop dancers in the 2020s tend to wear bigger-sized, gender-neutral clothing, like sweatpants and hoodies, that potentially expand the volume and visual size of movements due to the space and air between the body and fabric. While an exceptionally thin body (like that of Girls' Generation's Yoon-ah) is perfect for a two-dimensional photo that displays a clear, bony line, a voluminous muscular body is more suitable for a three-dimensional effect. In fact, the former could look like they lack stamina and a three-dimensional effect in space as their bodies might appear too flat and narrow. This could be one of the reasons why K-pop girl groups' dances appear more impactful in their two-dimensional music videos with edited camera work, even though they often appear too small and even weak in their live performances.

Backup dancers also can increase the volume of the performance. To highlight a clear, picturesque body line in point choreography, backup dancers can be distracting. But to highlight the volume and energy of movements, backup dancers can contribute significantly. The official music video for "On" (2020) exemplifies how backup dancers can expand the size of the body collectively. It stages a large scale of backup dancers and percussion musicians who maximize the visual, physical, and sonic impact of the performance.

A perfect ratio of the human body has been one of the core elements of aesthetics, like in the case of Michelangelo's *David* sculpture. Jungkook exemplifies a perfect dancer's body, not just a K-pop body. His body is relatively average, not too big, too small, or too lean. While he often struggles with diet, his body, which has an average amount of fat, adds volume to his dance. Twerking, a fast, repetitive bounce of the lower hips, exemplifies the impact and vibration of the flesh itself as an extension of movement, as a part of the dance. In dance, a ratio is not just about a better look but also about functionality. His iconic handstand movement in "Blood Sweat & Tears" (2016) demonstrates his balanced, coordinated body with enough strength and flexibility. He slowly descends to the floor from a handstand position and lands smoothly from his chest, abdomen, pelvis, and legs, waving his entire body in a regular tempo. He also has naturally expressive facial features with bold eyes. The body is the source in dance, like the ingredients in cooking. As arched feet themselves can be a merit that extends movement capability, an attractive face itself can diversify the capability of emotional expression. BTS member V's face, who is often named as the "most handsome man in the world" is an example (Ke). As fans and media often say, his face itself is a stage effect with a remarkable stage presence; the audience is naturally drawn to focus on his face while watching his performance even when he performs sitting in a chair due to injuries (star-struck).

BTS as Korean Folk Dancers and Global Activists

BTS blurs not only classical and popular dance, but also brings to it traditional Korean dance, reflecting the trend of reviving traditional Korean dance in the

2020s. BTS' "Idol" (2018) uses a computer-generated, traditional Korean pavilion and integrates traditional music. BTS' Suga and his "대취타 (Daechwita)" (2020) solo as Agust D is also set to a setting inspired by Joseon, the last dynastic kingdom of Korea, and its court music, along with hip-hop and rap music. Inspired by *Buchaechum*, a neoclassical Korean fan dance, Jimin presented a solo to the music of "Idol" (2018) at the 2018 MMA. Clad in a modernized *hanbok*, a traditional Korean outfit, he dances using a fan along with a group of male dancers who make beautiful patterns with fans. Swans have been a symbol of femininity, and so has the Korean fan dance largely been performed by women. BTS successfully adapts traditionally feminine codes with their gender-bending performances. Jimin's solo to "Idol" (2018) evoked a rising interest in fan dance, and a dance organization that preserves *Buchaechum* as intangible cultural heritage gave him a plaque of appreciation (Park). Jungkook lifting Jimin in a duet at the 2019 MMA is another example of gender-bending. In the intro, they showcase airy, angelic, dreamy movements. From ballet to cheerleading, lifting is highly gendered. Usually, men lift, initiating the movement of the female dancers whose bodies, in turn, are dependent on their male partners. BTS' duet, contrarily, evocatively challenges the gendered binary since both are sharing weight, initiating each other's movements, lifting, and being lifted, and sharing agency and vulnerability.

At the 2019 MMA, Jimin presented a solo that combined modern dance, ballet, acrobatics, and Korean folk dance. He wears a light, slightly see-through white garment that is commonly found in traditional Korean folk dance concerts. The performance is set to a tender, grandiose ballad version of BTS' song "I Need You" (2015). He holds a long white scarf, the main prop in *Salpuri*. *Salpuri* is a traditional folk dance that originates from the exorcism in a shamanic ritual. Han Sung-Joon, the father of modern Korean dance discussed in Chapter 2, contributed to developing neoclassical modern Korean dance in the late nineteenth to the early twentieth century, including *Salpuri* and the crane dance addressed below. In *Salpuri*, dancers wear a white *hanbok* and dance with a white scarf. The scarf is carefully choreographed in synchronization with the dancer's movement, whose sustained, throwing motions signify the release of sadness and sorrow. The scarf enhances the effortless, heavenly, and angelic image of Jimin's performance. It becomes an extension of his movement and body. When he lands on the floor from a jump, the scarf descends later, temporarily held in the air, creating a much bigger, higher line above him. Because of the scarf lingering in the air, he looks like he is flying while jumping. His delicate and airy beauty resonates with the long legacy of androgyny in dance history, exemplified by the legendary male dancer Vaslav Nijinsky in the early twentieth century, best known for his beauty and effortless jump among his fans.

The solo also includes influences from other Korean dance traditions. With airy, fluid, and balletic upper-body movements, Jimin gracefully moves across the stage. He jumps, spreading his arms to the side as if he is a flying bird, contracting his torso inward and getting his knee closer to his face. The jump resonates with the iconic image of *Dongrae Hakchum*, a traditional folk dance that originated from an area named Dongrae. *Hak* means a crane, and *chum* means dance. Dancers wear *hanboks* and imitate the flowing movement of cranes. Yet, Jim's adaptation has a modern interpretation. Unlike the classical version where dancers wear traditional shoes, Jimin dances in bare feet. Further, in Korean folk dance, dancers barely fully stretch out their limps and joints as the straight lines can contradict the circular shape of the nature reflected in yin and yang. Contrarily, his arms reached to the side are more aggressively, sharply, and directly stretched out. Then Jimin draws a large circle on the stage, turning and jumping simultaneously with spiral leaps. The movement technique derives from *Pungmul*, a type of traditional Korean folk music, drumming, and dance where performers dance while manipulating *sangmos* through acrobatic turning and jumping around a circle. *Sangmo* is a folk art ribbon hat with feathers or long paper streamers that create an arch in the air with the dancers' motion. In the end, Jimin glides on the floor, subtly popping his chest as if he is broken and dying like the final scene of the classical ballet *The Dying Swan*.

Conclusion

With their constant evolutions transgressing disciplinary boundaries, BTS advocates for global activism. Their song "Permission to Dance" (2021) shares optimistic lyrics:

> We don't need to worry
> 'Cause when we fall, we know how to land
> Don't need to talk the talk, just walk the walk tonight
> 'Cause we don't need permission to dance.

According to *Forbes*, the MV shares "the Post-Covid message the world needs right now" (McIntyre). The choreography is filled with a cheerful, happy vibe with easy-going, accessible steps, hand swings, bright smiles, and playfully cavorting feet. Their "Permission to Dance" (2021) performance at the United Nations General Assembly with various groups of citizens is notable, as it aims to draw the audience's attention to "sustainable development" and "inspire action" for the pandemic, food systems, climate change, energy, employment, and social protection, among other issues. As Chapter 1 explains, the viral dance challenges during COVID-19 exhibit the functions of dance as a source of self-expression, fostering physical and psychological wellbeing. The symbolic meanings of dance – freedom, liberation, and political activism – are fully explored in Chapter 6, which is based on Thai refugee teen cover dancers.

Note

1 The original lyrics combine English and Korean. The translation comes from their official music video.

References

"20's Choice_Hyuna (현아) 'Bubble Pop!'" YouTube, uploaded by Mnet K-POP, 15 July 2011, https://www.youtube.com/watch?v=X9Ya-tjPAfA&t=161s.

Anderson, Crystal S. *Soul in Seoul: African American Popular Music and K-pop.* UP of Mississippi, 2020.

Banes, Sally. *Dancing Women: Female Bodies Onstage.* Routledge, 1998.

"[BANGTAN BOMB] 'IDOL' Special Stage (BTS focus) @2018 MMA - BTS (방탄소년단)." YouTube, uploaded by BANGTANTV, 10 December 2018, https://www.youtube.com/watch?v=ayGl-igrwy8.

Billy Elliot. Directed by Stephen Daldry, Universal Pictures, 2000.

Black Swan. Directed by Darren Aronofsky, Fox Searchlight Pictures, 2010.

"BTS (방탄소년단) 'Black Swan' Art Film Performed by MN Dance Company." Directed by Yong Seok Choi. YouTube, uploaded by HYBE LABELS, 17 January 2020, https://www.youtube.com/watch?v=vGbuUFRdYqU.

"BTS (방탄소년단) 'Black Swan' Official MV." Directed by Yong Seok Choi. YouTube, uploaded by HYBE LABELS, 4 March 2020, https://www.youtube.com/watch?v=0lapF4DQPKQ.

"BTS (방탄소년단) '피 땀 눈물 (Blood Sweat & Tears)' Official MV. YouTube, uploaded by HYBE LABELS, 9 October 2016, https://www.youtube.com/watch?v=hmE9f-TEutc.

"BTS (방탄소년단) 'ON' Kinetic Manifesto Film: Come Prima." YouTube, uploaded by HYBE LABELS, 21 February 2020, https://www.youtube.com/watch?v=gwMa6gpoE9I.

"BTS (방탄소년단) 'ON' Official MV." YouTube, uploaded by HYBE LABELS, 27 February 2020, https://www.youtube.com/watch?v=mPVDGOVjRQ0.

"BTS – 'Permission to Dance' Performed at the United Nations General Assembly | SDGs | Official Video." YouTube, uploaded by United Nations, 20 September 2021, https://www.youtube.com/watch?v=9SmQOZWNyWE.

Burt, Ramsay. *The Male Dancer: Bodies, Spectacle, Sexualities.* 2nd ed., Routledge, 2007.

"[CHOREOGRAPHY] BTS (방탄소년단) 'Black Swan' Dance Practice." YouTube, uploaded by BANGTANTV, 7 February 2020, https://www.youtube.com/watch?v=fTS1jAhWPbw.

Craig, Maxine Leeds. *Sorry I Don't Dance: Why Men Refuse to Move.* Oxford UP, 2013.

Daly, Ann. "The Balanchine Woman: Of Hummingbirds and Channel Swimmers." *The Drama Review: TDR*, vol. 31, no. 1, 1987, pp. 8–21. *JSTOR*, https://doi.org/10.2307/1145763.

Delgado, Sara. "BTS 'ON' Music Video: 'Game of Thrones,' 'Lion King,' 'Maze Runner,' and More." *Teen Vogue*, 27 February 2020, https://www.teenvogue.com/story/bts-on-music-video-game-of-thrones-lion-king-maze-runner.

Desmond, Jane. "Dancing out the Difference: Cultural Imperialism and Ruth St. Denis's 'Radha' Of 1906." *Signs*, vol. 17, no. 1, 1991, pp. 28–49. *JSTOR*, http://www.jstor.org/stable/3174444.

Dodds, Sherril. "On Watching Screendance." *The International Journal of Screendance*, vol. 10, 2019, pp. 141–145. http://dx.doi.org/10.18061/ijsd.v10i0.6726.

"[EPISODE] BTS (방탄소년단) 'ON' MV Shooting Sketch." YouTube, uploaded by BANGTANTV, 2 March 2020, https://www.youtube.com/watch?time_continue=368&v=bYdDxEa3us8&feature=emb_title.

Foster, Susan Leigh. *Choreographing Empathy: Kinesthesia in Performance.* Routledge, 2010.

Foster, Susan Leigh, ed. *Worlding Dance.* Palgrave Macmillan, 2009.

Fraleigh, Sondra Horton. *Dance and the Lived Body: A Descriptive Aesthetics*. U of Pittsburgh P, 1987.

Franko, Mark. *Dancing Modernism/Performing Politics*. Indiana UP, 1995.

Freedman, Russell. *Martha Graham: A Dancer's Life*. Clarion Books, 1998.

Grindstaff, Laura, and Emily West. "Cheerleading and the Gendered Politics of Sport." *Social Problems*, vol. 53, no. 4, November 2006, pp. 500–518. *Oxford Academic*, https://doi.org/10.1525/sp.2006.53.4.500.

Juhasz, Suzanne. "Queer Swans: Those Fabulous Avians in the *Swan Lakes* of Les Ballets Trockadero and Matthew Bourne." *Dance Chronicle*, vol. 31, no. 1, 2008, pp. 54–83. *Taylor and Francis Online*, https://doi.org/10.1080/01472520701860623.

Ke, Bryan. "BTS' V named 'Most Handsome Man in the World in 2021' by Two Publications in the Same Week." *Yahoo News*, 6 October 2021, https://news.yahoo.com/bts-v-named-most-handsome-170309470.html.

Kealiinohomoku, Joann. "An Anthropologist Looks at Ballet as a Form of Ethnic Dance." In *Moving History/Dancing Cultures: A Dance History Reader*, edited by Ann Dils and Ann Cooper Albright, Wesleyan UP, 2001, 33–43.

Kim, Ki-yoon. "BTS Choreographer 'Sienna Lalau,' Praised as 'A Musical, Not an Idol Choreography.'" *Dong-A Ilbo*, 9 July 2019, https://www.donga.com/news/Culture/article/all/20190709/96393549/1.

Kwan, SanSan. "When Is Contemporary Dance?" *Dance Research Journal*, vol. 49, no. 3, Dec. 2017, pp. 38–52. *Cambridge Core*, https://doi.org/10.1017/S0149767717000341.

Lindner, Katharina. "Spectacular (Dis-) Embodiments: The Female Dancer on Film." *Scope: An Online Journal of Film and TV Studies*, vol. 20, June 2011, pp. 1–18. *STORRE*, http://hdl.handle.net/1893/3703.

Magic Mike. Directed by Stephen Soderbergh, Warner Brothers Pictures, 2012.

Maher, Erin K. "Ballet, Race, and Agnes de Mille's *Black Ritual*." *The Musical Quarterly*, vol. 97, no. 3, 2014, pp. 390–428. *Oxford Academic*, https://doi.org/10.1093/musqtl/gdu009.

Manning, Susan. *Modern Dance, Negro Dance: Race in Motion*. U of Minnesota P, 2004.

Martin, John. "The Dance: Martha Graham She Returns in Triumph after Season's absence—Notes from the Field." *New York Times*, 2 January 1944. Retrieved from the Library of Congress, <www.loc.gov/item/ihas.200153424/>.

McIntyre, Hugh. "BTS's 'Permission To Dance' Is Officially The Biggest Song In The World." *Forbes*. 19 July 2021, https://www.forbes.com/sites/hughmcintyre/2021/07/19/btss-permission-to-dance-is-officially-the-biggest-song-in-the-world/?sh=5509880b74f3.

"[MMA 2019] 방탄소년단 (BTS) | Full Live Performance." YouTube, uploaded by 1theK, 1 December 2019, https://www.youtube.com/watch?v=b9cG4DzpL_c.

Murray, Lydia. "Meet Sienna Lalau, the 19-Year-Old Who Has Choreographed for K-Pop Superstars BTS." *Dance Magazine*, 9 January 2020, https://www.dancemagazine.com/sienna-lalau2644465284.html?rebelltitem=2#rebelltitem2.

"[MV] GAIN (가인) _ Paradise Lost." YouTube, uploaded by 1theK, 11 March 2015, https://www.youtube.com/watch?v=4i32ANEa5mk.

Oh, Chuyun. "Queering Spectatorship in K-pop: The Androgynous Male Dancing Body and Western Female Fandom." *The Journal of Fandom Studies*, vol. 3, no. 1, 2015, pp. 59–78. *Ingenta Connect*, https://doi.org/10.1386/jfs.3.1.59_1.

Park, Hyun-taek. "Fan Dance Preservation Society Gives an Appreciation Plaque to BTS Jimin for 'Raising the Status of Fan Dance.'" *Edaily*, 28 February 2019, https://www.edaily.co.kr/news/read?newsId=01213606622394784&mediaCodeNo=258.

Russo, Gianluca. "Sienna Lalau: The Dynamite Dancer and Choreographer Helping BTS Make Magic." *Dance Spirit*. 4 May 2021, https://dancespirit.com/sienna-lalau/.

Sheets-Johnstone, Maxine. *The Phenomenology of Dance*. 2nd ed., Dance Books, 1979.

Shin, Nara. "'Bubble Pop' Barefoot on the First Stage … Cried After (HyunA)." *Dispatch*, 4 September 2017, https://www.dispatch.co.kr/880621.

Song, Myoung-Sun. *Hanguk Hip Hop Global Rap in South Korea*. Palgrave Macmillan, 2019.

star-struck. "Global Media Members Praise V's Powerful Stage Presence in Their Review of BTS's Online Concert, 'Permission To Dance On Stage.'" *Allkpop*, 28 October 2021, https://www.allkpop.com/article/2021/10/global-media-members-praise-vs-powerful-st age-presence-in-their-review-of-btss-online-concert-permission-to-dance-on-stage.

Spiegel, Jennifer Beth. "Amateur Performance and the Labour of Love or Cultural Repro-duction 'After' the Collapse of Capitalism." *Performance Research*, vol. 25, no. 1, 2020, pp. 121–124. *Taylor and Francis Online*, https://doi.org/10.1080/13528165.2020.1747270.

"Sunmi (선미) '24 hours (24시간이 모자라)' M/V." YouTube, uploaded by JYP Enter-tainment, 20 August 2013, https://www.youtube.com/watch?v=2UmDrsMlXXg.

Taleb, Nassim Nicholas. *The Black Swan: The Impact of the Highly Improbable*. 1st ed., Random House, 2007.

Thoms, Victoria. "Martha Graham's Haunting Body: Autobiography at the Intersection of Writing and Dancing." *Dance Research Journal*, vol. 40, no. 1, summer 2008, pp. 3–16. *Cambridge Core*, https://doi.org/10.1017/S0149767700001339.

Tsai, Addie. "Magic Mike, Dirty Dancing, and the (Empty) Promise of Heteromasculinity." *The International Journal of Screendance*, vol. 9, 2018, pp. 98–117, http://dx.doi.org/10. 18061/ijsd.v9i0.6040.

"TWICE 'TT' M/V." YouTube, uploaded by JYP Entertainment, 23 October 2016, http s://www.youtube.com/watch?v=ePpPVE-GGJw.

PART II

K-pop Dance Fandom

4

K-POP COVER DANCE AS INTERCULTURAL PERFORMANCE

Introduction[1]

A group of college students is dancing to upbeat K-pop music in a campus gym. The music is loud enough to be heard by pedestrians passing by. More students have just arrived. After a moment of hugging and catching up, they soon join in practicing the K-pop cover dance. Some are so focused on dancing that they do not even notice the new members who have just arrived. It is a summer Friday evening in San Diego, California. The practice lasts more two hours. They are completely immersed in making the movement right: accuracy. In a group dance, they try to match each angle of their feet on the floor and the lines of their bodies, the direction their shoulders are facing, spatial formation, and timing as each dancer enters and walks off the stage, as well as precise facial expressions and lip-syncing according to the music. Among approximately 50 dancers, only a few are Korean. They repeat the practice over and over again until everything is perfectly synchronized. They are drenched in sweat throughout but still seem rejuvenated. The room is full of community, youth, and joy.

I draw this scene from a K-pop collegiate dance team's practice at a state university in San Diego. This chapter focuses on nine collegiate K-pop cover dancers from three K-pop dance teams I interviewed from 2019 to 2020: two teams are in San Diego, and one is in Seoul. The nine participants are Latinx, Chinese American, white American, Filipino American, Korean American, and Korean. Six are women, and three are men. Their sexual orientations vary from heterosexual to gay and bisexual, and their ages range from late teens to late 20s. They often compete with other K-pop dancers on and offline, work professionally as dancers, and socialize as fans. The chapter interchangeably uses terms such as dance team, crew, club, and group, reflecting interviewees' different word choices.

This chapter approaches K-pop cover dance as a kind of intercultural communication – a communication across different cultures and social groups – and more

DOI: 10.4324/9781003212188-7

specifically, intercultural performance. Responding to the transnational adaptation of K-pop dance, such as PSY's "Gangnam Style," Marcus Tan noted that "The moving body, driven by rhythm, becomes the site of the global intercultural performative" (Tan 88). In December 2020, *Time Magazine* recognized the K-pop boy group BTS as the Entertainer of the Year. It introduced two K-pop fans, an African American and Asian American, who wholeheartedly supported the group as fans and as racial minorities in the US. While there is an abundance of research on ethnic minority K-pop fans in the US, the extant research does not fully address differences *within* ethnic minority communities. Further, comparative analysis of K-pop dance fandom between Korea and the US is limited. Despite its global popularity, there is also scarce research on intercultural performances of K-pop cover dance such as learning, producing, and performing K-pop cover from a dancer's perspective.

The body is a core site of intercultural communication. A critical integration of performance can re-center the body that has often been marginalized in intercultural communication (Calafell). As I demonstrated in my previous research ("From Seoul"; "Identity Passing"), from renting a dance studio to preparing a show (music, set, lighting, costuming, choreographing, rehearsing, recording, and promoting), cover dance requires institutional support, diligent physical labor, and continuous bodily discipline. An analysis of K-pop cover dance can deepen our understanding of intercultural performance because K-pop cover dance *embodies* a transnational adaptation and appreciation of culture.

Employing performance ethnography (Madison), this chapter analyzes embodied labor in the intercultural performance of K-pop cover dance. Joni L. Jones noted the significance of embodiment in defining cultural authenticity. As explained later, this chapter suggests bodily effort to distinguish cultural appreciation and transformation from cultural appropriation. The interviewees' stories disclose the unequal distribution of resources, discrepancies between racial and ethnic minority groups, and the (in)ability of identity passing based on what scholars have called "intersectionality" (Crenshaw; Collins) such as age, race, ethnicity, class, education, family, geography, and citizenship. At the same time, obstacles in reality further inspire fans' dreams to be like K-pop idols.

K-pop is for Everyone

Olivia is a 21-year-old Chinese American woman born in California, double majoring in linguistics and psychology at a state university in California. She began her professional ballet training with parental support, when she was five years old and continued until age 17. She got into K-pop through fan fiction and was shocked when she first saw a K-pop boy group's dance on YouTube: "I've never seen boys dance like them before," she recalled. Her K-pop dancing started when she was 16. During her first year of college, she found a K-pop dance team and became a staff member. She is currently leading most of the dance workshops for the team.

When I first met Olivia, I could easily recognize her; she was tall and athletic and looked like a ballet dancer. She wore a hoodie with the name of her university, one of the most prestigious universities in California. Her polished makeup and bright lipstick reminded me of K-pop girl groups. "When I was a kid, my parents, like a lot of Asian parents, made me do a bunch of different classes and stuff. So, I started doing ballet," she said confidently. She did not like the rigid ballet structure because she struggled with flexibility and found the restrictive practices painful. Contrarily, she found K-pop dancing "very free." She added, "You have a lot of options. You can dance in whatever style you want. You can change the choreography to fit your style better." In university, she found K-pop a "stress relief" hobby to express herself. The determined, hard-working ethics of K-pop idols also inspired her: "These idols have nothing, and then all they want to do is dance and sing. It's almost like they're an example, even though I might not want to dance for my career."

To Olivia, K-pop is all about "inclusiveness." The K-pop dance team she is involved in is one of the biggest dance teams at the university. Approximately 70 members regularly participate in their weekly workshops and gathering. The team aims to provide "a home" for all K-pop fans. Her dance team is a community where "everyone is just welcome, and everyone can do it." She explained:

> We do not discriminate against age, gender, race, skill, or anything. We take everyone. Our personal goal is to make K-pop something that everyone can feel comfortable liking or feel comfortable being a fan of. I think many people do not look like they could like K-pop, but the point is that K-pop transcends language and cultural barriers.

Given the many Asian Americans on the dance team, K-pop "for everyone" reflects a utopian pan-Asian identity and a sense of community among Asian ethnic and racial minorities as an alternative subculture against the US mainstream media. Like the Southeast Asian refugee teens discussed in Chapter 6, Asian Americans on Olivia's dance team create a sense of belonging and "feeling at home" in the transpacific pop culture of K-pop (Balance 147). Olivia's dance team also makes a statement regarding positive inclusivity by accepting all students regardless of dance training, body type, race, or ethnicity. Indeed, whenever I visited their practices, the room was filled with a diverse student group consisting of different body types, races, ethnicities, sexual orientations, and cultural backgrounds.

To many, the K-pop dance team opened an educational gateway to learn about and be exposed to other types of dance beyond Western concert dance. Amber is Chinese American on the K-pop dance team who used to be a dance major. Like Olivia, she studied dance from an early age. She recalled an experimental choreography class she took from the Dance Department, "'Close your eyes... feel the air... shake your arms.' I don't know what that means." The esoteric style of postmodern dance was quite different from what she expected. She later switched to a dance minor, and now fulfills her passion for dancing on student dance teams including K-pop. As Chapter 1 explained, social media allows an infinite stage beyond academia for members of a young generation who do not hesitate to claim their voice and preference beyond the Western canon. The invisibility of Mexican, Asian, and African dance classes in higher education could be another reason that discourages minority students to study dance.

Throughout K-pop dance, many interviewees further diversify and refine their interests and skills in dancing. Many wanted to dance in high school but could not because of other more urgent matters, such as preparing for university entrance exams. Another thing frequently mentioned among the participants was the high school dance culture, mainly cheerleading dance, and its association with typical racial and gender stereotypes and social life, which they felt did not include them. During my research process, I noticed that some students from the K-pop dance teams had moved to other dance teams such as urban and hip-hop dance. Some of them also began to take formal dance courses at the university, such as introductory jazz and contemporary dance classes that they had never tried before. As a result, they gradually gained more confidence in dancing and their movements through the gateway of K-pop dance.

Korean American Joel is a freshman majoring in molecular and cellular biology. He joined the same K-pop dance team with Olivia in his first year without formal dance training. He expressed how excited he was when he first got a chance to perform. "Because, you know, I just wanted to do a K-pop cover, any cover. But then, the only group that was looking for people and accepting new members was for a 'Fancy' cover, so I was like, 'I'll do Fancy!'" "Fancy" is the girl group TWICE's song, and as girl group choreography, it was even less familiar to him. Yet, he successfully finished his first cover dance within a few months, during which he not only deepened his friendships but also gained confidence in dancing in general. After his dance experiences on the K-pop dance team, Joel said that he was planning on taking more dance classes from the university's dance department. "I am not very good or dedicated enough to do an actual dance team yet," Joel elaborated. While he implies that K-pop dance is different from "actual dance," he soon told me about the complicated process of making a K-pop cover dance.

Joel's comparison between K-pop dance versus "actual dance" resonates with Olivia's concern. She said other dance teams often dismiss the K-pop dance team because it does cover dance, not choreography, and thus lacks creativity. The criticism implies that K-pop dance is a mere imitation, and therefore does not have artistic value. As a former ballet dancer, she expressed her discomfort toward the comments, saying that if repeating a repertoire makes a dance not an actual dance, classical ballet should not be a dance because ballet relies on repertoires such as *The Swan Lake* and *The Nutcracker*. Collegiate dance team members usually have majors other than dance. It is rare to find dance majors on collegiate dance teams. Amber's K-pop team performed at Fusion Hip-Hop Dance Competition, one of the biggest collegiate hip-hop dance competitions on the West Coast, along with nearly 100 participants from other teams. I asked her how many of them are actual dance majors. She said, "Maybe one or two, I'm not gonna lie." Extensive rehearsal hours, schedule conflicts, or different stylistic preferences between students and dance faculty can be reasons for the lack of dance majors on collegiate dance teams. When most collegiate dance teams are extracurriculars, neglecting K-pop as not an actual dance and mere imitation seems to reflect racial prejudice against K-pop and Asian American dancers and the notion of racialized authenticity, as was explained in the Introduction. In fact, based on my observation, most of their cover dance live performances had creative interpretations, including modified formations, movements, costumes, edited music, and lighting, among others.

The K-pop dance team stands out among many other university dance teams because of its balance between socializing and dancing. The team is "demanding enough to force you to get better at dancing, but it is not like so demanding that you can't sleep," Joel said. His comment reminded me of my interview with "Sleepless Collective," an urban dance team at his university, where collegiate dancers literally stayed up until late at night to dance, sacrificing their time to sleep for dancing. According to my interviewees, new K-pop dance teams and clubs have been created on campus with a stricter and more exclusive audition process to bring in skillful and experienced dancers. Yet, to Olivia and Joel, their K-pop dance team, which is one of the longest-running and largest K-pop dance teams on campus, is unique with its mission that embraces anyone interested in and passionate about K-pop. Wearing a smile, Joel said, "The dance team is like I have a kind of family that I sweat with." White American Aelin shared a similar idea. She is on the same dance team as Olivia and Joel. "It is a dance team, but it is a social club as well. We do things like just go bowling together and hang out, watch movies, and support each other."

While the dance team serves as a social club, its function as a K-pop cover dance team requires more labor than socializing. Identity passing requires more than the enthusiasm of an individual. When identity passing occurs through physical performance, structural and material support is necessary for becoming. Olivia and Joel's K-pop dance team consists of student staff members and committees specialized in specific areas: dance, media, and promotion. Within this infrastructure, their cover dance productions are neatly organized. Students first apply for a dance they want to cover and find group members. Then, the dance committee assigns a dance coordinator to help with learning the choreography. Participants are expected to practice at least two hours a week, and then the dancers choose a potential film date. Next, the media team videotapes the performance, edits, shares the draft with the dancers to determine whether an additional shooting is needed, and finally releases it on its official YouTube channel. Olivia said that her work would not be possible without the media team's support. "They edited the cover and put little touches, like the clips here with the palette on the bottom, directly inspired by the original video, [which] made the cover feel more real and connected to the original," she said.

Equipment and venue support from the university further eases the team members' practice. They hold their dance workshops in a clean, spacious gym they can use every week. They can also occasionally use dance studios overseen by the university's Dance Department. When I came to observe their rehearsals, the workshop always started on time and dancers went through multiple hours of practice with clear instructions by skillful dance instructors on the team. The filming is usually done in various locations, including a fancy recording studio equipped with state-of-the-art technology and is led by a couple of videographers from the media team. For equipment purchases, such as the camera, they have received funding from the university's student council as well as from fundraising events and the subscription fees for the dance team.

Nathan is on the same K-pop dance team with Olivia. He is a Filipino American and majoring in communication and political science. He wants to be an immigration lawyer. "I am inspired by my parents because they had so many difficulties, so I want to lessen people's burdens," he said. One day, he invited me to an early Saturday morning rehearsal. Opening the building door, he greeted me with smile. His face was covered with sweat. After practice, they took a group photo, each holding banana-flavored milk and posing in front of the camera like models. I asked a member why they drank the sweet and thick banana milk instead of water after a vigorous dance practice. Smiling, he replied that they had gotten sponsorship from a local Korean market selling the product.

The high production quality of the dance team's cover of BLACKPINK's "Kill This Love" demonstrates the resources available to Olivia and her dance team. The entire process takes around ten weeks with the collective team effort. Three of the dancers in the video are Chinese American, and one is Vietnamese American. All the dancers are light-skinned and have black hair and visually approximate typical K-pop idols. Most of the members have had professional movement training, from martial arts to ballet. Their execution of choreography, synchronization of the group dance, and articulation of movements are precise. Their costumes and makeup match well with the flirtatious yet bold and rebellious concept of the original music video. They lip-sync to the song in Korean quite smoothly. The video was filmed at Balboa Park in San Diego with multiple camera angles and the final product was well-polished and had their logo superimposed on the images. Amber, another dancer who performed in the video, told me a story of a young girl who watched the filming from the beginning. When one of the dancers spoke to the girl, the child ended up crying because she thought they were celebrities. Indeed, because of their successful execution of the dance moves and their synchronized look from the choreography to the costumes, they could easily be mistaken for professional dancers, and in this case, pass as K-pop idols.

The K-pop Dance Team without Koreans

During the ethnographic research, I discovered that Olivia's K-pop dance team had few Koreans or Korean Americans. When I asked about this, Olivia responded:

> Many people ask us, "Are you guys Korean? Do you guys have a lot of Koreans?" I am like, "No. We are just normal people. Our race or ethnicity does not really matter." We actually do not have that many Koreans. We have two or three, but most of our team are from all over. We have Chinese people, we have Vietnamese, we have Hispanic.

During the interview, she often used some Korean words. I asked whether she is of Korean descent or has a connection with Korean culture. Being mistaken as a Korean, she laughed with excitement and proudly responded that she learned Korean while attending a study abroad program at one of the top three universities in Korea. Because the Olivia's team is all about inclusivity, it is worthwhile to consider the apparent lack of Korean and Korean American dancers. During the research process, I found that the team had only one Korean member. Korean and Korean American students found the club a little uncomfortable because they felt "Othered," according to a Korean international student who used to be one of the few Koreans on the team.

Joel is one of the few Korean Americans on the dance team. He was born in the US and stayed in Korea until he was six years old. "I speak Korean like a first-grader, basically [laughs]," he said. He first started dancing in high school to BTS songs and watched their music videos on YouTube to have fun with his friends, who were mostly Asian Americans. He wanted to learn more about Korean culture as he realized that he knew nothing about Korean history compared to his knowledge of American history. In his first year in university, he found a club on campus for Koreans, which he identified as a club for "Korean Koreans, not Korean Americans." In the club, he felt different because to him, Korean international students in the club seemed to expect more hierarchical relations depending on age. When he met the K-pop dance team handing out fliers at the university library, he saw a "bunch of Asian students dancing." He recalled, "I thought there would be Korean people in the dance team, so my first impression was, there are no Koreans here [laughs]." He soon found that it was the exact opposite of what he had expected. "Even though I am Korean, everyone else knows more about K-pop than me." He then shared a sense of the Othering he had witnessed in college:

> This is just something I have noticed, but some people fetish[ize] a Korean even if the Korean isn't attractive. They'll just be like, "Well, you're Korean, you're so attractive." Or they'll associate what the idols with, like just the regular people who look nothing like the idols. I find it all interesting.

There can be an internalization of Orientalism even among Asian racial and ethnic minorities (Eguchi 38). The body is a "text" that needs intercultural translation, often through dominant discourse (Chávez 23). When K-pop becomes an outlet for Asian Americans with its increased visibility, there is the potential for Korea to be Orientalized by those who might seek an authentic Korean experience, which Eguchi might call a "nostalgic fantasy" toward Asia (Eguchi 39).

In addition to the exoticization of Koreans, K-pop seems to be more than music to some cover dancers. Joel said that to him, K-pop is "just the music, pretty people, and interesting choreographies." He found, however, that this was not the case for his non-Korean, K-pop fan-dancer friends. He compared K-pop with Japanese anime. "For a lot of my friends, anime is really cool, and like it's interesting to watch and has a good storyline. But then for actual Japanese people, it's often looked down upon, almost like what kids watch and things like that." While he thinks K-pop is mostly a genre of music, he noticed that K-pop played a much bigger role to non-Korean, K-pop cover dancers. He said K-pop was more like a "lifestyle" to some of his friends. Many of the dance team members were passionate and dedicated fans of Korean dramas, reality television shows, and music and truly enjoyed talking about it together. "They are more invested than the other Koreans and me," he added. As scholars have argued, K-pop has been a platform for racial and ethnic minorities in the US, especially Asian Americans, given the lack of positive media representations of Asians in the US. As K-pop and Chinese American Olivia are both racial Others in the US, solidarity can arise, given the pan-Asian unity among Korean Americans and Chinese Americans (Kibria).

Indeed, Chinse American Shawn, a sophomore engineering major, said that he became a K-pop fan and started dancing to K-pop in high school after seeing BTS at the MTV Video Music Awards. Watching BTS on a mainstream American stage, he felt proud of himself as Asian. Joel agreed with Shawn and said he believed that one of the driving forces in K-pop dance fandom in the US has been that "they see there are cool people [Asians], and they want to be more like them." But as a Korean American, Joel thinks differently from other Asian American fans. While Joel also thought that many K-pop singers are "hot" and "pretty," he did not necessarily feel the need or desire to identify with K-pop or Korea, perhaps because he is already ethnically Korean.

Despite the apparent benefit of K-pop being supported by and making visible Asian American communities, the lack of Koreans on Olivia's K-pop dance team speaks to a larger structural issue. From its initial emergence to the nation-branding strategy by the Korean government, K-pop is a cultural product from Korea. The ethnic and national specificity of K-pop is often erased in Olivia's moment of identity passing. Indeed, the absence and meanings of the "K" in K-pop has been the subject of scholarly debate (Yoon 3). The lack of Koreans on the dance team appears to be filled by other ethnic and racial minority students, including other Asian Americans, mostly Chinese Americans.

Toward Cultural Appreciation and Transformation

When majority cultures take those of minorities, whether through a racial, ethnic, or diplomatic hierarchy, the roots of minority cultures are often diluted or erased. Regarding hip-hop, Tricia Rose pointed out that "because the world can share it," people believe that "it has no origin" and the primary innovators of hip-hop – "Jamaicans, Puerto Ricans, Dominicans, Cubans, African Americans, and other [ethnic] groups" – are erased in commercialization of hip-hop for white consumers. A consideration of ethnicity and citizenship vis-à-vis colonial history can deepen our understanding of ethics in intercultural performance of K-pop dance. Historically, South Korea has been placed in an uneasy battlefield between China and North Korea and between Japan and the US. The previously subordinated position of South Korea under the US's modern influence has created a sense of postcolonial anxiety in Korean society (Moon).

While Asian Americans are racially Asian, they can be marked as (white) American to Koreans. Given Asian Americans' citizenship and cultural and linguistic belonging to the US, there can be a sense of neocolonial exploitation among Koreans when they encounter Americans. The power dynamics between the US and Korea partially explain the lack of Koreans or Korean Americans on Olivia's dance team. The ethnic and national positionality of Olivia as a Chinese American could provide her a double-layered privilege, allowing her to easily put on and wear the mask of K-pop idols: for citizenship, the influence of the US's neocolonial modernity in Korea, and for ethnicity, China's past dominance over Korea during the premodern era. Yet, social media complicates the geography and race-oriented identity. Even if Asian Americans in the US can uphold US imperialism as US citizens, many often relate to Asian culture, such as K-pop. While their country (the US) has a history of colonial invasion, their ethnic root reflects those of colonized (Asian). The transnational space of social media opens a diasporic formation of identity beyond a fixed race, geography, and ethnicity. The utopianistic statement of K-pop being "for everyone" opens a space for a discussion about cultural appreciation and appropriation when embodying a new cultural identity. As Dwight Conquergood reminded us, the belief that asks, "Aren't all people really just alike?" or what he referred to as "The Enthusiast's Infatuation" can be problematic. This is because even with a positive intention, identifying with the Other too easily and eagerly can trivialize and generalize the Other to the point of superficiality (Conquergood 6).

Nevertheless, Olivia's case is further complicated because her team advocates for the Other in the US. The other significant difference is their sincere bodily effort to embody K-pop dance over the years. What they do is not that different from the dance majors I teach. At my current institution, dance majors take Western techniques (namely, ballet, modern, and postmodern) as well as hip-hop and Capoeira. Sometimes, they take additional classes over years, like Advanced Technique 200 and 300 to graduate. It seems difficult to say that dance majors' learning hip-hop for years is a cultural appropriation. This is mainly because we know of the students' sincere bodily effort, dedicated time and energy, yearlong embodied training, and possibly, good intention to learn the dance (even if they take the courses to graduate). Interestingly, African, Asian, and Latin American students taking ballet or modern dance rarely induce the conversation about cultural appropriation. This reveals the significance of race and colonial history when defining the ethics of cultural appropriation. It is hard to imagine someone happily dancing voluntarily and passionately if they are not genuinely interested in it. Such dedicated, continuous bodily effort can distinguish cultural appreciation and intercultural performance from mere cultural appropriation. What Olivia's dance team does is as enthusiastic and labor-intensive as those of dance majors, if not more, because the dancers' effort is voluntary and genuine, not for credit or grade.

Undoubtedly, their dedication to K-pop dance may or may not be extended to a broader understanding of history, culture, and political context. An "untheorized celebration of access" of dance in globalization can be dangerous as it could flatten and mistranslate a culture (Chatterjea 9). Increasing visibility does not equate to increased power for those historically marginalized (Phelan). Yet, exposure is still better than absence. An action with real sweat has more potential than empty words of promise. An embodied exposure, physical experience in action can be a beginning of appreciating difference. This initiation can become a continuous, dialogical performance along with the possibility of cultural transformation.

K-pop is Just "Music"

While K-pop is often consumed as a piece of exotic Asian pop music in the US, this is not the case in South Korea. As people in the US are less likely to call pop songs "American" pop songs, K-pop, too, is a generic term, simply referred to as "pop songs" or "songs" (*gayo* in Korean) in Korea. Unlike the ethnicization of K-pop in the US, K-pop is the mainstream music genre in Korea. Lee Min is a Korean student attending a university in Seoul. She is a fan of the K-pop boy group EXO and is currently a member of a dance team at her university. She does not have any formal dance training. She briefly learned dance in elementary school and then took adult dance classes, including a K-pop dance class, to lose weight during high school. "In my university, we mostly perform at festivals and events on campus with some popular songs of the months," she said. During the interview, she did not even say the word "K-pop" and merely said "songs." When her dance team is dancing at a college festival targeting young audiences, they play trendy and popular songs for the youth, mostly K-pop.

Korean American Joel expressed a similar point of view on K-pop as simply "music." Recalling his childhood in Korea, Joel said, "Because I am [ethnically] Korean and I grew up in Korea, like K-pop wasn't really K-pop in Korea. K-pop was just music that you listened to, right? I didn't really think of it as like … I didn't really idolize it." When he later came to the US, he realized that "a lot of people, especially Asians that aren't Koreans, would kind of idolize K-pop." Joel's word choice of "idolize" implies that in the US fandom K-pop idols are likely at the center of attention through which fans desire to be like K-pop singers.

In addition to the different societal perceptions and naming of K-pop, Lee Min's dance team in Seoul does not show any effort in identity passing. Just like common collegiate cheerleading or dance teams in Korea, Lee Min's dance team does not lip-sync when dancing to K-pop. This is different from the US-based, non-Korean cover dancers whose major challenge is lip-syncing in Korean. Further, although Lee Min's team plays K-pop songs and imitates the original choreography or creates similar choreographies, the members do not necessarily consider it a "cover dance." Rather, it is as common as any collegiate students' activities – just playing popular songs and dancing to them. There seems to be no pressure to sing or look like a Korean while dancing. They also do not wear spectacular clothes, glamorous makeup, or dramatic facial expressions like those of K-pop idols. Since they are already Korean, there is no need to pass as Korean.

The nearly flawless level of identity passing of K-pop cover dancers in the US, from their dance moves to lip-syncing, often surprises Lee Min. Responding to the rapidly rising popularity of K-pop across the globe over the last decade, she said that she did not expect K-pop groups, including EXO, to become that popular when she first became a fan. Seeing EXO's fans and their cover dance videos worldwide made her feel like she was "losing them [EXO]" to foreign fans to some extent. Notably, many of the K-pop cover dance groups on YouTube are not Koreans but rather fans from all over the world. "How can they even do that, and why? I always wonder whenever I watch foreigners' K-pop cover dance videos." Her comment mainly refers to the similarity of K-pop cover dances to the originals, not to mention a large amount of hidden labor behind the video productions. She was amazed and curious to know how foreign fans could sing in Korean and dance, dress, and look like K-pop idols so well. Her surprise and slight discomfort came from more than the dancers' virtuosity and skills in identity passing.

On a deeper level, as a native Korean, the ethnic and racial majority in Korea, she may or may not have had the experience of being a racial Other. In this case, Koreanness operates as the essentialized and even neutral, unmarked ethnicity that is so pervasive it often remains unseen. This hegemonic privilege of the monolithic notion of the "pure blood" myth has upheld "pure blood" ethnic nationalism (Shin 38). Such hegemonic ethnicity in a local context is challenged by global, non-Korean cover dancers who dance, move, sing, and speak like Koreans, and thus, reveal racial, ethnic, and national identity as constructed performances.

K-pop versus "Real" America

Jun is a Korean international student who joined Olivia's K-pop dance team during his one-year study abroad program in San Diego. He joined the K-pop dance team as one of the few Koreans. He made it clear that he does not feel like he dances like K-pop idols when doing a cover dance. "I just dance to their music and choreography. But I think it also depends on how my team members want to represent themselves." When I watched his cover dance video of BTS's "MIC Drop," he was the only Korean in the video. On their YouTube video, the rest of the team members use stage names that sound Korean. He lip-syncs like the rest of the K-pop cover dancers. As he is the only one who speaks Korean, apparently, his lip-sync seems easier and more natural compared to the other dancers on the team. As a Korean, he not only sees K-pop as a non-racialized genre, but he also spends less bodily labor to pass as a K-pop idol. He seems to not care about whether he looks Korean.

He began to listen to K-pop during his military service. He listened to K-pop girl group songs with friends while serving in the US Army in South Korea. "In the military, no one listens to boy group songs [laughs]," he added. Then, he recalled his unexpected encounter with the K-pop dance team in San Diego when a student gave him the K-pop dance team's flier in the university library:

> When they said it is a K-pop club, I was like, "what? K-pop? [grimaces] Why do you even like K-pop?" I joined the study abroad program because I wanted to learn American culture more and develop my English skills but ended up spending more time with Asians [laughs].

He did not necessarily expect that there could be a K-pop club for university students because he believed that K-pop was for teenage girls. His somewhat cynical attitude also implied an assumption that K-pop was perhaps not likable for people in the US based on colonial inferiority, which I will explain further.

It appears that Korean international students tend to racialize not only K-pop but also American culture. When I asked Jun about what other Korean international students think about him being on the K-pop dance team, he hesitated for a second and shared his thoughts: "Some of them said that 'you should experience real America! Why do you have to go and hang out with Asians even in the US?'" He also said many of his international friends want to experience "Black culture," such as being invited to a party by African American friends or being on a hip-hop dance crew because they think Black culture is "cool." He said it was quite common among his Korean international friends to brag about how they had experienced the "real" American culture at least once. Contrarily, they tended to have a strong negative perception of "Asian culture" in the US. Many of them assumed that Asian culture was not sophisticated, fancy, trendy, or "cool enough" and even thought of "Otaku" culture. This Japanese term refers to avid anime and manga consumers, often in a negative way.

Jun's comments indicate that the "real" America mainly refers to White and Black cultures for some Korean international students. Interestingly, when they idolize Black and White cultures, they tend to generalize and even neglect Asian culture as lesser than American culture. It was unclear whether the Korean international students distinguish Asians from Asian Americans. Often, Korean youth participating in US study abroad programs internalize postcolonial inferiority and thus believe that Western culture is superior to the East's. Black culture plays a particularly interesting role here. Although African Americans are a racial minority in the US, to Korean international students, Black culture is associated with the hegemonic "cool American" mainstream culture. In terms of power dynamics associated with nationality, Black culture is whitened to some extent in the eyes of the Korean international students who see American citizenship and nationality more than race.

The Korean international students' perception of Asian culture likely reveals their internalization of Asians as Other. When the "real" America is dichotomized as either Black or White, Asians and Asian Americans are omitted, reproducing the persistent stereotypes and marginalization of Asians as "foreigners" in the US. Yet, K-pop has now become part of American culture as much as being a part of the global youth culture: K-pop books are sold at American bookstores; BTS miniatures stand next to Wonder Woman miniatures at children's toy stores; K-pop singers appear on popular US shows from the Billboard Music Awards to Jimmy Kimmel Live; and K-pop singers' interviews are broadcast on Apple Music Radio 1. But for some Korean international students, the presence of K-pop in American culture is incomprehensible because "real" Americans should be White or Black. The Korean international students become the Other who is Othering Asians, and thus, K-pop in the US. It is unclear, however, whether they are aware that they are, as Koreans, part of the Asian culture that they dismiss.

If there is a sense of internalized racism and postcolonial inferiority in Korean international students, this might better explain why they "brag" about their experience in "real" American culture; that is, being part of either a Black or White community reassures them that they do not belong to the Asian community, and thus, could potentially pass as White or Black culturally. Simultaneously, while their fascination with "real" America could be a sign of postcolonial inferiority, it could also be another way of exoticizing and romanticizing a foreign culture. Like the American students in the US who exoticize K-pop, Korean students in the US exoticize American culture. Just as American K-pop fans dream of being like K-pop idols, at least on the cover dance stage, Korean international students desire to be like Americans, at least during their study abroad in the US.

Jun's understanding of K-pop changed depending on his geographical and, thus, cultural belonging. In Korea, he used to believe that K-pop was songs for teenage girls or young men in the military. In the US, being a member of a K-pop dance club proves aspects of his positionality to himself as an Asian and his advocacy for other races, ethnicities, and sexualities. Jun distinguishes himself from conventional masculinity and social norms in Korea:

> I think I am not a typical Korean. I even went to the American military in South Korea. The South Korean military is the place where Korean men learn conventional masculinity and norms. I had Black friends, friends from Southeast Asia, and I also support the LGBTQ community.

He continued by explaining his discomfort with Korean society's discrimination against skin color. Korean society has a long history of preferring light skin as a beauty standard, not to mention the society's favorable treatment of Caucasian immigrants and expatriates. Jun's reference to "conventional masculinity" refers to a militarized, hegemonic masculinity tied to Korea's patriarchal, heterosexual, and ethnocentric nationalist agendas. To him, being a member of the K-pop dance team meant that he was open to meeting various races, ethnicities, and sexualities by which he distinguished himself from conventional Korean masculinity and social norms. In fact, the American military in South Korea is less likely an egalitarian site compared to the Korean military, given the long history of neocolonial violence, transnational crime, sex trafficking, and the US military's exploitation of locals and Korean women (Hughes et al.; Soh). Although military masculinity is not the focus of this chapter, Jun's binary juxtaposition between Korean and American masculinities based on his military experience reveals how he might idolize American culture as more liberatory and progressive. His perception reflects the rhetoric of postcolonial inferiority that perceives America as a "symbolic father" vis-à-vis the heroic white masculinity (Joo 200). Interestingly, it was his K-pop dance team that bridged his desire to be more of a part of American culture with his resistance against conventional Korean masculinity.

After his study abroad program, Jun returned to Korea. Interestingly, in Korea, his memory of K-pop dance became nostalgic as he experienced code-switching in a diasporic sense of identity. He found it bothersome when people constantly asked him to eat more even after he said he was full. He said that he missed the individualism in the US and briefly expressed his interest in coming back to the US. Even though it had been a few months since he had returned to Korea, I noticed that his Facebook cover photo was still a group photo of the K-pop dance team in the US. He was one of the few Koreans in the photo. He somehow romanticized his time in the US with his experience of K-pop dance, which unconsciously and gradually turned into a pivotal part of his memory about American culture.

Dancing itself further fostered his nostalgia. Before going to study abroad in the US, Jun wanted to take dance classes at his university in Korea. But taking a dance class was not common, and he did not find many options. During his one-year stay in the US, he found more introductory dance classes for non-majors, while he also joined the K-pop dance team. He might have felt more liberated and freer because the network he had created would last only a year, and he may have worried less about others' societal perceptions about him dancing. Including his study abroad experience, he has now spent five years as a university student. He said that he is already worried about his career and that listening to "bright and happy" K-pop songs is too childish and no longer relevant to what he is doing. It is possible that to him, the K-pop dance team in the US was a touristy, exotic destination where he discovered and tried something new. The K-pop dance team served like an extended period of his youth when he still had the luxury of time to discover his hobbies and cultural identity.

While Jun tended to idolize American culture, he felt more distance from than proximity to Korean Americans. He said that he could easily recognize whether Korean students he saw on campus were Korean or Korean Americans, no matter their fluency in speaking English. He could tell their national origin by the ways they moved and spoke, how they dressed, and often, simply by how they looked. When I asked what he thought about Korean Americans during his study abroad in the US, he said that he did not meet many Korean Americans and could only name one Korean who also happened to be on his dance team. He found Korean Americans more American than Korean due to cultural differences and linguistic barriers.

K-pop is Something Even People Like Me Can Try

Emily is a 27-year-old woman. She graduated from a small community college in California in 2015 where she studied graphic art. She is a Latinx American born in California, and she began dancing when she was 18. She first got into K-pop in high school because it seemed different from mainstream cheerleading dance. She is a self-taught dancer, who practices at home and produces K-pop cover dance videos by herself. Her father passed away, and she and her brother take care of her mother.

When I met her for the interview, Emily walked into the classroom holding her mother's hand; her mother was quite aged and seemed to have difficulty walking. She asked to schedule the interview for Sunday because parking is free on campus during the weekend. Emily stood out and was distinguishable from general students on campus because she dressed like a K-pop idol, if not a fashion model. She wore an oversized blue jacket, pink eyeshadow, pink earrings, and white ankle boots.

Emily approaches K-pop as a "creative outlet" for diversity. "We bring a lot of different cultures and people and bring them together for K-pop," she said. When I asked her if she is of Asian descent or connected to Asian culture, she responded, "I wish," looking down, wearing a shy and somehow unconfident smile. "I don't have a lot of Asian friends. Mostly because they're usually busy … but the main reason is that we're dark-skinned, so it's very hard to find people like that too." Her experience contrasts with Olivia's, who could easily be mistaken for Korean due to her lighter-skinned East Asian phenotype as Chinese American. Olivia also had the privilege of learning Korean in a university and interacting with other Asian Americans and Asians on the dance team.

In today's globalized world, mobility becomes a privilege. Today, migration is no longer limited to working-class immigrants and enslaved people who migrated overseas to work voluntarily or through force. Urban, upper-class, and educated people, who ethnographer Smitha Radhakrishnan (2011) called the "transnational class" (Radhakrishnan 3) have more access to travel the world with an increased mobility as privilege like Indian professionals in in Silicon Valley. Many of the collegiate K-pop dancers from the dance team at the state university in San Diego have received an opportunity to participate in a study abroad program. While their ethnicities are not limited to Indian nor their majors to technology, some of their transnational mobility reflects the emergence of the "transnational class" who have more choices in performing identities through structural resources, economic networks and capital, as well as cultural, educational, and linguistic privileges. Unlike Olivia, Emily has neither traveled nor studied outside of the US. She also has not had a chance to study Korean in university.

Another difference from Olivia is that Emily did not begin dancing at a young age. "It is very silly. The first class I went to was in a small, little hip-hop class, where I was 18 years old, and everyone else in the class was six," she recalled wearing a shy smile on her face:

I wish I started dancing way earlier… I am still working hard through my barrier, and I am finding it even harder to overcome. Many fans and friends of mine say I am improving! It's great to hear that my hard work is paying off. Unfortunately, I don't seem to be gaining new viewers or support.

Based on my observation of her performances, Emily was as skillful as many renowned K-pop cover dancers. Her lack of popularity seemed related more to the fact that she has neither a label nor collaborators who can take care of videography, promotion, reserving space, or editing. Performance is a multi-disciplinary work. Professional dance companies work with musicians, cinematographers, lighting designers, costume designers, marketing teams, fundraisers, etc., so that dancers can focus on dancing. Emily's difficulties do not necessarily arise from a lack of skill but rather a lack of infrastructure and institutional support.

Unlike Olivia, who professionally studied ballet, a dance genre in the "high arts," Emily is self-taught and began with hip-hop, which has a long history of serving marginalized communities. She discovered K-pop in 2010 and that sparked her interest in becoming a professional K-pop dancer: "Back then, I was a really shy, little girl. But I would love plays and theater, but I never got to try it." K-pop looked like musical theatre to her due to its "happy" visual elements and its storyline and lyrics that matched the choreography. "If the singers say something like, 'I hear you,' they'll do like this." She put her hand around her ear. "K-pop looked like something I could try … you know?" she added. Her attitude was humble and hopeful. The gestural choreography that often matched the lyrics in K-pop created an easier entrance for her to start learning K-pop dance.

As media scholar Kyong Yoon articulated, social media, albeit seemingly free and open to everyone, is not necessarily "a neutral space" but is instead impacted by existing hegemony (Yoon 10). On the surface, Emily and Olivia seem to have a similar approach to K-pop dance: It is something everyone can do. Although both Emily and Olivia thought K-pop was about inclusivity and implied the democratic applicability of K-pop, the nuance between the two dancers was different. In addition to linguistic, racial, and ethnic marginalization and privileges within this ethnic minority fan community, Emily and Olivia perceived K-pop differently in their life paths. Olivia felt at ease in K-pop dance compared to her formal, "high arts" training in ballet. K-pop was a fun hobby and escape compared to her experiences in the strict practices of ballet and discipline of schoolwork. Comparatively, Emily looked at K-pop as a possible gateway where she could dream about an alternative life. Like the refugee teen dancers discussed in Chapter 6, for Emily, K-pop dance was a refuge where even a person who does not have formal training or resources could dream of and start being a dancer.

Like the refugee dancers and many other cover dancers, Emily solely relied on YouTube and social media to learn the choreography. Most K-pop songs have dance tutorial videos. "That's what I love about YouTube. It has it all. It helps a lot of people like me," she said. YouTube is free, and access to these videos means that Emily did not need to pay for dance classes. Unlike Olivia, however, Emily did not have peers who could provide feedback. She mostly covers solo dances because she does not have team members. While K-pop on YouTube is accessible to everyone, the results are different based on access to socioeconomic resources and members of the community.

Emily's process of making Red Velvet's "Zimzalabim" cover dance demonstrates the multilayered effort needed for identity passing due to a lack of resources. The original dance consists of five performers, but Emily performs it alone by modifying the original choreography because she did not have others to join her. Although her costume does not perfectly match the original music video's futuristic concept, it visually suits the amusement park where she filmed the video. The video is edited moderately well, but her powerful movement and charisma are strong enough to make her performance mesmerizing.

There is labor hidden behind the sleek final video production. When I asked where she practices, Emily responded:

> I have a cool closet mirror in my room, so I am able to look at myself and practice at home. I am very lucky to have mirror closets. But sometimes I can't jump or something because I am on the second floor, and it's going to be too loud... When I am actually out filming it, that's when I try to practice the actual energy and going all out and actually do it.

As a former dancer, I could only imagine how many barriers she confronted. As she cannot practice with full energy during a rehearsal, and presumably has limited space in her room, the first time she can try the choreography in public is on the date of filming.

Unlike Olivia, who scheduled the filming months ahead of time, Emily filmed the "Zimzalabim" cover dance by chance. The process was spontaneous and somewhat chaotic. One day, her friend gave her tickets to the San Diego County Fair at the Del Mar Fairgrounds. Though she had not planned to go, Red Velvet released its new music video "Zimzalabim" the day after she received the tickets. The video features playful and futuristic images of an amusement park. Emily realized that she could recreate this at the fair. No dance tutorial videos were available on YouTube, but Emily was able to obtain an unofficial version of the dance with the help of her friend:

> When the music video comes out, they have a showcase. If you look hard enough, you can find the fancams. That was hard to find because the entertainment agent tries to hide it as much as possible. Another friend of mine, she was learning from that one. I was like, "Oh, help me out. I need it."

The unpredictable schedule of a K-pop video release was not the only barrier Emily faced. She had no one to help her film. The fair did not allow large tripods, so she asked her brother to come. "I learned the dance the night before going to the fair because my brother could only go the next day," she elaborated. During the performance, Emily acted both as a director and dancer, simultaneously providing her brother with the instructions he needed: "We did it very fast. I tried to help him direct, like which angle to go at because he doesn't know how to do videography. I was like, 'Hold the camera,' 'Move it this way.'" The filming lasted only an hour and a half, and Emily spent three hours editing the video that night.

Such structural and institutional barriers engender a lack of further opportunities. In 2019, a Korean church in San Diego invited Olivia and her dance team to an annual charity concert. When I arrived at the church, I saw about 100 audience members waiting for the show, including children, parents, and churchgoers. The stage was neat and spacious, equipped with fancy lighting and decorative flowers in the background. Their dance performance was presented during the climax of the concert after a series of classical music performances with instruments such as piano and violins. A group of teenage boys was sitting next to me. When a middle-aged woman said hello, they responded with excitement, saying, "We are here to see hip-hop dance!" It was interesting to me that the young boys understood K-pop as hip-hop. The audience greeted the dance team's performance with big cheers after the show. The church provided a nice socializing dinner for the dancers and the audience members. The team was paid after the show. In contrast, Emily had recently performed at a Korean culture festival in a small community school attended by a much smaller audience. She presented her performance in a small classroom surrounded by a couple of students. "My friend, she works there, and she knows about my stuff, so she's like, 'Yeah, come perform. It will be fine. There's free food,'" she recalled.

Emily did not have instructional, institutional, or familial support for her career. This lack of resources was compounded by the fact that she also did not have a regular income:

> It's very hard…I actually don't have a job right now, but I did have a job, and I always found myself dancing in the back when I'm not looking at the customers [laughs]. I do want to focus more on making dancing more of my career. And then I also take care of my mom, so it's a bit harder.

The intercultural negotiations of identity are not simple processes but "on-going complex and paradoxical dialectics of life struggle" (Asante and Eguchi 183). While Olivia's dance career and school life seemed inseparable from her parents' lifetime support, Emily has had to support her mother from an early age. She said that her brother is always busy, as he also has had to support the family financially after her father passed away. She also told me that she came to the interview with her mother because she could not leave her alone at home.

The fact that Emily is in her late twenties further creates a certain level of anxiety for her. She said she often feels disempowered and loses confidence because she kept thinking that it could be too late for her to be a dancer. Interestingly, age is a rather common issue among K-pop cover dancers who want to debut, and many are already anxious about their age. Indeed, many K-pop idols debut when they are teens or even as young as 10 years old. The anxiety about age certainly motivated Emily to practice harder and helped her develop her dance skills faster. "A lot of my friends are saying that I am improving really fast," she said. But Emily had a bigger goal than being a K-pop cover dancer on YouTube. She wanted to be a professional dancer/singer in the K-pop industry. When I asked her whether she considered applying to K-pop auditions or sending music agents her dance videos, she seemed hesitant but interested. One of her concerns was also the fact that the K-pop industry is driven by the idol system, and music agents prefer young trainees. At the end of the interview, I told Emily that she looked so youthful in her dance videos. She laughed and said, "That's why I put 16 in my YouTube nickname! I wanted to look like 16 years old."

When I went back home after the interview, I stopped by a café for lunch. I saw that Emily was practicing on the café terrace. The choreography consisted of an energetic body wave and chest popping movements. Her dance was rich, powerful, exuberant, highly expressive, and beautifully articulated. She videotaped her practice with her smartphone, reviewed it, danced, and recorded it again. Every time she reviewed her video, she corrected her gestures and movements by herself so that she made the choreography right in the next filming. She repeated this process of recording, reviewing, correcting, and performing repeatedly until I finished my meal. It was a bright, hot August Sunday in San Diego. The campus was full of visitors, new students, and parents. A lot of people who passed Emily observed her dance with curiosity, often staying for a while and even turning back to see her when they walked away. She took off her jacket, wiping off the sweat. She wore a short white top and tight jeans. Watching her dancing on the terrace reminded me of what she had just told me about the limited space she has at home. The roomy marble outdoor café terrace became a stage for her to practice, given her limited resources. Further, it was obvious that she enjoyed the public's attention.

Emily's readiness and interest in performing in public contrasted with the university dance team's interests, many of whom expressed a preference for K-pop cover dance videos over K-pop dancing in public. Emily seemed to have a stronger charisma and presence while dancing live in public than in her dance videos. Perhaps this was because she has been performing K-pop dance mostly as a solo dancer who needs more charisma. Or maybe her videos fail to show her charisma due to the lack of multiple shoots taken by multiple cameras, edited by multiple people. At the same time, I could not help but think that all the hardships she has had to go through, in fact, gave her resilience and persistence. Persistence and resilience are fundamental qualities required for any dancer given the physically demanding, and thus mentally challenging, training process.

Working-class girls often employ dance to overcome socioeconomic barriers and dream of an alternative life (McRobbie 130). Emily's story resonates with the notion of the "dreamy girl" in dance. Throughout the interview process, she was the most passionate interviewee. Her experiences are the opposite of many college students' and even dance majors' who started dancing at an early age and then quit dancing to pursue a higher-paying job.

In February 2020, I had a follow-up interview with Emily. She looked more confident and mature. In the last year, she had launched her own cover dance group. Unlike Olivia's dance team, which consisted of predominantly East and Southeast Asian students, Emily's dance team consisted of African American and Latinx dancers in their late twenties. I have noticed that Emily's cover dance videos are getting more views. Her June 2019 cover of "Zimzalabim" had more than 3,000 views by February 2020, which is quite huge even compared to other more well-known cover dance teams. Emily's video has a lot of comments, and she likes every single comment made by the audience with a heart button and responds to each of them.

Certainly, the number of views is not the singular source to define the merit of performance. A dancer's experience is not necessarily quantifiable because for dancers, dancing itself can generate a sense of empowerment, self-achievement, and emotional satisfaction and reward regardless of audience reception. Above all, in dancing there is a sense of intrinsic value, like a ritual. Further, there are numerous factors that affect the popularity of the content, including the popularity of the original content since online search engines automatically suggest similar content. Given that both BLACKPINK and Red Velvet are representative of K-pop female groups, it is equally possible that both Olivia's dance team and Emily's could benefit from the original songs' established popularity. Yet, the major difference between Olivia and Emily is the different levels of resources. Emily's success over time sheds light on how much additional effort and labor she has given to build her career as a K-pop cover dancer online.

A Structural Irony of Fandom

The cover dancers addressed in this chapter feel and experience K-pop dance in various ways: K-pop dance for everyone regardless of ethnicity or skill, K-pop just as a piece of music, K-pop as a bridge to "real" American culture, K-pop as not an actual dance, K-pop dance as an outlet to dream of a professional career. Although their stories do not represent the full spectrum of K-pop cover dance in Southern California nor in Seoul, they offer a multiplicity of the fandom's positionality and a nuanced understanding of why people of color affectively invest in K-pop as a space of "mediated imagination" (Yoon 6). Future studies can further theorize growing African, Latin American, and LGBTQ+ cover dancers and their resistive identity formations.

Fandom provides an alternative space to dream of what is otherwise unobtainable. Despite the barriers, it was Emily who wanted to pursue a professional career in K-pop dance. Her lack of opportunity and intersectional hardship motivated her more profound fan labor and affective investment. As critical scholars have noted, fans' mediated imagination is "not mere fantasy or escape but rather a social practice involving the cultural dynamics of dominance and resistance" (Yoon 6). The fan dancers' multi-layered privilege and marginalization reveal a structural irony of fandom – the more fans are marginalized, the more they desire to be like the stars, despite a lesser chance of obtaining the dream. Emily's story resonates with those of the refugee teens discussed in Chapter Six, who had the least resources but the biggest dreams and passions in a K-pop refuge.

Note

1 An earlier version of this study was published in 2020. "Identity Passing in Intercultural Performance of K-pop Cover Dance," Chuyun Oh, *Journal of Intercultural Communication Research*, copyright © 2020 World Communication Association, reprinted by permission of Taylor & Francis Ltd, http://www.tandfonline.com on behalf of World Communication Association.

References

Balance, Christine Bacareza. "How It Feels to Be Viral Me: Affective Labor and Asian American YouTube Performance." *WSQ: Women's Studies Quarterly*, vol. 40, no. 1/2, 2012, pp. 138–152. doi:10.1353/wsq.2012.0016.

Calafell, Bernadette Marie. "The Critical Performative Turn in Intercultural Communication." *Journal of Intercultural Communication Research*, vol. 49, no. 5, 2020, pp. 410–415. https://doi.org/10.1080/17475759.2020.1740292.

Chávez, Karma R. "Embodied Translation: Dominant Discourse and Communication with Migrant Bodies-as-text." *Howard Journal of Communications*, vol. 20, no. 1, 2009, pp. 18–36. https://doi.org/10.1080/10646170802664912.

Chatterjea, Ananya. "On the Value of Mistranslations and Contaminations: The Category Of 'Contemporary Choreography' in Asian Dance." *Dance Research Journal*, vol. 45 no. 1, 2013, pp. 4–21. https://www.jstor.org/stable/23524723.

Collins, Patricia Hill, and Sirma Bilge. *Intersectionality*. John Wiley & Sons, 2020.

Conquergood, Dwight. "Performing as a Moral Act: Ethical Dimensions of the Ethnography of Performance." *Literature in Performance*, vol. 5, no. 2, 1985, pp. 1–13. https://doi.org/10.1080/10462938509391578.

Crenshaw, Kimberle. "Mapping the Margins: Intersectionality, Identity Politics, and Violence Against Women of Color." *Stanford Law Review*, vol. 43, 1990, pp. 1241–1299. https://www.jstor.org/stable/1229039.

Eguchi, Shinsuke. "Queer Intercultural Relationality: An Autoethnography of Asian–Black (dis) Connections in White Gay America." *Journal of International and Intercultural Communication*, vol. 8, no. 1, 2015, pp. 27–43. https://doi.org/10.1080/17513057.2015.991077.

Eguchi, Shinsuke, and Godfried Asante. "Disidentifications Revisited: Queer(y)ing Intercultural Communication Theory." *Communication Theory*, vol. 26, no. 2, 2016, pp. 171–189. https://doi.org/10.1111/comt.12086.

Hughes, Donna M., Katherine Y.Chon, and Derek P.Ellerman. "Modern-day Comfort Women: The US military, Transnational Crime, and the Trafficking of Women." *Violence Against Women*, vol. 13, no. 9, 2007, pp. 901–922. https://doi.org/10.1177/1077801207305218.

Joo, Eunwoo, "Under the Gaze of the American Other," *Korea Journal*, vol. 44, no. 1, 2004, pp. 199–220.

Jones, Joni L. "Performance Ethnography: The Role of Embodiment in Cultural Authenticity." *Theatre Topics*, vol. 12, no. 1, 2002, pp. 1–15. doi:10.1353/tt.2002.0004.

Kibria, Nazli. "The Construction of 'Asian American': Reflections on Intermarriage and Ethnic Identity Among Second-generation Chinese and Korean Americans." *Ethnic and*

Racial Studies, vol. 20, no. 3, 1997, pp. 523–544. https://doi.org/10.1080/01419870. 1997.9993973.

Madison, D. Soyini. *Critical Ethnography: Method, Ethics, and Performance.* Sage Publications, 2011.

McRobbie, Angela. "Dance and Social Fantasy." In *Gender and Generation (Youth Question),* edited by Angela McRobbie and Mica Nava, 1984, Palgrave Macmillan, pp. 130–161.

Moon, Seungsook. *Militarized Modernity and Gendered Citizenship in South Korea.* Duke UP, 2005.

Oh, Chuyun. "From Seoul to Copenhagen: Migrating K-Pop Cover Dance and Performing Diasporic Youth in Social Media." *Dance Research Journal,* vol. 52, no. 1, 2020a, pp. 20–32. https://doi.org/10.1017/S0149767720000030.

Oh, Chuyun. "Identity Passing in Intercultural Performance of K-pop Cover Dance." *Journal of Intercultural Communication Research,* vol. 49, no. 5, 2020b, pp. 472–483. https://doi.org/10.1080/17475759.2020.1803103.

Phelan, Peggy. *Unmarked: The Politics of Performance.* Routledge, 2003.

Radhakrishnan, Smitha. *Appropriately Indian: Gender and Culture in a New Transnational Class.* Duke UP, 2011.

Shin, Gi-Wook. *Ethnic Nationalism in Korea: Genealogy, Politics, and Legacy.* Stanford UP, 2006.

Tan, Marcus. "K-Contagion: Sound, Speed, and Space in "Gangnam Style." *TDR/The Drama Review,* vol. 59, no. 1, 2015, pp. 83–96. https://doi.org/10.1162/DRAM_a_00430.

"Tricia Rose on "Hip Hop, Mass Media and Racial Storytelling in the Age of Obama." YouTube, uploaded by SocialJusticeNOW, 13 November 2012, https://www.youtube.com/watch?v=rbAVa8ndepk.

Yoon, Kyong. "Postcolonial Production and Consumption of Global K-pop." In *The Korean Wave: Retrospect and Prospect,* edited by Dal Yong Jin and Tae-Jin Yoon, Rowman & Littlefield, 2017, pp. 1–13.

5

A WHITE K-POP FAN-DANCER IN JAPAN

Introduction

Chapter 4 discussed different spectrums of Latinx, Asian American, and Korean K-pop cover dancers in San Diego and Seoul. This chapter focuses on Aelin, a white American K-pop cover dancer in the same K-pop dance team in Southern California discussed in the previous chapter. Aelin was born and raised in California. She had been dancing on the K-pop dance team for two years, starting her freshmen year. She was a fan of Japanese anime in high school and later discovered K-pop. In university, she turned her fandom into academic endeavors with a major in Japanese studies and a minor in Korean studies. Among many interviewees, she was one of the few cover dancers who was formally majoring in Asian studies and later got a job in Asia.

As scholars have noted, fans construct alternative racial, gender, ethnic, linguistic, and sexual identities via K-pop. Her position as a white woman who studied abroad adds another layer to her identity formation. As a white international student in Japan and a K-pop fan in San Diego, she experienced conflicted identity formations across borders due to her fannish, racial, and spatial orientation. I derive the adjective "fannish" from Francesca Coppa's widely cited 2008 article "Women, *Star Trek*, and the Early Development of Fannish Viding." In the essay, Coppa discussed female fanfiction videos that remix pop music with original *Star Trek* footage using a fannish, or fandom-oriented, creative investment.

Compared to the research on ethnic minority K-pop fandom, white K-pop fans often remain understudied, despite their increasing visibility. My previous research on white Canadian expatriates, "Eat Your Kimchi" (EYK), Canadian expatriate K-pop fans and YouTube bloggers, and white Danish girls are some of the few studies on this topic ("From Seoul"; "White-Expat-Fans"; "Vlogging White Privilege").

DOI: 10.4324/9781003212188-8

Moreover, there has been little research on white K-pop fans who have experienced geographical and spatial relocation. Today, migration is no longer limited to people from developing worlds moving to the so-called "First World." With the rapidly changing global economy, an increasing number of immigrants, expatriates, academics, and students migrate from the West to East for education, business, and job opportunities (Cranston; Croucher; Lan; Lundström). According to SanSan Kwan (2011), space is not neutral but racialized; performing race is performing geography (Kwan 126). She wrote, "Whoever has the power to organize social space gains the privilege to define race" (Kwan 121). Spatial belonging impacts a (re)formation of racial identity. Korean K-pop idols, for example, are ethnic minorities in the US, but ethnic majority in Korea. The line across race, ethnicity, citizenship, and cultural belonging becomes more fluid and often complicated because of the easy access to global cultures on and offline in globalization.

White K-pop fans outside their home countries disclose a unique reconstruction of spatial and diasporic identities that often resettle their whiteness. My previous research on "Eat Your Kimchi" (EYK) in Korea (later "Eat Your Sushi" in Japan) articulates the complex formation of racial, spatial, and fannish identities. As David Oh and I ("White-Expat-Fans") theorize, their whiteness often contradicts their fandom and complicates their relationship with K-pop and local Korean communities. As K-pop fans, EYK identified with and subordinated themselves to the K-pop idols they admired. But as whites, they assumed that they had a more objective view of Asia than local Koreans in Korea or younger K-pop fans who they often degraded as fanatic and irrational, thus replicating colonial tourists' logic of racial superiority. As expatriates, offline, they searched for recognition and a sense of belonging from the local Korean community in Korea. As follow, they showed hostility when they were called foreigners in Korea. But online, they highlighted their positions as white expatriates and foreigners for commercial profits, so that they could benefit from YouTube viewers who preferred white users and from non-Korean K-pop fans abroad to whom they promised "secret information" about K-pop idols in Korea.

When their white privilege was challenged, they understood it as "reverse" racism. To compensate for their sense of marginalization, they used social media to increase their visibility and gradually evolve from (less visible) K-pop fans and English teachers to (hypervisible) white micro-celebrities and full-time bloggers on YouTube. Eventually, as white-expat-fans, they selected being white over being expatriates and K-pop fans because whiteness is the most privileged category among the three.

This chapter applies the framework of white fans abroad to Aelin's case. While Aelin's case differs from that of EYK, they share some similarities in terms of affiliations in education, as well as racial, fannish, and geographical belonging. This is not to generalize white K-pop fans. Instead, it aims to extend the framework of white–expat–fans through a close analysis of Aelin's case and her temporal, racial, spatial, and fannish experiences in Japan and Korea to illuminate the complicated positionality of white K-pop fans abroad.

The chapter first reviews bell hooks's notion of "eating the Other" and Edward Said's theory of Orientalism. Intersecting critical race and performance studies theories, the chapter closely reads Aelin's racial, spatial, and fannish orientation. Aelin's fandom certainly drove her to imitate and perform K-pop cover dance. Her spatial and racial position, however, complicates her fannish orientation. As a white fan surrounded by Asians or Asian Americans in her US K-pop dance team in the US, and as a foreign exchange student on a Japanese K-pop dance team, she felt a sense of marginalization. This sense was exacerbated in Japan because of the linguistic barrier and her visual difference as a white American.

Whites Eating the Other

In her groundbreaking book *Black Looks: Race and Representation,* bell hooks argued that the mainstream US culture commodifies ethnic and racial differences and Otherness for capitalist profits (hooks 39). The issue here is the trivialization of the Other as a mere exchangeable and "palatable" commodity for white consumers who eat, consume, and then forget the Other, or what hooks called "consumer cannibalism" (hooks 39). The action of eating the Other for self-exploration and pleasure repeats the history of oppression since the colonial era and the systemic exploitation of ethnic and racial minorities. To hooks, eating the Other is an act of privilege because white consumers do not experience stigmas imposed on racial and ethnic minorities whose cultures white consumers conveniently wear and then discard. Yet, those white consumers eating the Other often appear "progressive" (hooks 24) as they seemingly support plurality, even if what they actually do is maintain the long history of white people appropriating minorities' cultures without facing the real consequences, discrimination, and structural violence the Other has experienced.

White female dancers reveal an interesting intersection of race and gender in intercultural performance. As women, they could be marginalized and resist conventional gender norms, but as whites, they are privileged and could reproduce racial hierarchy, which has been the common pitfall of white feminism. Ruth St. Denis and Martha Graham are seen as empowering because of their contributions to the women's rights movement and visibility in society. Their Orientalism and cultural appropriation, however, have received less attention, and are overshadowed by their status as pioneers of American modern dance. White women in the US believe that they are liberal and can "free" Arab and Muslim women by domesticating belly dance, while what they actually do is to reduce anxiety toward Middle East after 9/11 through a "guilty pleasures of U.S. imperialism" (Maira 341) and Orientalism that perceives Middle Eastern women as feminine, timeless, passive Other who needs liberation through Western intervention and democracy. Even if white female dancers' adaptations of non-Western cultures serve as an alternative site of resistance to Western patriarchy in a local context, at the intersection of race, gender, and colonialism, their liberation and self-actualization can oppress women of color in a global context.

In the Introduction, I discussed whites' adaptations and appropriations of Latin, Cuban, African, and Asian dances. Because of their whiteness – often viewed as the universal human race – the "unmarked" racial privilege of whites guarantees freedom in appropriating the Other (Dyer 45; Phelan 2, 5). Whites' privilege is not limited to dance but rather extends to culture in general. Amara Lindsay Miller claimed that "white, thin, acrobatic, female, [and] heterosexual" women have become the dominant image of "authentic" yogis, which marginalizes other ethnicities and body types in the yoga industry (Miller 1). The Indian historical and cultural origins of yoga have been erased through the superficial consumption of yoga as a commodity for white mainstream consumers. Accordingly, yoga now symbolizes a "skinny white girl yoga culture" in the US (Berger 40).

As seen through the lens of hooks' theory of eating the Other, Asians and Asian Americans are primarily "eaten" through the West's long legacy of Orientalism (hooks 39). Edward Said developed the term "Orientalism" based on his research on the colonial relations between the Middle East and Europe. Europe has framed the Middle East as the deviant, irrational, exotic, feminine, and inferior Other as compared to the logical, masculine, superior European colonizer. Though the term Orientalism originated from a Middle Eastern context, in the US the Orient also refers to East Asia, including Korea, Japan, and China (Weinstein 145). As demonstrated by pervasive ethnic stereotypes, from media to daily life, the Oriental gaze is still deeply rooted in a Western society with neocolonial imperialism. It remains a "systematic discipline" that justifies Western dominance, colonial violence, and invasions, thus maintaining racial, ethnic, and gendered hierarchies that extend into the contemporary era (Darnell 1004).

When referring to marginalized racial and ethnic minorities in the US, I use the "Other" in reference to its use in critical race, gender, and postcolonial studies. As Trinh T. Minh-Ha articulated in *Woman, Native, Other: Writing Postcoloniality and Feminism*, unlike others, the Other in capitalization refers to the genealogy of colonialism and structural violence against non-white, non-European or non-American, colonized groups of people. Colored women are doubly marginalized due to their race, ethnicity, and gender. They have been objectified and dehumanized as the mysterious, dangerous, and illogical Other since the colonial era to justify the white Western colonizers' discipline, surveillance, and imperial invasion.

The Hypervisibility of Whiteness in Japan

When I first met Aelin at the university library in Southern California, her purple hair was noticeable from a distance. She has blue eyes and pale skin. With her bright makeup and purple hair, she looked like a Japanese manga character to some extent. She had some dance training in high school, including ballet and modern dance, but stopped dancing before entering university. During her freshman year, she wanted to take dance classes, but the classes open to non-majors were too competitive. In the meantime, she joined the K-pop dance team to satisfy her passion for dancing.

She discovered K-pop later in high school through the K-pop boy group GOT7 and the girl group TWICE. Since then, K-pop is the genre she listens to the most. She loves watching K-pop music videos and dance practice videos online, which inspired her to learn more about Korean culture as a whole. She declared biology as her major during her first year but was not sure if she could work as a full-time biologist. Following her passion, she switched her major to Japanese studies with a minor in Korean studies. When I met her, she was taking a TEFL course for the professional certificate to teach English in Korea and Japan in the future.

A year ago, she went to a yearlong study abroad program at a university in Japan. In high school, she and her friends thought Japanese kimonos and festivals were "cute," which later sparked her interest in Japanese language, food, and culture in general. Before studying abroad, she was exposed to Japanese culture through mediated platforms only, such as viewing anime and J-pop videos online or class-room discussions in the US about Asian culture. Her image of a "cute" Japan, however, changed when she started living in Japan. Attending pop music concerts and meeting people in Japan, for example, "felt very different than just having listened to it online or on my phone" and was "definitely a bit harder," she recalled.

In Japan, she experienced code-switching and the transition of her mediated image of Japan into reality. While watching J-pop online, she said it was always nice to listen to the songs even if she did not understand the lyrics. However, when she attended a concert in Japan, she learned that there were so many things she needed to know, such as the etiquette within the venue and how to interact with people. She discovered that most of the audience at a female idol's concert were mostly men. "It's all guys. It's like we're surrounded," she recalled. She also did not know how to do the "fan chant" because she had only listened to the songs online before. Because she mostly learned Japanese in an academic setting, her Japanese would "get a lot worse" when she got nervous in everyday conversations.

The most challenging thing about living in Japan was, of course, the language. She said that although people in Japan and Korea are getting used to hearing other languages because of the growing number of foreign residents and tourists, she still felt a sense of being other in Japan. She said:

> When speaking Japanese, whatever accent I have, there is definitely a bit of a shock. You can still see people's faces. They are very comfortable with someone else who is Japanese when they see you come up. But to me, they're like, "Oh, I'm going to have to speak in English now," and they start freaking out. If I then speak in Japanese, they're probably not expecting it. So, the first time they don't hear it, because they're expecting English. Then they hear Japanese, they don't really understand it.

What she said revealed her multi-layered discomfort, including discomfort about the language barrier and people's different reactions to her, when she encountered

Japanese people. During the interview, she did not mention her race, ethnicity, or American citizenship. However, those positions certainly played an essential role in visually positioning her as a white American foreigner in her encounters with the Japanese.

From a spatial dimension, her discomfort in Japan first came from the new geographical location and cultural environment, including the primary language spoken in that space. When space is racialized, one's racial privilege can be resettled. Aelin started her formal education in Japanese language after entering the university in Southern California and was still learning and practicing Japanese when she went to Japan. Her Japanese sounds different from native Japanese speakers in aspects such as accent and fluency. In addition to Aelin's language barrier, from a spatial and racial dimension, in Japan she was marked as not Japanese but white. Although whiteness functions as the unmarked, universal "human" race, it is also hypervisible as white. As Reddy described, "Whiteness and heterosexuality seem invisible, transparent, to those who are white and/or heterosexual; they are simply norms. In contrast, whiteness makes itself hypervisible to those who are not white" (Reddy 55). Her body appeared visually different from Japanese bodies, which she became more fully aware of based on people's reactions to her, such as the different facial expressions directed at her. Being seen as the Other is an ordinary daily life experience for ethnic and racial minorities in the US. However, as a white American, this could have been Alien's first experience racially and thus, physically being marked as different.

Surely, her feeling of being different derives from her racial privilege and speaking North American English in the US. As scholars have observed (Cranston; Croucher; Lundström), white Americans can uphold privilege in Asia due to the neocolonial influences of the West. Kubota pointed out that English operates as a hegemony even in some developed countries in Asia (Kubota 305). In Japan, British and American English serve as a Western communication model and often subjugates local people who do not know or who are still learning English (Kubota 300). It is thus possible to suggest that her white race vis-à-vis English language hegemony in Asia "freak[ed] out" Japanese people.

In the US, white privilege operates through systemic and structural racism and from regulations concerning the law, housing, class, and education that benefit white people, which George Lipsitz referred to as "possessive investment" of white (Lipsitz vii). Precisely because white privilege is rooted in an institutionalized power structure, it often remains invisible for white Americans in the US. However, Aelin's whiteness and the structural privilege that had remained likely invisible to her became suddenly hypervisible in Japan because of her positionality as a non-Japanese, white person. Despite the structural privilege of being white in Asia, white people outside their homelands can suffer from emotional marginalization and nostalgia for their home countries (Puga 72). In Japan, Aelin's racial and linguistic privileges did not always generate enjoyable feelings for her because of her lack of spatial belonging – she was in a foreign country where whiteness and English are the other, and the Japanese race, ethnicity, and language are the norm.

Just being hypervisible would not be an issue if the visibility came from positive shared connotations through a communal cultural group. In this case, being highly visible might give them a feeling of empowerment because they are at the center of the community's attention. Aelin's hypervisibility as white in Japan is different from that of her visibility in the US because in Japan she was a foreign international student. An international student is a temporal resident. She is expected to leave as soon as the study is over. She is not the Other but certainly "other" compared to local citizens, permanent residents, and the ethnic majority in Japan. International students may have fewer infrastructural supports or human networks because of their lack of inside knowledge about the local community, which affected Aelin's fan labor in the dance studio as explained in the next section.

The White Fan's English Language as Power

In Japan, Aelin had to negotiate power dynamics as a white K-pop fan–dancer and international student. In the university where she studied in Japan, there was a K-pop dance team that she wanted to join. However, she could not join the team because they only accepted Japanese students and did not allow international students. Her fannish investment in K-pop dance seemed to be discouraged until she found an international dance club with multiple branches, such as K-pop, Bollywood, and American swing dance groups. In the dance club, there were students from Germany, India, the US, and South Korea and two Japanese leaders who did not speak English. The leaders' Japanese friends often came to the practice. When I asked if she enjoyed dancing in the club, she said, "Yes, although it was a mix."

In the beginning, the club had a male student who had just returned to Japan after staying in the US for seven years. He was fluent in both Japanese and English. "He was like, 'Listen, like even if you only speak English, this group is meant for you. I'll translate anything you need,'" Aelin recalled. Unfortunately, after a couple of weeks, he spoke in Japanese only, and Aelin and other international students tried to translate Japanese instructions by themselves. She felt that while people on her dance team in California had a "true passion for dancing and teaching and helping others," the leaders in the dance club in Japan "wanted to have a stage to dance on themselves and put themselves in all the solo roles." She said that she went to every dance practice, but international students, including her, were only assigned two songs out of the three songs they practiced. She was told that there was not enough room on stage for the third song, although she thought the stage looked roomy enough. She said that the experience was "unfair."

> I felt the only English speakers kind of felt excluded. The longer the practice went on, he [the leader] could only speak in Japanese, and then we [the international students] would have to translate. I understand that we're in the Japanese country so we shouldn't expect them to fully conform to us, but it was a bit hard. It's like they didn't really speak in English. And I'm not going

> to be like, "You need to learn real quick to make yourself more easy for me to understand," but with him, he was fully fluent in English. For him to not speak to the girls who only spoke English, I felt he was a bit rude.

Her point was that international students had a disadvantage because they did not speak Japanese and she blamed the Japanese student who could speak both English and Japanese. Her frustration is understandable given her passion for performing on stage. In fact, it would be most dancers' dream to dance at the center.

Unlike the mediated, somewhat romanticized imagery of Japan she imagined in the US, the dance studio experience was more visceral and less pleasant than what she expected before she came to Japan. The performance experiences happened through actual physical interactions with the local (Japanese) people and student dancers. She sensed the feeling of marginalization physically and visually on stage. Dancing behind the Japanese dancers, thinking about how she might look from the audience, all these physical experiences were nothing but real. Such corporeal, palpable experiences would leave no room for her but to accept her socially and culturally marginalized position with a slight sense of the de-mystification of Japan. Her consumption of Japan as a mystical image turned into an actual physical competition with Japanese dancers.

At the same time, her comment on unfairness speaks to more than a dancer's personal feeling of disappointment from not performing more prominent roles. As she admitted, she knew that she would not "expect [the Japanese] to fully con-form" to her, meaning an English speaker. Nevertheless, while Aelin could also speak both Japanese and English, she felt the Japanese student was "rude" when he did not speak English. Her expectations reveal that she may have perceived English as the common language of all international students regardless of different nationalities. As the team consisted of students from many different countries, the other international students may or may not have been fluent in English. Further, because they came to the study abroad program in Japan, they may have been interested in learning more about the Japanese culture and language than English and would have taken courses offered in Japanese. Although it was possible for her to emotionally identify with English speakers more closely, the generalization of English as the universal language could be problematic on a structural level. English can operate as "linguistic imperialism" (Phillipson 1) vis-à-vis the constant dominance of white British and American English speakers in Asia and beyond. When English is assumed as the norm, it can reinforce linguistic neocolonialism and racism (Guo and Beckett) and English as the sign of modernity in East Asia (Lan; Lee, Han, and McKerrow).

In addition to her hostile attitude to the Japanese students, her feeling of "unfairness" reveals the higher degree of expectation she might have had when it came to the convenience of using a language that was more familiar to her. Although the Japanese student, unfortunately, stopped his voluntary translations, it is also understandable that he would be there as a student dancer, not as a translator serving English speakers. Before pursuing my PhD, I performed professionally and internationally with different dance companies across South Korea, Japan, Germany, the US, and Austria. As a dancer, we followed the conventions of the dance companies. Whether big or small, each group or company had its rules. If I did not fully understand what the director or other dancers were saying in the studio, that was my limitation. It was my job to catch up, not the others' responsibility to translate German, Japanese, or English to Korean for me, regardless of their fluency in Korean, the language with which I am more familiar. I have seen some professional companies hire translators, but it would be too much to expect such generosity for a student dance club.

In fact, a dancer who does not fully speak the primary language, either the director's or the dance company's, will be unlikely to get the best part. Language is important in dance practice because dance not only involves physical practice or instruction but also communications among dancers and the director. Examples of such communication include verbal discussions of musical timing, synchronization, the role being played, spatial allocation and composition, costume choices, execution of detailed movements directed, nuanced emotional expression, and scheduling. Although the K-pop dance club in Japan may not need the meticulous details required for professional companies, verbal communication would remain key in preparing stage performances.

When I watched Aelin's actual performance video from the dance club in Japan, I noticed that she mostly performed at the center. The performance is a cover dance of the K-pop girl group IZ★ONE's "La Vie en Rose." The cover dance video consists of about 15 female students, mostly Asian and a few white, and four male students who, according to what Aelin said, were the leaders' friends. Throughout my research, I have seen her change her hair color often to colors like gold, purple, blue, and green, which are quite common colors among Japanese manga characters (Kawashima 170). In this video, her hair is a golden blonde. She visibly stands out as the typical image of a blond, white girl. In "point choreography," she dances in the first row. The next scene is the climax where five dancers from the group present a short solo. They dance under a bright spotlight while all the other dancers are in darkness. In one sequence, a dancer starts her solo in the center on the first row. She stands in front of Aelin in the front row as the lead dancer who walks first onto the stage to start the show. Her solo is powerful and eye-catching, composed of light, quick, and sharp jumps and precise, twirling arms with nimble steps, which makes the recorded audience gasp and cheer with awe. Then Aelin and another dancer do their solos on the second row, and then two other dancers present their solos on the third row. During her solo, Aelin presents a turn with some powerful, flowy upper-body movements.

Knowledge is a power that regulates and disciplines an individual's societal and even physical behaviors through the internalization of power and hierarchy (Foucault; Hall). When someone does not fully understand what others are saying, the person might feel they have lost authority, presence, or power in the group. As critical theory scholars have noted, white people often claim "reverse" racism when their privileges are denied and demand special attention and more respect

than other racial and ethnic minorities (Piper 25). In addition to the white privilege that exists in Japan, Japanese pop culture "idealizes" white beauty, like pale
skin and blond hair of characters in Japanese manga, which resemble Caucasians
(Kawashima 170). It is possible that Aelin might expect higher and more positive
recognition as white, knowing her privilege as a white American.

Scholars have explained the (re)constructions of white privilege in various terms,
such as "white fragility" (DiAngelo 54), a "crisis in White identity" (Yousman 375),
"reverse" racism (Piper 25), and white victimhood (Nelson et al.; Bartlett), all of
which have escalated even further since Donald Trump's successful presidential
campaign. Aelin's sense of marginalization seems to reveal the taken-for-granted
privilege of being white. Because of her privilege, she assumed the Japanese student
should have provided constant attention to her and the other English speakers
throughout the dance rehearsals and that she should have performed more prominent roles on center stage. Her feeling of potential victimization could have been a
way of inserting hegemonic white American English to the Japanese students, so that
she could better negotiate and orient her spatial marginalization as a non-Japanese,
international student. By claiming her treatment was "unfair," she could compensate
for her feeling of marginalization and expect a degree of "preferential treatment" and
respect and thus reclaim white privilege (Wasserstrom 581).

"I am Not a Koreaboo"

When I first asked her how she got into K-pop, Aelin started answering the
question by talking about Japanese anime. "It was the same kind of thing where it
started off with just the music." While her main interest in Japanese culture started
with anime, her main interest in Korean culture started with K-pop. Like her
interest in Japanese anime, her interest in K-pop soon extended to Korean food,
language, and culture. To Aelin, what distinguished K-pop from J-pop or American pop is the strong bond and connection between fan clubs and idols. Like
many other K-pop fan-dancers, she also liked K-pop's dance-centric nature. She
said that compared to J-pop, which emphasizes uniformity, K-pop has more varied
compositions, such as having one member singing and dancing a solo dressed in
different outfits. "There's a lot more technique involved in K-pop dance,
where J-pop is supposed to be kind of more cutesy. They'll do kind of simple, just
kind of like hand movements and stuff like that."

As Chapter 4 discussed, Korean collegiate dancers in Korea perceive K-pop
simply as a music genre, but K-pop is often racialized and exoticized in the US as
an exotic Asian culture. When Aelin first started listing to K-pop in early high
school, K-pop was less known in the US and listening to K-pop was "a bit taboo."
"Whenever I mentioned K-pop to people in high school, they'd be like, 'Oh,
you're one of them.' And I was like, 'What does that mean? I just like their music.
What's wrong with that?'"

As a white K-pop fan, Aelin consciously resists the potentially negative racial
stereotypes of K-pop. Yet, during the interview, I noticed that she often said

"Japan or Korea" in an indistinguishable way. She took Korean culture classes and was on the K-pop dance team during her study abroad at a Japanese university. She said that she was interested in teaching English in Japan but would go to Korea first. She also mentioned both Korea and Japan often interchangeably when describing her travel experiences and pop culture in Asia. Mentioning the stigma put on K-pop fans, she mentioned "weeaboo" as "the Japanese version of koreaboo," a term that will be explained later in this chapter.

Her K-pop fandom motivated her to keep pursuing activities related to K-pop while studying in Japan. Simultaneously, it is possible that she was trying to understand Korea through Japan and vice versa. Nonetheless, it appeared that she often conflated the two countries too easily. Both the Japanese and Koreans are lumped together as Asian in the US Japanese Americans and Korean Americans can share a pan-ethnic identity and solidarity as minorities in the US However, this is not the case when it comes to Koreans in Korea and Japanese in Japan. While Japan and Korea are geographically proximate, the two have different languages, ethnicities, and customs, not to mention the colonial history between the two nations.

Japan's colonial legacy and the resultant trauma remain and affect people living in the two countries. In Japan, it is common to see xenophobia, anti-Korean sentiments, and hate speech against Koreans, including K-pop idols. These practices became more evident starting in the early 2000s with a surge of Japanese nationalist movements, referred to as the Action Conservative Movement, attacking Koreans on the internet (Ahn and Yoon; Lie; Yamaguchi). Koreans in Japan are ethnic minorities and experience a high level of discrimination and violence from housing to education. Koreans have no nostalgic or romantic memory when it comes to Japan's colonial history. Instead, they remember the brutal reality of genocide, ethnic cleansing, and culture annihilation. In Japan, K-pop, or even Korea at large, is the Other due to the imperial and ethnic neocolonialism that treated colonized citizens and countries as "unsophisticated" and "raw" and the colonial logic that has justified the exploitation of people and cultures across the world over centuries.

Aelin's somewhat too easy conflation of Japan and Korea resonates with the Orientalism that conflates East Asia under the umbrella concept of the Orient. Whereas K-pop and J-pop could be "the same kind of thing" from an Orientalist framework, this easy conflation can be alarming given the colonial history and the invariant residues of it today. In Aelin's experience, Korea seems to belong to Japan, and the specificity of Korea and the nation's resistance since the colonial era appears to be erased. Korea is doubly Othered in her imagination, as an Oriental Other and as the Other from the reproduction of the Japanese colonizers' eyes.

In her fannish orientation, however, Aelin is aware of the Orientalism concerning K-pop idols. During the interview, many of her fan experiences focused on not being a "Koreaboo." According to Urban Dictionary, a crowdsourced online dictionary, Koreaboo is a slang word that refers to someone who is "obsessed with Korean culture so much they denounce their own culture and call themselves Korean" and who is "mentally ill and need [*sic*] help." While the definitions on Urban Dictionary change over time, this definition gives a glimpse of how K-pop fans are viewed in general, including how K-pop fans view themselves and how K-pop is viewed in mainstream US culture. Urban Dictionary differentiates K-pop fans from Koreaboos who are rather "fanatics" and have an overdramatic association and identification with Korean culture. It defines K-pop "fangirls," meaning fan girls, as "little creatures who scream like animals at concerts for their biases/male idols" and who "constantly dream about this [*sic*] dream men and being their wife and write extremely interesting fanfictions."

During the interview, Aelin distinguished herself from a Koreaboo. She understands a Koreaboo as someone who does not have enough knowledge about Korea.

> A Koreaboo is someone who wants to speak in Korean but doesn't actually learn Korean. They don't actually educate themselves about Korea or anything outside of K-pop. They won't know the history of Korea or fully learn the language. They will just learn the basic words and throw them into American conversations. It's uncomfortable to watch because it can be potentially maybe racist or just kind of ignorant things that people are saying.

To her, using Korean words without an in-depth understanding of or education about Korea's language, culture, or history can lead to a superficial cultural appropriation, and this would be a sign of a Koreaboo. She also distinguished herself from other fans who say, "I am learning Korean, but I am not doing it." Her criticism of "not doing" refers to non-Korean K-pop fans who casually use short Korean words in everyday conversations. Her distinction of herself from the majority non-Korean K-pop fans through her emphasis on education reflects her positionality and values as an Asian studies major. She will undoubtedly spend more time educating herself in the Korean language and culture in academia.

Based on my observations, cover dancers on her K-pop dance team in California frequently used Korean words. The main leaders and dancers were mostly Asian American students of Southeast and East Asian descent with few Hispanic or African American students. The large proportion of Asian American dancers probably reflects the culture in the region. The university is in California, which has a large Asian American population. Indeed, the university has one of the largest Asian and Asian American populations who make up nearly half of the entire student body. Whenever a practice ended, the team members casually said goodbye in Korean, like their own convention.

As a native Korean, I felt that their use of Korean words was a tribute to their fandom and a way of showing an effort to get to know more about the Korean language and culture or at least recognizing or getting familiar with Korea. The superficial use of language could indeed be offensive, like when a white yogi says "namaste" at the end of a yoga class, while the entire class and the names of each pose were taught in English. At the same time, however, it would also be strange to not use the local or native language at all when someone is learning or performing other ethnic or cultural groups' traditions or practices. Of course, a nation with an imperial history has an advantage. For example, ballet is widely taught in French terms, while yoga, Asian dance, or Asian martial arts classes in the US barely adapt the languages from where those practices originated.

Among the many interviewees from the dance team, Aelin was the only one who brought up Koreaboos. Her somewhat passionate but precarious approach to K-pop showed her apprehension of "yellow fever." Compared to her mixed, often ambivalent understanding of the self, including her racial and linguistic privilege in Japan, Aelin seemed to have a clearer understanding of her position as a white K-pop fan in the US. Her resistance to speaking Korean in dance practice, which reminds her of Koreaboo, distanced her from the majority Asian and Asian American cover dancers on the dance team, who share pan-Asian identities as discussed in Chapter Four. Indeed, Aelin was one of the few white students on the large dance team.

Many of her friends who were not K-pop fans often automatically assumed K-pop fans were "extreme" or "cringy," and they often did not distinguish K-pop fans from Koreaboos. She elaborated:

> I have been called a "koreaboo" and been asked if I only date Koreans. [...] Some girls would be like, "I just want to marry a Korean guy" and kind of fetishize Korean idols. It's fine if they want to date someone who's Korean, but they should date him because they like him and his personality, not just because he's Korean.

She was critical of Koreaboos because they tend to generalize and exoticize Korean men. She continued, "I am not trying to pretend I am Korean or cultural appropriation [sic]. Ultimately, I simply like the music and dance for what it is and think Korean idols are very talented." She then explained how diverse her music taste is.

> I also have Spanish, French, German, and Japanese music on my phone. Usually, I find that I don't really need to understand the lyrics to enjoy the music, which is why I think I listened to so many different types. I listen to Spanish, and I don't speak Spanish, and I listen to French.

She explained that she listens to multiple types of global and ethnic music, even if she does not speak the language. She is not alone as many of the audiences listening to K-pop enjoy the melodies and vibes of the music itself even if they do not fully understand the lyrics. Yet, her idea about consuming various types of ethnic music without needing to understand the language contradicts her previous point of view, which highlighted the importance of learning the foreign language to avoid a superficial cultural appropriation.

Not only is her music taste diverse but also her knowledge of language and culture in general. "Although I'm not learning any other Asian languages other than Japanese and Korean, I still also find things like Chinese culture and Thai culture and all of that to be very interesting," she added. On the one hand, her comment could signify an inclusive and open attitude to global cultures. On the other hand, however, such a perspective and her wide, open-ended interest in Asian and global ethnic music, foods, and languages resonates with what bell hooks called "eating the Other," where ethnic minorities' cultures become a "spice" for the "dull" (white) American culture and an exchangeable commodity for white people's self-exploration.

"I Simply Like the Music"

Aelin's phrase "I simply like the music" (or "I just like their music") opens up multiple interpretations on the ambivalent position as a fan. Surely, K-pop is a music genre, and it is possible for any fan to like K-pop because of its sound. In fact, it is quite common to see fans or audiences saying, "I just like their music." Examining the phrase "I simply like the music" in its rhetorical usage is not meant to dismiss fans' appreciation of music and sound itself. Yet, unpacking the phrase "I simply like the music" as a rhetorical term can reveal the multi-layered and often conflicting positions of white US fans about racialized stigma on K-pop fandom in the US.

On the surface, "I simply like the music" could be reminiscent of how Korean Americans in the US and Korean dancers in Korea say that K-pop is just a music genre. As discussed in Chapter Four, Koreans and Korean Americans do not necessarily "exoticize" or see K-pop as racially marked Korean or Asian music. Their ethnicity or citizenship is already Korean, and thus, K-pop is simply nothing but mainstream pop music in Korea to them. While the idea of "I simply like the music" first appears to take the same approach as the Korean and Korean American dancers' perception of K-pop simply as pop music, Aelin's case can be interpreted differently. Unlike Koreans and Korean Americans who do not necessarily need to prove why they like K-pop, Aelin appears to have a more complex relationship to K-pop, often expressed in a slightly defensive attitude, such as declaring her colorblindness. It appeared that she had to put in extra energy to prove to herself and others why she liked K-pop.

To some extent, the phrase "I simply like the music" could be an attempt to de-racialize K-pop by mainly referring to it as just music. While K-pop is music performed by Koreans, when fans refer to it as music that may mean that K-pop is a sound that can be universal. This phrase prioritizes and draws attention to the music itself, separates it from the performers, and thus, implies that the fans are not necessarily interested in K-pop idols or the idols' visuality, physicality, or personality. It also avoids any association with a bigger cultural context. Thus, in addition to de-racializing, "I just like their music" tends to de-humanize K-pop as just sound to some extent. By evading a potential racialization of K-pop, the phrase negates Western fans' anxiety of being mistaken as a Koreaboo. Given the long legacy of the racialization of Asians in the US, it also negates fans' fear of having "yellow fever" and the social stigmas around biracial romantic relationships and potential attractions.

Nevertheless, since K-pop is a dance-centric visual genre, it would be nearly unavoidable for fans not to "see" how the music is performed. Further, as elaborated in previous chapters, in dance, it is easy to conflate dancers with their dances; when audiences like a dancer, it is likely that they like her/his dance, dance movement, and even their body. The potential conflation between dancer and dance derives from the fact that in dance, the person and her/his body become the artistic, expressive medium of dance. As K-pop is visual centric, for K-pop fans, it could be even harder to draw a line between the sound of the songs and the visuality of the idols, such as their bodies, appearance, fashions, dance movements, stage personae, charisma, personal charms, and characteristics.

Moreover, a clear distinction between music and performance may be nearly impossible for K-pop fan-dancers because the affective fan labor is already embodied with cover dance's emphasis on the body and visuality. Aelin's position as a K-pop cover dancer may have enhanced her fear of being called a Koreaboo or a cultural appropriator. K-pop fans listening to music in a foreign language could be less apprehensive. However, K-pop cover dance differs from passive appreciation or consumption; it is a creation. K-pop cover dancers do not merely listen to music. K-pop cover dance is a physical response, (re)presentation, production, and embodiment of the music. The music and dance become one through the dancers' bodies.

In relation to her apprehension about cultural appropriation, Aelin seemed less interested in "passing" as a K-pop idol than her dance team members of Asian descent whom I discussed in Chapter 4. When I asked about their favorite cover dance, most interviewees chose edited versions of cover dance videos. Typically, cover dance videos present sleek, polished makeup, costumes, and fancy performances like K-pop idols with well edited footage. In contrast, Aelin picked a K-pop medley dance practice video. In the video, more than 40 students perform five different K-pop song choreographies in multiple groups. Most of them appear to be of Asian descent with a handful of Hispanic, African American, and white students. Nearly half are men and half are women. During the performance, Aelin occasionally appears and performs at the center with others. Some compositions are modified in the cover dance performance because of the different number of dancers from the original music video, but they adopt similar facial expressions and point choreographies from the original music videos. Because it is a dance practice video filmed on campus, however, the dancers barely wear any makeup and wear rather casual purple T-shirts and black jeans. Many of the students do not even bother to keep wearing their eyeglasses while dancing. There are no specific stage settings, lighting, or backgrounds. The video also seems less edited with fewer camera angles compared to the dance team's other cover dance videos.

What is unique about this practice video is that it highlights the dancers and their body movements because there are no other visual signs that might distract viewers' attention. The video reminded me of what Aelin said about acting versus dance. She took acting and dance classes in high school and learned that she was more comfortable in dancing because she felt shy about using facial expressions. A cover dance video's goal is to replicate the original as much as it can, including the use of perfectly matching facial expressions for the close-up camera angles. Contrarily, with its looser structure, a practice video allows more freedom in facial expressions because it focuses more on the dance itself, rather than the cover dance choreographed for the camera. The composition of the original choreography was also modified to be performed by a larger group of dancers than in the original video. Therefore, for her, there would be less needed to "choreograph" the precise details of her face for a solo section with a close-up shot.

The video well exhibits the dancers' labor and visibly noticeable passion. During the seven minutes of the compilation video, dancers' faces begin to sweat. Some students begin to tremble and miss the tempo as they get exhausted. Nevertheless, they, including Aelin, complete their performance successfully. In the climax of the performance, some wear a smile of catharsis that seems to come naturally. Their spontaneous and somehow awkward smiles are different from the perfectly choreographed, presentational smiles that match the lyrics for a typical cover dance. The practice video feels more alive than the sleek, final production of a cover dance video in which many of the dancers are so flawlessly polished that they often appear artificial. Aelin said, "Many of my close friends were chosen for the piece, and I felt that all of our energies combined made for a fabulous cover." It is indeed the collective energy and liveness of the dancers that make the video stand out.

Like many other K-pop cover dancers, her K-pop dance team in California was a home for her, although not everything was perfectly harmonious. Christine Balance explained how the global explosion of K-pop on YouTube explicates an "interplay between the virtual and material" in the digital era where marginalized communities find "home" through the mediated consumption of K-pop (Balance 146). When she was dancing with the K-pop dance club in Japan, where she did not feel very welcomed, she noticed that her K-pop dance team in California kept releasing cover dance videos: "It allowed me to connect with them even though I wasn't there. Like I would always watch it online and comment on the videos. I'm like, 'Oh you guys do really good. Sorry, I couldn't be there to support you.'" With her shifted racial and fannish identities and enhanced diasporic identity in Japan, social media was a place where she felt at home and communicated with her friends in the US, keeping the sense of community.

From Fantasy to Reality

Aelin recently graduated. On her Instagram, she has her name written both in Japanese and Korean. She shares her photos taken in Korea and Japan, including a photo of her wearing a rented traditional Korean dress in a palace in Seoul. Many of her past photos represent her happy memories with the K-pop dance team in California, such as socializing, making Asian food, and being on stage with her friends.

Looking back, to me, being a university student was one of the most grateful moments in my life. I was able to explore not only new academic subjects but also different world cultures in general, whether through fashion, food, music, or dance. As a freshman, I was often not aware of the deep historical meanings of cultural appropriation and the complicated politics regarding colonialism, racism, and sexism. Yet, those moments of my first exposure to these subjects were fully filled with genuine curiosity and excitement.

In 2010, I came to the US as an ambitious PhD student at UT Austin. I imagined that my life would look like that of Carrie Bradshaw in *Sex and the City*. Of course, I ended up spending five years, mostly staying up all night in a library with greasy hair and eating food truck breakfast tacos and coffee next morning, which by the way, is one of the best things in Austin that I still miss. Although my actual experience had nothing to do a fancy brunch in Central Park or the glamorous image from the mainstream media, without those initial, mediated experiences and fantasy, my life would be completely different. As Judith Butler said, fantasy is a part of (psychic) reality, which can later turn into an actual segment of reality. As a university professor, now I am grateful that the naïve passion and fantasy that emerged in college have motivated my life, guided me to a direction that I did not imagine, and still fuels my pathway as an academic on a diasporic journey between the US and Korea.

It would be too early and presumptuous to judge young dancers' passion as mere cultural appropriation. No one is ever perfect. One of the beauties of such imperfection is the ability to keep trying despite our flaws. It is possible to fall in love in a fleeting moment – meeting each other's eyes, holding hands, ephemeral or superficial fantasy, or even ruse. Nevertheless, those moments can lead us to a lifelong journey, relationship, and dedication. The audience perhaps never knows what really happens in the dance studio, during the late-night practices and rehearsals, and in fan-dancers' lives. The only clue the audience has is likely the sleek dance videos on social media, and it is not enough to talk about ethics in performing the Other with that alone.

References

Ahn, Ji-Hyun and E. Kyung Yoon. "Between Love and Hate: The New Korean Wave, Japanese Female Fans, and Anti-Korean Sentiment in Japan." *Journal of Contemporary Eastern Asia*, vol. 19, no. 2, 2020, pp. 179–196. https://doi.org/10.17477/jcea.2020.19.2.179.

Balance, Christine. "How It Feels to Be Viral Me: Affective Labor and Asian American YouTube Performance." *WSQ: Women's Studies Quarterly*, vol. 40, no. 1/2, 2012, pp. 138–152. doi:10.1353/wsq.2012.0016.

Bartlett, Bruce. "Donald Trump and 'Reverse Racism.'" *SSRN*, February 2016. *papers.ssrn.com*, http://dx.doi.org/10.2139/ssrn.2726413.

Berger, Michele Tracy. "I Do Practice Yoga! Controlling Images and Recovering the Black Female Body in 'Skinny White Girl' Yoga Culture." *Race and Yoga*, vol. 3, no. 1, 2018, pp. 31–49. https://doi.org/10.5070/R331034199.

Butler, Judith. "The Force of fantasy: Feminism, Mapplethorpe, and Discursive Excess." *Differences: A Journal of Feminist Cultural Studies*, vol. 2, no. 2, 1990, pp. 105–125.

Conquergood, Dwight. "Performing as a Moral Act: Ethical Dimensions of the Ethnography of Performance." *Literature in Performance*, vol. 5, no. 2, 1985, pp. 1–13. https://doi.org/10.1080/10462938509391578.

Coppa, Francesca. "Women, Star Trek, and the Early Development of Fannish Vidding." *Transformative Works and Cultures*, vol. 1, no. 1, 2008. https://journal.transformativeworks.org/index.php/twc/article/download/44/64?inline=1?inline=1.

Cranston, Sophie. "Expatriate as a 'Good' Migrant: Thinking through Skilled International Migrant Categories." *Population, Space and Place*, vol. 23, no. 6, 2017, pp. 1–12.

Croucher, Sheila. "Migrants of Privilege: The Political Transformation of Americans in Mexico." *Identities: Global Studies in Culture and Power*, vol. 16, no. 4, 2009, pp. 463–491.

Darnell, Simon C. "Orientalism through Sport: Towards a Said-ian Analysis of Imperialism and 'Sport for Development and Peace.'" *Sport in Society*, vol. 17, no. 8, 2014, pp. 1000–1014. https://doi.org/10.1080/17430437.2013.838349.

DiAngelo, Robin. "White Fragility." *International Journal of Critical Pedagogy*, vol. 3, no. 3, 2011, pp. 54–70.

Dyer, Richard. *White*. Routledge, 1997.

Foucault, Michel. "Power/Knowledge." In *The New Social Theory Reader*, edited by Steven Seidman and Jeffrey C.Alexander, Routledge, 2008, pp. 73–79.

Guo, Yan and Gulbahar H.Beckett. "The Hegemony of English as a Global Language: A Critical Analysis." In *Education and Social Development: Global Issues and Analyses*, edited by Ali A.Abdi and Shibao Guo. Sense Publishers, 2008, pp. 57–69.

Hall, Stuart. "Foucault: Power, Knowledge and Discourse." *Discourse Theory and Practice: A Reader*, edited by Margaret Wetherell, StephanieTaylor, and Simeon J. Yates. Sage, 2002, pp. 72–81.

hooks, bell. *Black Looks: Race and Representation*. South End Books, 1992.

Kawashima, Terry. "Seeing Faces, Making Races: Challenging Visual Tropes of Racial Difference." *Meridians: Feminism, Race, Transnationalism*, vol. 3, no. 1, 2002, pp. 161–190.

Kubota, Ryuko. "Ideologies of English in Japan." *World Englishes*, vol. 17, no. 3, 1998, pp. 295–306. https://doi.org/10.1111/1467-971X.00105.

Kwan, SanSan. "Performing a Geography of Asian America: The Chop Suey Circuit." *TDR/The Drama Review*, vol. 55, no. 1, 2011, pp. 120–136. https://doi.org/10.1162/dram_a_00052.

Lan, Pei-Chia. "White Privilege, Language Capital and Cultural Ghettoisation: Western High-skilled Migrants in Taiwan." *Journal of Ethnic and Migration Studies*, vol. 37, no. 10, 2011, pp. 1669–1693.

Lee, Jong Hwa, Min Wha Han, and Raymie E.McKerrow. "English or Perish: How Contemporary South Korea Received, Accommodated, and Internalized English and American Modernity." *Language and Intercultural Communication*, vol. 10, no. 4, 2013, pp. 337–357. https://doi.org/10.1080/14708477.2010.497555.

Lie, John. *Zainichi (Koreans in Japan): Diasporic Nationalism and Postcolonial Identity*. U of California P, 2008.

Lipsitz, George. *The Possessive Investment in Whiteness: How White People Profit from Identity Politics*. Temple UP, 2006.

Lundström, Catrin. *White Migrations: Gender, Whiteness and Privilege in Transnational Migration*. Springer, 2014.

Maira, Sunaina. "Belly Dancing: Arab-face, Orientalist Feminism, and US Empire." *American Quarterly*, vol. 60, no. 2, 2008, pp. 317–345.

Miller, Amara Lindsay. "Eating the Other Yogi: Kathryn Budig, the Yoga Industrial Complex, And the Appropriation of Body Positivity." *Race and Yoga*, vol. 1, no. 1, 2016, pp. 1–22.

Minh-Ha, Trinh T. *Woman, Native, Other: Writing Postcoloniality and Feminism*. Indiana UP, 1989.

Nelson, Jacqueline K., et al. "Witnessing Anti-white 'Racism': White Victimhood and 'Reverse Racism' in Australia." *Journal of Intercultural Studies*, vol. 39, no. 3, 2018, pp. 339–358.

Oh, Chuyun. "From Seoul to Copenhagen: Migrating K-Pop Cover Dance and Performing Diasporic Youth in Social Media." *Dance Research Journal*, vol. 52, no. 1, 2020, pp. 20–32. https://doi.org/10.1017/S0149767720000030.

Oh, Chuyun and David Oh. "White-Expat-Fans' Performing K-pop Other on YouTube." *Text and Performance Quarterly*, 2022, pp. 1–22. https://doi.org/10.1080/10462937.2022. 2062441.

Oh, David C. and Chuyun Oh. "Vlogging White Privilege Abroad: Eat Your Kimchi's Eating And Spitting out of the Korean Other on YouTube." *Communication, Culture & Critique*, vol. 10, no. 4, 2017, pp. 696–711. https://doi.org/10.1111/cccr.12180.

Oh, David C. "K-Pop Fans React: Hybridity and the White Celebrity-Fan on YouTube." *International Journal of Communication*, vol. 11, 2017, pp. 2270–2287.

Phelan, Peggy. *Unmarked: The Politics of Performance*. Routledge, 2003.

Phillipson, Robert. "Linguistic Imperialism." In *The Encyclopedia of Applied Linguistics*, edited by Carol A.Chapelle. Blackwell Publishing Ltd, 2013, pp. 1–7.

Piper, Adrian. "Passing for White, Passing for Black." In *Out of Order, Out of Sight, Volume I: Selected Essays in Meta-Art 1968–1992*. MIT P, 1996. http://www.adrianpiper.com/docs/Passing.pdf.

Puga, Ana Elena. "Migrant Melodrama and the Political Economy of Suffering." *Women & Performance: A Journal of Feminist Theory*, vol. 26, no. 1, 2016, pp. 72–93. https://doi.org/10.1080/0740770X.2016.1183982.

Reddy, Maureen T. "Invisibility/Hypervisibility: The Paradox of Normative Whiteness." *Transformations: The Journal of Inclusive Scholarship and Pedagogy*, vol. 9, no. 2, 1998, pp. 55–64. https://www.jstor.org/stable/43587107.

Said, Edward W. *Orientalism*. *Vintage Books Edition*, 1979.

"Top Definition Kpop Fan." *Urban Dictionary*. https://www.urbandictionary.com/define. php?term=kpop%20fan.

Wasserstrom, Richard A. "Racism, Sexism, and Preferential Treatment: An Approach to the Topics." *UCLA Law Review*, vol. 24, no. 3, 1976, pp. 581–622.

Weinstein, John B. "The Orient on Ice: Transnational Cultural Portrayals by Asian and Asian American Figure Skaters." In *Transnational Performance, Identity and Mobility in Asia*, edited by Iris H. Tuan and Ivy I-Chu Chang. Palgrave Pivot, 2018, pp. 144–157.

Yamaguchi, Tomomi. "Xenophobia in Action: Ultranationalism, Hate speech, and the Internet in Japan." *Radical History Review*, vol. 2013, no. 117, 2013, pp. 98–118. https://doi.org/10.1215/01636545-2210617.

Yousman, Bill. "Blackophilia and Blackophobia: White Youth, the Consumption of Rap Music, And White Supremacy." *Communication Theory*, vol. 13, no. 4, 2003, pp. 366–391. https://doi.org/10.1111/j.1468-2885.2003.tb00297.x.

6

A REFUGE FOR REFUGEE TEENS

Introduction

In November 2016, Donald Trump was running for president. Hatred against refugees and racial and ethnic minorities was soaring, including from those in conservative religious groups. As that hostility rose, there was also advocacy against it. On February 10, 2017, the Refugee Solidarity Rally was hosted at Utica's Oneida Square. At the rally, a few hundred people gathered, carrying placards with slogans such as "Ban Wars, Not the Victims," "A Daughter of an Immigrant - #Stand with Refugees and Immigrants," and "No Human Is Illegal." Many local community members were supportive of the rally, but not all. Some drove past shouting "Go home!" and displaying obscene gestures.

I draw the scene as a participant in the protest. In fall 2016, I was a Visiting Assistant Professor at Hamilton College. Along with my colleagues, students, and civil rights activists, I participated in the rally with community members from the Midtown Utica Community Center. MUCC is a grassroots refugee-serving community in Utica, New York. Before the rally, I stopped by MUCC. We created colorful placards, and some painted their face and bodies for the protest. Some of the children at MUCC asked me how to write "no hatred but peace" in Korean. We noted that together on one of their placards.

My ethnographic fieldwork with K-pop cover dancers first began with Thailand refugee teens at MUCC in 2016. Chris Sunderlin, the founder and executive director, established the Center to provide social services for ethnic minority children and refugees in Utica, a city with a long history of immigrant settlers and communities. The Center offers study mentorship, English tutoring, and an arts and culture festival, among other services. MUCC has a teenage K-pop dance crew consisting of approximately five members who, historically, have been primarily male. As Karen refugees from Thailand,[1] the dance crew is a leading

DOI: 10.4324/9781003212188-9

FIGURE 6.1 Refugee Solidarity Rally at Oneida Square on February 10, 2017
Source: Photo by the author.

refugee artist group at MUCC that inspires their friends and community members and teaches them K-pop dance. With the increasing popularity of the K-pop dance crew in the local community, girls began to make a female version of the group. The crew performs at local music festivals, museums, schools, and universities. When I first met the group in 2016, they had more than 3,000 fans and followers on their Facebook and YouTube homepages. Their unique background draws positive media attention.

Back then, I was teaching a performance ethnography class and looking for a local community center for a student field trip. Drs. John Bartle and Thomas Wilson, valued friends and mentors at the college, told me about MUCC and its famous K-pop dance crew. A few months later, I got a chance to visit MUCC. The Center was using a building donated by a church. The building was pretty big, with multiple rooms. It was old and quite worn-out but neat and warm. When I walked in, I saw boys and girls having snacks in the kitchen, and a middle-aged woman greeted me with a smile. Next to the kitchen there was a big hall with a wooden floor and mirrors, which looked like a dance floor. The K-pop crew dancers were surrounded by community members while they practiced K-pop. Director Chris introduced me to the crew and invited me to watch their performance of a song by K-pop boy group BTS. They were not the only group dancing, although they were clearly at the center of attention. Nearly 20 girls and boys were playing K-pop and practicing dance.

FIGURE 6.2 MUCC K-pop dance crew performing at the Refugee Artist Program on March 22, 2017 at Jones Elementary School in Utica, New York
Source: Photo by © Alex Cooper – USA TODAY NETWORK.

On that day, strangely enough, I felt at home. It was a freezing winter in upstate New York. The Center, however, was filled with joy, warm smiles, and the exciting energy of young children. As a native Korean and international faculty member working in the US, I was missing my home and family. Refugees are different from immigrants; many want to return to their home countries but cannot because of sociopolitical or religious reasons such as war and genocide. I am not a refugee, and I cannot even imagine the difficulties they encounter. Nevertheless, as a racial and ethnic minority, non-US citizen, I felt connected with refugees regarding the sense of diasporic home – a home without a home – shaped by music, dance, and the food they temporarily share, not by a geographical or permanent physical location that resides in a country. I was curious about how these young people from different places could build such a strong bond and community. In addition, I was struck by the K-pop dance crew's dance skills and passion. I admit that I had not expected refugee teens to dance to K-pop. Where did they learn to dance, and why? I wanted to know how the teens at the Center came to K-pop despite their different languages, cultural backgrounds, and societal circumstances.

Over the next few months, they invited me to their fundraising performances at local events and rallies. We quickly became friends on Facebook. I brought my students to the Center for volunteer work. Many of my students were theatre and dance majors, so they offered dance, acting, and singing classes for the children at

MUCC. I began to volunteer by providing a weekly dance and movement workshop. I visited the Center twice a week and sometimes during the weekends just to celebrate some of the children's birthday parties. Later, some of the children asked me if I could teach them Korean. I am a native Korean, but I had never taught the language before. I asked about their favorite K-pop songs and began to teach them the lyrics. Simultaneously, I learned that some of the K-pop dance crew members were seriously considering pursuing their careers in the dance and pop music industry and preparing for an upcoming K-pop audition. SM Entertainment, one of the biggest agencies in K-pop, was about to hold an SM Global Audition in New York. I helped them prepare their dance improvisation and solo performances for the audition.

At MUCC, the process of "building rapport," an essential part of ethnographic fieldwork (Madison 39), came naturally. I have no doubt that the main reason was the warm, inviting openness at the Center and being surrounded by such an amazing group of people, local volunteers, and the director, who was almost a fatherly figure to the refugee community. He lived across the street from the Center and often invited the refugee children to his house to watch their dance videos together over the dinner table. Initially, I was not planning to conduct formal research. Not having a predetermined research goal might have helped me build rapport easily. I simply enjoyed spending time and being with the community.

As Judith Hamera reminded us, performance ethnography is "doing" critical theory (Hamera, "Performance Ethnography" 208); it differs from viewing, listening, or reading theory. It turns ethnographic fieldwork and field notes into an artistic presentation and performance, often in collaboration with community members and research participants. Performance ethnography offers researchers "a vocabulary for exploring the expressive elements of culture, a focus on embodiment as a crucial competent of cultural analysis" converging theory and practice (Hamera, "Performance Ethnography" 207).

As Shakina Nayfack aptly pointed out, a seemingly failed ethnography project could be an opportunity to write "an ethnography of failure" (Nayfack 96). My ethnographic fieldwork has been frustrating and demanding as much as it is filled with unexpected joy and gratefulness. I mostly felt failure. The more genuinely I put my heart into performance ethnography projects, the more I felt hopeless afterward, no matter how good the final performance ethnography looked on stage, and no matter how much applause I received from the audience.

To turn my "failed ethnography" to "an ethnography of failure," this chapter analyzes *Love Means Love,* which I choreographed and performed with the K-pop dance crew at MUCC along with ethnographic fieldwork and in-depth interviews from 2016 to 2018, as an example of what Dwight Conquergood might call "dialogical performance" (Conquergood 9). As Paul Scolieri observed, dance serves multiple roles in refugee communities worldwide from Iraqi to Cambodian, "as a form of cultural currency, survival strategy, movement therapy, political activism, and social service" (Scolieri xii). This chapter discusses how the refugee teens utilize K-pop dance to overcome trauma and negotiate diasporic identities. Applying Friedrich Nietzsche's notion of Zarathustra, a dancer, I argue that their resistance resonates with the liberatory history of dancers who have fought against oppression and dance bans.

"Doing" Performance (Auto)ethnography: *Love Means Love*

Between Aesthetics and Ethics

In making a political statement, arts are a double-edged sword. In her essay about how art depicts suffering published in *The New Yorker*, Susan Sontag (2002) refers to the "inauthenticity of the beautiful," the concept that the visual aspects of art can turn the audience's attention to the medium itself with "mixed signals." While audiences are aware of what the art piece is addressing, such as wars, they could be distracted or even forget about the message because the art piece can be visually beautiful. When applying Sontag's notion of "inauthenticity of the beautiful" to dance, on the one hand, because of its aesthetically pleasing or spectacular nature of moving bodies, dance shares this assumption and can be negated as mere entertainment. On the other hand, because dance is visually attractive, it can be used to approach topics that are not easily discussed, such as trauma, suffering, and dislocation. In his analysis of a performance about wars, Matthew Reason argued that dancing allows survivors to see "their experience *at a distance*" [original emphasis], which can be "less shocking and less immediate" and "abstracted, beautiful, theatrical, and thereby suddenly very articulate" (Reason 90). Perhaps, for performers, the medium of dance – the dancing body – is not only a possible distraction to be heard, but also a possibility to speak.

In early spring 2017, I was invited to present choreography at an annual faculty dance concert. As I was regularly visiting MUCC to offer movement workshops, the dance faculty's request reminded me of the resources I had. Through the College's dance program, I had access to a spacious, pleasant, and well-maintained dance studio as well as a large, fully equipped theatre run by professional staff members. Though my primary responsibility was to work with students in the dance program in college, I could not help but think about the refugee teens and their circumstances at the Center.

The students at MUCC were either the same age or slightly younger than the students at Hamilton College. What I saw, however, was a drastic difference. Hamilton is a private college, and my students were predominantly upper-class and white. Some students in my class skipped the final weeks of their last semester because they had already secured jobs at prestigious law firms or businesses run by their families. At MUCC, on the other hand, I saw teenagers who had witnessed war, death, and loss, and whose families often relied on food stamps. I wanted to share my resources with the refugee teens and give them the opportunities they deserved. The hostile political climate against refugees also made me aware of the importance of working with refugee artists by utilizing performance as a site of civic engagement.

In ethnographic fieldwork, empathy often comes even before the analysis begins because, as Conquergood beautifully encapsulated, "Opening and interpreting lives is very different from opening and closing books" (Conquergood 2). Whether my decision was inspired by the refugee teens' passion for K-pop dance or came from my desire to integrate practice and theory as a researcher, I felt that I had no choice but to work with the young artists at MUCC. Most importantly, I hoped to inspire the refugee teens so that they might apply to college as dance majors. If they were interested in applying to a college, I thought that performing at an annual faculty concert would make their applications stand out. Therefore, I made an unusual decision and asked the dance faculty if I could work with students outside the college. They kindly accepted my request.

With the warm and generous support from the Dance and Movement Studies and Asian Studies Departments, in March 2017, I premiered *Love Means Love* (http s://www.youtube.com/watch?v=5z19y-5Egik) at the Wellin Hall in Schambach Center in New York in collaboration with two members from MUCC's K-pop dance crew, Hyun and Way. Della Pollock suggested an "immersive" approach where the researcher and object of research become "cosubjects" (Pollock 325). The researcher is "entangled with, even ravished by the cocreative process," and the researcher's subjectivity is "diffused and often disappearing into the others' bodies in the field" (Pollock 325). This approach is self-reflective. Instead of the hidden "I," who assumes an objective position, immersive performance (auto)ethnography reveals the researcher's position, often confessing one's privilege, such as "I am white, female, sub/posturban…" (Pollock 326). It invites readers to "feel" the researcher's passion, grace, and even the limitations of her/his position. Writing this chapter has been a performative (auto)ethnography from the stage to the page as "writing as performance and performance as writing" (Madison 220) through which I have reflected on my limitations and positions. This fieldwork opened my eyes to the global youth's diasporic construction of identity through their bold, audacious, and often desperate dream to be K-pop idols, which later evolved into this book.

Jill Dolan described a transformative experience in theatre as a "utopia in performance" (Dolan 2); the communal, sensory feeling of watching performance can guide the audience to a more harmonious space, distancing them from explicit political debates, albeit temporarily. *Love Means Love* was a testimony of how a performance transgresses ideological barriers across ethnicity, religion, and citizenship to create a space for what scholars referred to as "kinesthetic empathy." It is a moment when the audience feels empathy by observing dancers' bodies and movements that directly influence "*how* one felt another's feeling" (Foster 129; J. Young 97; Reason and Reynolds 53). It is a physical, visceral, emotional, and ideological connection in dance when the audience can mirror dancers' feelings through empathy. I hoped that audiences and my students can meet refugee artists instead of merely hearing their stories from newspapers or television news. This 20-minute performance ethnography combined personal narrations, shamanic ritual, K-pop, Christian worship dance, and modern dance. It shared my ethnographic research as a form of staged performance with members of the community.

The performance begins with my speech explaining the yearlong performance ethnography process. It then showcases a duet choreographed by Hyun and Way and then a trio with me. The opening duet was an autobiographic narration in a physical form that exhibits a slice of their life. For the duet, they devised movements from K-pop with which they were already familiar. Dancers are subject to being objectified as corporeal objects when their bodies are displayed without spoken words. The teen dancers' positions were doubly vulnerable because of their status as refugees. To minimize such danger and to add their humane, personal stories, a voice recording of them narrating what dance means to them is played in the background. To devise the scripts played in the background, they first wrote out what dance means to them. I asked if they preferred saying it aloud on stage or playing a pre-recorded sound. They chose the latter. They were not fully fluent in English and often looked shy speaking in English. They recorded the narrations at home using their smartphones and sent me the recordings and scripts, which I later edited with music. Way wrote:

> I do love to dance more than I love school. I want to live, to do things that I love, and dancing is what I love. I am not good with words, but I do know how to express my feelings through dance. Love comes in many languages, and dancing is my language.

Hyun wrote about how miraculous it was when he first formed and danced with the K-pop dance crew under the support of MUCC. Reading their stories, I felt how many unspoken words the teens would keep in their hearts.

Besides the voice recording, they chose the song "Blinded" by Emmit Fenn for the duet. The song has a cosmic, airy vibe combined with a slightly nostalgic and gloomy melody along with simple repetitive lyrics that say, "Don't need this like I used to 'Cause I feel blinded, blinded by you." Their choice of the song seemed to signify their passion for dancing, even if they knew the limited resources they had. The title of the performance, *Love Means Love,* originated from the first fieldnote that disclosed the teen dancers' unconditional love for K-pop dance wherein they were so passionate that they willingly blind themselves.

When their narration is played, they lie on the floor under the dim blue light. On stage, they heard their stories at a distance. Their voices resonate in the air of the beautiful, large Wellin Hall. As the narration ends, they jolt, bounce their chests, and gradually stand up, as if they are reborn, wake up, and resist. Once they fully recover themselves from the floor, they lurch forward in a robotic manner like breakdancing and staggering with heavy feet, covering and uncovering their eyes with their hands. They shove, bumping their chests rhythmically, jolting and stomping their feet, as if bursting their emotion. The duet ends with Hyun covering his eyes while facing front. Way stands behind him and reaches his arms in front of Hyun's face. He gently takes Hyun's hands and uncovers his eyes. They switch the position and repeat the movement of uncovering each other's eyes. Based on what they shared with me during a studio rehearsal, this ending scene signifies that they will assist each other when they see and confront reality and eventually will shine together.

Trauma lingers as trauma because it fails to recognize time already passed (Levan 81). To overcome trauma, survivors need to "work through" it (Corey 123–124; LaCapra xii). Dancing and performing trauma can a "beautiful" space, as it can channel anger, re-write survivors' stories with a sense of agency, and return the silenced, absent bodies in the past to survivors in the present (Corey 123, Park-Fuller 24). The presence of the audience can further empower the survivors (Cristobal 80; Park-Fuller 27). In the duet, they hear their stories emerge from traumatic memories at a distance, reclaim their will and resilience through dance in the present, and recognize the time passed in front of the audience who became witnesses of their testimony.

The next scene is my solo. I include my solo not to represent refugees but to do "doing" (Hamera, "Performance Ethnography" 208) performance ethnography. Some of the movements in the solo directly came from my previous experiences in Christian worship dance, modern dance, and Korean folk dance, salpuri. Salpuri is a Korean folk dance that originated from ancient shamanic rituals and exorcism (Lee and Kim 25). I employed salpuri as a way of performing ritual to mourn and honor stories of survivors across borders. I first learned salpuri at home from my mother, who was a nationally known dancer during her era. After entering Ewha Woman's University in Seoul, South Korea, I also learned Christian worship dance as a dance major along with the Graham and Limón Techniques. Established in the late nineteenth century by Christian missionaries, the university established the nation's first dance department. As a leading institution of dance in higher education in Korea, the university offers Korean dance, modern dance, and classical ballet majors. The university presented a Christian worship dance every semester choreographed by dance faculty.

The combinations of modern, Christian worship, and classical Korean dances came naturally from improvisation, a tool that is often considered to devise an "authentic" movement (Reason 84). Interestingly, the movements brought back my memories associated with the movement from childhood to college. The solo became autobiographical, while it also aimed to speak with others. My memories were embodied and as diasporic as the hybrid training itself.

As Johannes Birringer (1986) argued, repetition can combine entertaining and ritualistic aspects of dance with its transformative, emotional capacity. My solo used repetition, such as brushing hands with eyes closed, which resonated with ritualistic cleansing. With purified, simple, gestural movement, the solo aimed to find distance from potentially decorative, often seemingly empty, spectacular movement technique. I brought four candles on stage because of their visual and emotional resonance with a ritual. Each candle signifies an individual who went through traumatic events I met through my fieldwork with refugees.

Under the dim light, I kneel on the floor and show airy fluid arm gestures, taking a bow to each candle. I then walk across the stage, reaching my arm to the side as if I put my arms on my family member's shoulder. I continue walking

FIGURE 6.3 The author in her solo in *Love Means Love* (2017)
Note: Choreographed by the author.
Source: Photo by Claudette Ferrone at Hamilton College.

toward the diagonal with a dreamy gait and gradually hunch my back, falter, sinking to the floor until I nearly crawl. While crawling and tottering on the floor, my right arm continually jolts and falls, and my left arm lifts it over and over again. The scene aims to deliver a sense of mourning and resilience, while refugees move across borders, supporting each other.

During the process of making *Love Means Love*, I struggled to balance aesthetics versus ethics and theatricality versus activism. As a performance ethnography, it was significant to create a platform where the teens genuinely felt comfortable and shared their stories on stage. But as a staged show, it was also crucial to make the performance accessible and relatable to general audiences by using aesthetically and sonically pleasing material if needed. Minimum theatrical devices are often imperative on stage, including working with music, sound editing, costumes, lighting design, movements, choreographic routines, and a possible narrative or a storyline throughout the performance. Above all, a stage performance, whether it is performance ethnography or concert dance, is a staged performance. Performance may not be a performance without a properly rehearsed set of techniques that stage material in a more presentational way. Yet, performance itself, even theatrical techniques, do not necessarily contradict authenticity because performance is not a mere mirror of something, of "faking" it; instead, doing itself is "making" where unspoken truths can be further articulated and even physicalized through various artistic mediums (Turner 84).

Bryant Keith Alexander warned of the precarious line between *"performance as consciousness raising* and *performance as entertainment"* [original emphasis] (Alexander 110). Being aware of the fine line, nevertheless, once the show date was announced on a local newspaper, and the program pamphlet was sent out to the public, I found myself unconsciously switching from an ethnographer to a choreographer. To combine aesthetics and ethics, I made conscious choices as a choreographer. First, I decided to include my solo for stylistic reasons. In addition to my ethical responsibility of being a "co-performer" to challenge the colonial binary in ethnography, self/Other, text/body, researcher/participant (Denzin x), I thought of the general ambiance of the concert. Other pieces presented during the concert were modern dance and ballet choreographed by dance faculty with university students. Having only the teen K-pop dancers might make their performance appear not integrated to the rest concert program because of their visibly different dance style. Further, most pieces had a conventional concert dance scale, consisting of approximately ten dancers staged with grandiose props and classical costumes and lasting about 30 minutes. The K-pop crew mostly performs K-pop cover dance to short K-pop songs, and they have not had a full-length show in a conventional proscenium theatre. By adding my solo, I could not only make the length of *Love Means Love* more appropriate to the concert stage, but also add "classical" taste given my training in classical ballet and modern dance.

The music was also decided in negotiation between aesthetics and ethics. I played Jeff Buckley's song "Hallelujah" for my solo because of its subtle religious reference. I also chose the song because of its popularity and familiarity to the general public and iconic melody in American popular music. The solo is based on Korean folk dance and shamanic ritual, which might appear peculiar and unfamiliar to most audiences. The music could make the solo sonically proximate and thus less strange to the attendees in upstate New York, who were predominantly white.

The practicality of costumes and props was another thing to consider. Salpuri dancers wear a white hanbok, a traditional Korean garment. As salpuri inspired the solo, I wanted to wear a hanbok or a dress that resembled it. However, it was impossible to find a hanbok in upstate New York, and even if I ordered one from an online store, a hanbok would be too heavy to perform in. For the practicality of the theatrical presentation, I decided to wear a long white dress that felt light enough to move on stage. At first, Hyun and Way wanted to wear red plaid shirts. Once they tried the shirts on during a rehearsal and saw their video recording of the rehearsal, they found the shirts looked too casual for a conventional stage, not to mention the fabric that was not elastic. We decided to purchase plain white shirts, which I later bought from Target. For the stage props, real candles would have been nice, but I brought fake candles on stage for safety reasons.

A trio of Hyun, Way, and I followed the solo. They chose BTS's song "Young Forever" for this scene. The trio was a collection of the movement workshop outcome in addition to their K-pop-inspired choreography. In the scene, they used movements from the modern dance workshops I provided, such as floor movements, turns, and jumps, which would be more appropriate for a spacious proscenium stage. As they mostly practiced with K-pop dance designed for a music video or social media screen, their dance style's spatial use was limited. While choreographing *Love Means Love*, I asked them to devise one short movement, and then expand and explore it with a different space, time, level, and interaction. They also added a liberatory, free vibe inspired from the original song "Young Forever."

During the choreography process, I found that they were already aware of aging, which might explain their choice of BTS's "Young Forever." With the chorus line "Forever we are young," the song talks about BTS's will and dream for singing and dancing, even if the audience's applause will disappear someday. The lyrics "I want to be a boy forever"[2] implies BTS's youth, and possibly, their potentially limited career as idol dancers. Hyun and Way knew that as late teenagers they were already almost too old to debut as K-pop idols and make that dream a reality. Their music choice signifies how the teens identify with BTS in terms of the transient nature of the stage, and despite the short fleeting moment of youth, like dancing, their continuous will to pursue it.

In the climax of the trio, they chose to play the "Blinded" song again. They lay on the floor. Covering my eyes, I lean forward, bending my front knee and extending my other leg backward. I slowly drag my legs along and trudge toward the boys, hesitantly looking behind. Way grabs my ankle and holds on, still lying on the floor, as I heavily and gradually push myself to move forward. Hyun grabs Way's ankle and begins to trail along with us. Then, at the front, Way and I help Hyun stand up to walk with us in a row. We plod together, dropping our heads and dragging our feet. When one falls down, the others lift him up.

This movement signifies the teen dancers' burdens as they move across borders as well as the ways that they support each other through that trauma. When all three of us finally arrive downstage right, a list of people plays on the screen on stage. It contains people who came to the US as refugees and who changed the world, such as Sigmund Freud and Albert Einstein. The screen shares brief stories of why they were forced to leave their countries. The performance ends with the statement: "Being a refugee is not a choice. Supporting them to change the world is a choice."

The performance was well-received. As Judith Hamera observed, it was possible to create a celebratory site via performance where marginalized voices could be heard (Hamera, "Dancing Communities" 82). The audience came up to the stage after the show and celebrated the moment together. Albeit temporary, their warm cheers and supportive words reaffirmed the transformative power of performance. My most immense happiness came from seeing the members of the MUCC community in the auditorium. Director Chris told me that he cried watching the performance. He was one of the few people who truly knew how much hardship these children had endured and what dance means to them. He sent me a message on Facebook afterward: "Thank you so much for working with them. They really are my world, and I try so hard to get them as many opportunities as possible. And

FIGURE 6.4 *Love Means Love* (2017)
Note: Choreographed by the author. Wellin Hall, Schambach Center, Clinton, New York.
Source: Photo by Claudette Ferrone at Hamilton College.

it often feels impossible. And then people like you come along and help." While Chris expressed appreciation for what this opportunity meant to these refugee artists, I was the one who remained truly grateful. In performance ethnography, as Norman K. Denzin highlighted, speaking *with* others is an essential footstep to avoid speaking *for* them (Denzin 17). Being a "co-performer" is a core step toward speaking with the members of a community (Denzin xi). I humbly believe that *Love Means Love* exemplified a "dialogical performance" that brings different voices and cultural beliefs through a self-reflective, embodied, participatory, and collaborative process with the community, through negotiations between aesthetics/theatricality and ethic/activism of performance ethnography (Conquergood 9).

Dancing Ritual – Dancers as Zarathustra

After the performance, I continued volunteering at MUCC and began to interview the dance crew and other community members. Both Way and Hyun had started dancing at an early age. Way first learned traditional Karen folk dance in his home country and later developed other dance styles. In the US, he feels uncomfortable dancing in front of his parents and thus dances alone in his room late at night with the door closed. Hyun started dancing when he came to the US as a child. He first learned dance by watching videos on YouTube. One of the earliest videos he posted on Facebook was a short shuffle dance with nimble footwork filmed in a backyard. He said that during his early childhood in the US, "I wanted to do something that makes my parent proud of, so I picked up dancing." However, soon after, his parents separated: "When my parent [sic] separated, I was devastated. I felt alone. Not to feel like that, I danced until I wasn't angry at the world anymore." He then recalled the first day he came to MUCC:

> I didn't even have a place to practice except my room, so when I first step into MUCC, I laid an eye on it, and it was the most beautiful place I've ever seen. I wanted to dance there. I hardly knew back then I love dancing so much that it became a part of my life.

They both not only had limited resources for dancing but also had limited social networks at school. At MUCC, however, they can freely dance to K-pop: "To me, dancing means where I could feel my true feeling, who I am, and how I act," Way said. Whenever I visited the Center on an early Sunday morning, they were already there dancing.

For refugee teens, K-pop dance is a way of dreaming of an alternative life. One day, we were heading to a parking lot after rehearsal. I asked the teenagers why they like dancing so much. Way's response still lingers in my memory: "Just to get me out of here." Angela McRobbie (McRobbie, "Dance and Social Fantasy"; McRobbie, "Feminism") has argued that dance is often a tool to achieve a dream for working-class girls, such as upward class mobility. While the refugee teens are boys, McRobbie's idea is applicable given their lack of resources and structural marginalization in society.

Despite the stereotype of dance as an extravagant, bourgeois entertainment in modern society, throughout history dance has been used as a site for people who have been marginalized. Undoubtedly, a stylized concert dance often referred to as "art for art's sake" would have different expectations and require professional training and costly processes to make a show. However, before the emergence of elitism in concert dance in the modern era, dance in daily life has always been available to everyone. Capoeira is one of the many examples in which disenfranchised citizens used dance to amplify their voices. Dance history is a history of people who have migrated, been exiled and enslaved. Many of the legendary dancers in history were enslaved, working-class refugees and immigrants, or those exiled or marginalized because of their citizenship, race, ethnicity, sexual orientation, religion, gender, or political standpoint (Scolieri v–xx). Examples include Josephine Baker, Vaslav Nijinsky, Isadora Duncan, and Choi Seung-hee, an internationally known Korean dancer who was "the First K[orean]-Wave" (Atkins 147), to name a few.

The primary medium of dance – the body – might better explain dance's inclusive nature. The body in dance often enables socioeconomically marginalized people who do not have institutional support to dream of an alternative pathway in life. Many of the teenagers at MUCC had a chaotic childhood. Some of them fled from wars and genocide with empty hands. Most of their parents do not speak English and temporarily stay in Utica to work night shifts at a factory that pays minimum wage. Though financially impoverished, the teenagers have their bodies and dance allows them to use their bodies to express themselves, speak up, and showcase who they are.

Dance Ban and Resistance

Governments around the world have a long history of banning social dancing. Japan, for example, repealed a 67-year-old ban on dancing after midnight, which was established after World War II, in 2015 (Ripley). Spontaneous dancing in public is often illegal in Sweden except in a place that holds a "dance license" because "dancing creates disorder" according to police (O'Mahony). Palestine and Iran are some of the countries where people are arrested and punished for public dancing (Feranak; McDonald). In the US, Philadelphia banned public dancing in 2012, or "any theatrical performance relating to dance and the expression of [...] emotions through movement" because dancing, according to the police department, is "out of control" (Mulhearn). In 2017, Oklahoma City repealed a 40-year-old regulation that prevented dancing within 500 feet of church or school (Lim). New York City Council, too, repealed a 91-year-old cabaret law that prohibited public dancing because it related with interracial mingling at Harlem bars (Correal). When we dance, we claim our bodies, and thus, voice.

Such liberated bodies could threaten authorities. Kélina Gotman (2017) traced unruly movements of crowds in political protests and social revolts since the nineteenth century, called "choreomania," which imbued citizens with political power and agency via dancing. Anthony Shay (1999) examined solo improvised dance and its artistic and political impact. Improvisational solo dance is the most popular dance form in the Iranian world despite dance bans, which he called "choreophobia," oscillating between love and fear. As explained in Chapter 1, compared to concert dance that emphasizes technical skills, social dance is a voluntary and participatory activity. It has been a political tool for freedom of expression and re-claiming one's agency against the societal regulation and institutionalized bodily discipline.

In literature, dance has been a symbol of freedom. The common phrase of "dance like no one's watching" would be familiar to most readers. In philosophy, through the notion of "Übermensch," or "the Overhuman," in *Thus Spoke Zarathustra: A Book for Everyone and Nobody,* Friedrich Nietzsche inaugurated the phrase "*God is Dead!*" (Nietzsche 11). The phrase paved the way for the birth of postmodern philosophy, which he theorized through symbolic meanings of dance. He introduced a dancer, named Zarathustra, whose presence replaces the absence of the God:

> [...] the dancer, Zarathustra the light, who beckons with his wings, one ready for flight, beckoning to all birds, ready and prepared, and blissfully light-

hearted [...] You superior humans, the worst about you is: that none of you has learned to dance as one has to dance – dance away beyond yourselves! What does it matter that you have failed! How much is yet possible! So just *learn* to laugh away beyond yourselves! Lift up your hearts, you fine dancers, high! Higher!

(Nietzsche 257, 259)

He boldly described a dancer whose will for power transcends the ephemeral nature of the human condition in the most corporeal way, who is ready for an eternal recurrence of the same life (Nietzsche xviii). While the God represents the Apollonian logic and logos rooted in Plato's theory of ideas, Zarathustra signifies the spontaneous, corporeal, and emotional ecstasy of Dionysus, a god of theatre, wine, ritual, and festival from Greek mythology.

In a dance studio, I learned how to remain "light-hearted" and "dance away" beyond my body's limitation. I started my ballet training when I was seven years old at the Kirov Academy of Ballet in Washington, DC, and Seoul, South Korea, moving back and forth between the two institutions during the summer. Dancing was not only a strict and harsh bodily discipline but also an outlet to push my physical and, thus, mental and emotional limits. Even if I already knew I could not fly, I tried and practiced jumps as if I could fly like a bird. I practiced pirouette turns until midnight in an empty dance studio, falling, injuring, recovering, and trying it again. The next day, I happily went back to the studio, taping the bruised toenails, wrapping the feet, and massaging a pain relief gel on my sore back and knees. As a modern dancer later in my career, it was common to see dancers' blood under the thick calluses on their bare feet and elbows and bruises on their knees.

André Lepecki wrote "A dancer perfects movement by repeating and returning. Repeating and returning" (Lepecki 96). For dancers, the repetitive training is an everyday ritual in the dance studio. Ritual is a repeated action, a performance, in a community that shares mutual understanding, belief, and content and that accepts authenticity of each other's intention; because of such intrinsic validity, ritual has effect and affect (Alexander 527). As Victor Turner argued, ritual and performance are not a binary opposite, but share commonalities, such as intrinsic values, dramatic structure, transformation, and catharsis through rehearsed and repeated techniques. Through the endless bodily repetition and psychological discipline based on the norm of the studios, dancers are *Zarathustra* of their own who dream infinite possibilities with finite human bodies. The dancers go through a collective process of ritual with an intrinsic value; dancing itself is not necessarily needed to represent or mean something but doing so carried the validity within the community. If dancing and choreographing is a "system of control or discipline" within the control, dancers can mobilize agency (Clayton et al. 18).

Throughout the repetitive training, I felt more agency than restriction. It was nearly a perfect level of satisfaction and liberation that must be obtained through the disciplined, systematic, arduous bodily practice and endless repetitions. I was ready to go through the process over and over again, even if through an eternal recurrence of the same practice. In college, I decided to minor in philosophy after reading *Zarathustra*. My theoretical understanding of Nietzsche came much later by learning contemporary philosophers' interpretations of his theory. Yet, I still remember my very first encounter with Nietzsche's book on a dusty bookshelf in a library. When I first read *Thus Spoke Zarathustra*, it felt like a diary written by and for a dancer.

What I noticed working with the dance crew was the audacious hope of *Zarathustra* and endless will to continue their lives through dance, within which I spent my entire childhood and early career as a dancer. Metaphorically or physically, the refugee K-pop dancers' passion toward dance reflects the genealogy and the liberatory functions of dance and its humble roots in serving the community. They dance to K-pop because it is cheerful and entertaining, guiding them to move forward from their trauma. Like the Latinx dancer discussed in Chapter 4, the refugee teens can do K-pop dance with few resources as long as they have passion and their bodies filled with hope and dreams. As explained in Chapter 2, the digitalization of K-pop dance on social media and the democratization of dance education plays a vital role for the economically and socioculturally marginalized youth who are drawn to K-pop. Whenever I watched the dance crew practice, they always had their smartphones in hand, playing K-pop music videos, correcting each other, recording their practice, and comparing their dance routines with those on screen.

To the dance crew at MUCC, K-pop dance is a language that transcends verbal communication. When I first met Hyun, he did not meet my eyes during the conversation, a behavior that I noticed was habitual. He spoke in a low and quiet voice and often looked intimidated. I was able to better understand his communication style after hearing more about his family's traumatic story from senior volunteers and staff members at the Center. When he was dancing to K-pop, however, he transformed into a completely different person. He was expressive, outgoing, and highly energetic. He also recognized this different persona while dancing, telling me, "I am usually very calm, but when I am dancing, I can be like really aggressive." Through the language of K-pop dance, he was performing an alter ego, which I will further elaborate below.

Diasporic K-pop Dance: A Cultural Identity in Transition

Through K-pop cover dance, the dance crew at MUCC challenges racial, ethnic, and social stigmas of refugees. Hyun mentioned that refugees are stigmatized as being dangerous and leading miserable lives. "No one would imagine refugees dancing to K-pop," he added. He explained that the crew's name means something toxic, strong, and addictive. As K-pop is an emerging hipster culture of global youth, to them, dancing to K-pop makes a statement about how they are different from the prevalent stereotypes and how they enjoy their lives and claim voice through dance.

K-pop dance provides a rare platform for physical exercise and social gatherings for refugee teenagers at MUCC. The mental and physical health benefit of amateur social dancing has been well-recognized (Murcia et al.). For children, dancing develops commutative and collaborative skills and can therefore even lower school bullying rates (Robinson and Aronica). The youth community at MUCC exercise regularly and together via K-pop dance, where they get to mingle and know each other quickly. They dance every day, even during the weekends with friends. The Center has not only allowed them to hone their artistic talent but also to form a community and friendships. Frequently, they watch Korean dramas and talk about their favorite actors/actresses. These young refugees come from different countries, primarily in Southeast Asia and Africa, and speak different languages. While they hardly share a common cultural background, they use K-pop dance fandom to socialize, build more profound friendships, and create a sense of belonging, both verbally and physically.

The refugee teens' identities are in transit between maintaining their cultural roots and adapting to new identities in the US. Many of them have been ostracized because of their race, ethnicity, and language barriers, not to mention their social status as refugees. Hyun said of his experience when first arriving in the US: "...I felt new, and I felt like I could be somebody here. But I found out soon people can be cruel, not friendly to outsiders. Things they said destroyed me." While they are in the transition of learning a new identity, they feel homesick and confront discrimination. At the same time, they feel the pressure to assimilate into the mainstream (white) culture. As speaking English fluently is one of the main goals they seek to achieve, many take English classes at MUCC.

The teen refugees employ K-pop neither to complete their assimilation to US mainstream culture nor to retain their homeland's culture. This strategic adaptation is particularly evident among refugee teens from Southeast Asia, as in the case of the dance crew at MUCC. Way said that he likes US hip-hop, but often, the mainstream hip-hop lyrics are too explicit and heavily focus on drugs and sex. On the contrary, K-pop has hip-hop elements such as rap and dance style but also includes components that appeal to him more, such as soft and polite lyrics about teenage romance. Interestingly, the fact that they do not speak Korean helps the members of the K-pop dance crew better enjoy the rhythm and visually attractive images of K-pop music videos with additional room for imagination. As explained in Chapter 2, K-pop's integration of English lyrics, mostly simple words, and boundary-crossing style combining Asian and Western music and dance also make K-pop more adaptable to these teens.

There is a moment of racial identification in the dance crew's K-pop dance fandom. Although their ethnicity is Karen, as Asians in the US, Way and Hyun feel connected to and identify themselves with K-pop dancers. Way said that he wants to show his friends "how cool K-pop is." Hyun said that since the dance crew's local fan base has grown, people at school have begun to call him by his group name like a celebrity, instead of his real name, saying, "Look! There's TOX!" (pseudonym). Sharing an anecdote of how his friends now call him as his stage name, he wore a happy, proud smile on his face. His crew members are aware of the limited representations of Asians in US mainstream pop music and dance. Being a member of the K-pop dance crew elevates their self-esteem. Although their ethnicity is different, both K-pop idols and they are racially Asian, and positive peer recognition of K-pop seems to affect their perception of themselves. Even if they often get their clothing from local donations, at least on stage, they pass to the fancy, spectacular image of K-pop idols through dance. They destigmatize their status as refugees, facilitating and easing the process of embracing a new pan-racial identity as Asians in the US.

As I discussed elsewhere, performing an alter ego is one of the shared drives of K-pop dance fandom. When I interviewed Danish amateur K-pop fan-dancers, they said K-pop is like "drag" and an "alter ego"; an interviewee said, "It is so nice to be able to pretend like I am a total rock star for just a minute! Because I know that I will never be able to do what they do" (Oh 28). Growing up in a small town in Copenhagen, they did not have much chance to learn about Asian culture. Dressing like K-pop singers and dancing to K-pop in public was an outlet where Danish teenagers could distinguish themselves from mainstream Western pop culture.

The dance crew's identity passing to K-pop comes with cultural hybridity. They have appeared on local Karen television shows as an example of young Karen artists who promote their cultural heritage and visibility. A photo on their Facebook page comes from their performance at a Karen annual celebration festival in upstate New York. As the event team requested, they are wearing traditional Karen clothes while performing K-pop cover dances. The stage is decorated with Karen national flags and celebratory remarks written in the Karen language. As K-pop cover dancers, they also celebrate Koreanness in K-pop. In one of their photos on Facebook, the crew holds a large Korean flag to celebrate after a performance. Wearing masks was common for citizens of Seoul to due to air pollution long before COVID-19. K-pop idols also often wore masks with cute prints, and some of their photos have gone viral and become fashion trends. The dance crew at MUCC wore black masks when performing at the Karen festival as well as other local performing arts festivals.

In addition to fashion, language is another significant factor in identity passing. Many of the crew members have stage names that sound Korean. Due to K-pop cover dances' nature where the similarity with the K-pop idols matters, they lip-sync in Korean when filming a video. Most of the members were eager to learn the language. While learning English seemed like a burden or schoolwork, they appeared genuinely excited when I taught them Korean. They often said hello in Korean when they greeted me, and many of the teenagers at MUCC post on their social media in Korean. Frequently, their Facebook Korean seems out of context, which I attribute to its being generated through Google translate.

To the refugee dance crew, cultural identity is more fluid than ethnic identity. They willingly situate themselves in a liminal status combining American, Korean, and Karen cultures. Their identity passing is different from the assimilation or homogenization that many immigrants and second-generation immigrant children experience. Their identity passing through K-pop dance is a voluntary action and an active enactment on and offstage. Through the mediator of K-pop dance, they neither completely pass as Korean nor American but instead, temporarily construct a new mobile, fluid, spatial, and cultural identity through dancing.

From a racial dimension, I also noticed that some of the K-pop dance crew members identified with African Americans. In her research with Southeast Asian American refugee teens in South Philadelphia, Angela Reyes argued that instead of "act[ing] black," the teens adopt African American vernacular, stereotypical slang to affiliate with urban youth, subcultural style. By doing so, they construct themselves as "tough," authenticated slang speakers whose identities oscillate between "honorary whites [and] forever foreigners" (Reyes 527). While the residential area of the MUCC's dance crew differs from those of study participants, Reyes's research is relevant to the dancers, given their racial, ethnic, and social status. On the day of a stage rehearsal for *Love Means Love*, I asked them if they needed anything before the rehearsal. One of them texted me back, saying, "can u bring some snacks for this nigaa." Afterward, I explained what that term means, which he would certainly know, and asked him not to use it. He may identify with the urban youth African American subculture as a symbol of resistance. Simultaneously, this incident revealed how dynamic or, for lack of a better word, multifaceted was his sense of belonging and identity.

From 2017 to 2018, I made a transition from upstate New York to San Diego. In the meantime, the dance crew members went through multiple stages toward adulthood, auditioning to a K-pop agency and applying to a college as a dance major. The next chapter discusses (im)possibilities of dance and performance ethnography and still, the heuristic potential of it based on the refugee teens' year-long journey in K-pop dance – a home that is always there on social media, albeit an unobtainable mirage.

Notes

1 Karen is an indigenous ethnic group in Southeast Asia.
2 I translate the Korean lyrics.

References

Alexander, Bryant Keith. "Introduction: Performative Rhetorics of Desire, Resistance, and Possibility." *QED: A Journal in GLBTQ Worldmaking*, vol. 2, no. 1, 2015, pp. 109–111. https://doi.org/10.14321/qed.2.1.0109.

Alexander, Jeffrey C. "Cultural Pragmatics: Social Performance Between Ritual and Strategy." *Sociological Theory*, vol. 22, no. 4, 2004, pp. 527–573. https://doi.org/10.1111/j.0735-2751.2004.00233.x.

Atkins, Everett Taylor. *Primitive Selves: Koreana in the Japanese Colonial Gaze, 1910–1945*. University of California P, 2010.

Atkinson, Zakiya. "A Creative Response to the Holocaust, Genocide, and Injustice." *Dance Education in Practice*, vol. 4, no. 1, 2018, pp. 16–24. https://doi.org/10.1080/23734833.2018.1417211.

Birringer, Johannes. "Pina Bausch: Dancing across Borders." *The Drama Review: TDR*, vol. 30, no. 2, 1986, pp. 85–97. https://doi.org/10.2307/1145729.

Clayton, Michelle, et al. "Inside/Beside Dance Studies: A Conversation Mellon Dance Studies in/and the Humanities." *Dance Research Journal*, vol. 45, no. 3, 2013, pp. 3–28. https://muse.jhu.edu/article/541939.

Conquergood, Dwight. "Performing as a Moral Act: Ethical Dimensions of the Ethnography of Performance." *Literature in Performance*, vol. 5, no. 2, 1985, pp. 1–13. https://doi.org/10.1080/10462938509391578.

Corey, Frederick C. "When Performance Brings Us Through." *Text and Performance Quarterly*, vol. 34, no. 2, 2014, pp. 123–124. https://doi.org/10.1080/10462937.2014.887392.

Correal, Annie. "After 91 Years, New York Will Let Its People Boogie." *The New York Times*, 30 Oct. 2017, https://www.nytimes.com/2017/10/30/nyregion/new-york-cabaret-law-repeal.html.

Cristobal, Keira A. "Power of Touch: Working with Survivors of Sexual Abuse Within Dance/Movement Therapy." *American Journal of Dance Therapy*, vol. 40, no. 1, 2018, pp. 68–86. https://doi.org/10.1007/s10465-018-9275-7.

Denzin, Norman K. *Performance Ethnography: Critical Pedagogy and the Politics of Culture*. Sage Publications, 2003.

Dolan, Jill. *Utopia in Performance: Finding Hope at the Theater*. University of Michigan P, 2010.

Foster, Susan Leigh. *Choreographing Empathy: Kinesthesia in Performance*. Routledge, 2010.

Gotman, Kélina. *Choreomania: Dance and Disorder*. Oxford UP, 2017.

Hamera, Judith. "Performance Ethnography." In *The Sage Handbook of Qualitative Research*, edited by Norman K.Denzin and Yvonna S.Lincoln, SAGE Publications, 2011, pp. 317–330.

Hamera, Judith. *Dancing Communities*. Palgrave Macmillan, 2007.

Amidi, Feranak. "'I risked everything to dance in Iran.'" *BBC News*. 11 July 2018, https://www.bbc.com/news/world-middle-east-44777677.

LaCapra, Dominick. *Representing the Holocaust: History, Theory, Trauma*. Cornell UP, 1996.

Lee, Eun-Joo, and Yong-Shin Kim. *Salpuri-chum, A Korean Dance for Expelling Evil Spirits: A Psychoanalytic Interpretation of Its Artistic Characteristics*. Rowman & Littlefield, 2017.

Lepecki, André. "Dance Discourses: Keywords in Dance Research." *Dance Research Journal*, vol. 44, no. 1, 2012, pp. 93–99. https://muse.jhu.edu/article/473148.

Levan, Michael. "Folding Trauma: On Alfredo Jaar's Installations and Interventions." *Performance Research*, vol. 16, no. 1, 2011, pp. 80–90. https://doi.org/10.1080/13528165.2011.561678.

Lim, Stephanie. "Oklahoma Town Can Dance Again, 'Footloose' Ordinance Abolished." *Global News*. 22 Feb. 2017, https://globalnews.ca/news/3266820/oklahoma-town-can-dance-again-footloose-ordinance-abolished/.

Madison, D. Soyini. *Critical Ethnography: Method, Ethics, and Performance*. Sage Publications, 2011.

McDonald, David A. "Poetics and the Performance of Violence in Israel/Palestine." *Ethnomusicology*, vol. 53, no. 1, 2009, pp. 58–85. http://www.jstor.org/stable/25653047.

McRobbie, Angela. "Dance and Social Fantasy." In *Gender and Generation (Youth Question)*, edited by Angela McRobbie and Mica Nava, Palgrave Macmillan, 1984, pp. 130–161.

McRobbie, Angela. *Feminism and Youth Culture: From 'Jackie' to 'Just Seventeen.'* Palgrave, 1991.

Mulhearn, Jon. "URGENT: Dancing To Be Banned In Philadelphia." *The Dance Journal*. 1 April 2012, https://philadelphiadance.org/dancejournal/2012/04/01/urgent-dancing-to-be-banned-in-philadelphia/.

Nayfack, Shakina. "Dancing Communities: Performance, Difference, and Connection in the Global City (review)." *Dance Research Journal*, vol. 40, no. 2, 2008, pp. 94–97. https://www.jstor.org/stable/20527612.

Nietzsche, Friedrich. *Thus Spoke Zarathustra: A Book for Everyone and Nobody*. Translated by Graham Parkes, Oxford UP, 2005.

Oh, Chuyun. "From Seoul to Copenhagen: Migrating K-Pop Cover Dance and Performing Diasporic Youth in Social Media." *Dance Research Journal*, vol. 52, no. 1, 2020, pp. 20–32. https://doi.org/10.1017/S0149767720000030.

O'Mahony, Paul. "Sweden Keeps Ban on Spontaneous Dancing." *The Local*. 30 March 2015, https://www.thelocal.se/20150330/sweden-keeps-ban-on-spontaneous-dancing/.

Park-Fuller, Linda M. "Performing Absence: The Staged Personal Narrative as Testimony." *Text and Performance Quarterly*, vol. 20, no. 1, 2000, pp. 24–25. https://doi.org/10.1080/10462930009366281.

Pollock, Della. "Marking New Directions in Performance Ethnography." *Text and Performance Quarterly*, vol. 26, no. 4, 2006, pp. 325–329. https://doi.org/10.1080/10462930600828733.

Reason, Matthew. "Representing Soldiers to Soldiers Through Dance: Authenticity, Theatricality, and Witnessing the Pain of Others." *Dance Research Journal*, vol. 49, no. 2, 2017, pp. 79–95. https://doi.org/10.1017/S0149767717000213.

Reason, Matthew, and Dee Reynolds. "Kinesthesia, Empathy, and Related Pleasures: An Inquiry into Audience Experiences of Watching Dance." *Dance Research Journal*, vol. 42, no. 2, 2010, pp. 49–75. https://doi.org/10.1017/S0149767700001030.

"Refugee Dance Project: Love Means Love (2017)." YouTube, uploaded by Chuyun Oh, 17 April 2017, https://www.youtube.com/watch?v=5z19y-5Egik.

Reyes, Angela. "Appropriation of African American Slang by Asian American Youth." *Journal of Sociolinguistics*, vol. 9, no. 4, 2005, pp. 509–532. https://doi.org/10.1111/j.1360-6441.2005.00304.x.

Ripley, Will. "Japan Shakes Off 67-year Ban on Dancing after Midnight." *CNN*, 22 June 2015, https://edition.cnn.com/2015/06/21/asia/japan-midnight-dancing-ban/index.html.

Robinson, SirKen and Lou Aronica. "Why Dance Is Just as Important as Math in School." *TED Ideas*, 21 March 2018, https://ideas.ted.com/why-dance-is-just-as-important-as-math-in-school/.

Scolieri, Paul. "Global/mobile: Re-orienting Dance and Migration Studies." *Dance Research Journal*, vol. 40, no. 2, 2008, pp. v–xx. https://doi.org/10.1017/S0149767700000346.

Sontag, Susan. "'Looking at War' Photography's View of Devastation and Death." *The New Yorker*, 2 December 2002https://www.newyorker.com/magazine/2002/12/09/looking-at-war.

Turner, Victor. "Dramatic Ritual/Ritual Drama: Performative and Reflexive Anthropology." *The Kenyon Review*, vol. 1, no. 3, 1979, pp. 80–93. https://www.jstor.org/stable/4335047.

Turner, Victor. *The Anthropology of Performance*. PAJ Books, 1988.

Murcia, Cynthia Quiroga, et al. "Shall We Dance? An Exploration of the Perceived Benefits of Dancing on Well-being." *Arts & Health*, vol. 2, no. 2, 2010, pp. 149–163. https://doi.org/10.1080/17533010903488582.

Young, Jessica. "The Therapeutic Movement Relationship in Dance/Movement Therapy: A Phenomenological Study." *American Journal of Dance Therapy*, vol. 39, no. 1, 2017, pp. 93–112. https://doi.org/10.1007/s10465-017-9241-9.

EPILOGUE: (IM)POSSIBILITY OF DOING PERFORMANCE ETHNOGRAPHY IN K-POP DANCE

The Visible Dancing Body, The Invisible Structural Inequality

In 2017, I got a new job in San Diego, California. I was excited but felt bad that I would no longer be able to provide support for the MUCC community. I remembered one of the audience members who had attended *Love Means Love*. She is the director of a local dance academy for children in Utica, and universities across the nation have accepted her students. After watching the performance, she applauded the boys' dance skills and said, "They are doing real work." I contacted her and asked if the refugees could attend dance classes at her institution. After a few days, I received her response. She said it would not be possible because, according to her, it might make the students at her academy feel "uncomfortable."

The students at this dance academy are predominantly upper-class white girls. When I visited, I saw a group of middle-aged men and women waiting for their daughters outside the school in their BMWs and Mercedes Benzes. The director's intention may be nothing more than an effort to keep her students "safe," as she explained. Nevertheless, her response reaffirmed the racialized and classist stigma and criminalization of refugees, even children, as well as the structural inequalities in arts and dance education. Her reaction also appeared to reaffirm the juxtaposition between arts education and classism, which further marginalizes under-represented populations in dance. Unfortunately, kinesthetic empathy was not extended beyond theatre.

A few months before I left Hamilton College, I asked Hyun what he wants to do after graduating from high school. He responded:

> My dream is to become a dancer … you should never give up your dream. You shouldn't let other people control your dream either, don't let them to what to do. Just be who we are, and if you do that, in the near future, you will be happier in life.

DOI: 10.4324/9781003212188-10

Among the many dancers I have met, the cover dancers at MUCC were some of the most passionate and hardworking dancers. While working on *Love Means Love*, Hyun and Way finished choreographing their duet in just a few days. They seamlessly and effortlessly choreographed the beautiful autobiographical duet based on their struggle and support of each other through a dark period. As dancers, they were intuitive, considerate, and effective in their communication while devising movements. While Way was interested in being a singer as much as a dancer, Hyun was interested in dance more exclusively. His movements were accurate, executed cleanly with the right level of strength, rhythm, synchronization, and spatial awareness. He was not only a fast learner but also had excellent permeability. I taught him how to do a pirouette in the first dance movement workshop. He learned it along with a double turn in only a few minutes. As much as personal motivation plays a significant role in children's learning, it appeared that a lack of educational opportunity made him a better dancer to some extent. He was always eager to learn and passionate about learning more. Before I left upstate New York, I reminded Hyun and his dance crew that I could write them letters of recommendation if they applied for college as dance majors.

In January 2018 in San Diego, I received a Facebook message from the MUCC director Chris. In the message, he said that there had been a miscommunication between him and Hyun. He had taken Hyun to an orientation for future students at a state university in New York from which Chris had graduated. Hyun heard about the cost of tuition and lost interest in applying for college. At the time, however, the state universities in New York had begun to offer free education. Chris said that he was in tears because Hyun had decided to enlist in the military and asked whether I could nudge him to apply to college. I sent Hyun a Facebook message, and after a conversation, he changed his decision. Chris and I were genuinely excited not just because Hyun could receive an opportunity he deserves but also because education is one of the few ways to escape poverty. I began to research dance programs with diverse faculty profiles and inclusive coursework, including non-Western dance and pop dance, such as hip-hop. I then suggested a few universities and wrote a letter of recommendation.

I described Hyun's progress and his biggest strength in the letter, which is not his physical virtuosity or stage presence. It is his sincere effort and love for dancing. He already knew how to see himself through dancing and how to speak up about his identity through dance. Dancing was being himself. What I have witnessed is that only a few will continue their careers and remain in dance. Some students are drawn to dance because they like physical activities. However, such interest is not enough to continue dancing as a formal lifetime career. Unlike a science or engineering degree, it is often difficult to get a high-paying or full-time job as a dancer. Humanities departments across the nation are downsizing under the multinational capitalism, which has negative impacts on dance studies, which are often treated as a subfield of humanities (Clayton et al. 16–17). Aging and potential injuries are additional factors that hinder many dancers from continuing their careers. Many of the dance majors I have encountered at universities do not understand this yet, or do not fully develop this intrinsic connection between dancing and self-actualization. Many instead quickly switch their majors to more promising fields. Likely, those few who do stay are those who find their voice and experience self-growth through dance. In these cases, dancing becomes who they are, becomes part of their lives, and cannot be simply abandoned. In Hyun, I saw this rare, deep level of connectivity that turns a mover into an artist.

In February 2018, Christ sent me a photo on Facebook. It was the letter from the state university in New York to which Hyun had applied. In the letter, the dance department director wrote that though the Hyun's current skills did not meet the acceptance criteria, the committee believed that he showed potential. The committee "has taken into consideration the letter from your mentor," and thus, decided to give Hyun a chance. They invited him to attend the intermediate ballet, African dance, and an upper-level modern dance class for free for a semester and then to audition again in the spring 2019. The committee also wrote that there would be other performance opportunities for him in the meantime with student organizations and other dance teams on campus. I felt overwhelmed, happy, and deeply grateful. Hyun, Chris, and I immediately had a FaceTime call and cherished this unforgettable moment.

Writing Performance (Auto)ethnography

A few months later, however, I heard that Hyun had ultimately given up the opportunity. It turned out that there were too many barriers that he could not handle. First, the university is a few hours away from his house. His parent could not afford housing in a different city. Further, he felt that he did not belong at the university. He told me that he felt strange and uncomfortable at the audition and classes. Most of the students in the department were white girls wearing ballet leotards and slippers. He was the only boy and Asian (and refugee) wearing sweatpants, and I could easily imagine him wearing worn-out running shoes. The other barrier was the required SAT, with which even students attending private high schools often struggle. Hyun did not have any educational resources or parental support for his study other than voluntary tutors or the director who helped with his homework at MUCC.

The process of writing this book resonates with what Norman K. Denzin might call "performative writing" process (Denzin 94). Performance ethnography opens the "subjectivity of researcher-researched" (Pollock 326). Through the writing process, I became an "other" (Pollock 326) a self-subject, which led me to recognize how naïve I had been. Going back to the refugee teens discussed in Chapter 6, what I saw was Hyun's talent and potential as a dancer. However, I failed to see the structural inequality and inevitable limitations he faced. He did not have the minimum degree of institutional or parental support needed for him to grab the opportunity of a lifetime. I also had to admit another brutal truth. Even if he was eventually accepted, was this opportunity really the best choice for him? He is different from many college students who attend private liberal arts colleges or prestigious universities in New York. Not all, but most, dance majors begin their training early with parental support, come from affluent families, attend numerous competitions, and receive awards before they even start to college.

As a former professional dancer and dance professor with a PhD, I admit that my career would not have been possible without my parents' financial and emotional support and even sacrifice. When I was a teenager, my family encountered financial difficulties. I remember my parents took out a loan to pay the high fees for my dance lessons. They did my stage makeup for me whenever I performed, gave me rides to competition venues and carried the stage costumes for me, brought me lunch boxes and small gifts for my dance teachers. Without any of that educational, financial, or parental support, how would it be possible for Hyun to feel welcomed and accepted in some of the most privileged groups? More significantly, what would he do after graduation? Getting a high-paid, full-time job with health insurance is nearly impossible in dance. I have seen my fellow dancers and choreographers spend their own money to stage their performances. Explaining roles of social theatre, James Thompson and Richard Schechner wrote that "people in crisis need peace, food, water, medicines, shelter, and, sooner or later, jobs" (Schechner 15). But if dancing itself provides such utilities, it is a social work. A sustainable, secure infrastructure is desperately needed to fuel young dancers beyond the temporary sponsor-deal on social media.

K-pop dance was a site of resistance and a refuge for the refugee teens. However, without sustainable institutional support, dancing could be a temporal shelter for liberation but not a securely grounded space where they can thrive. What I could provide was a stage, but maybe dancing was nothing but a temporal, luxurious escape. What the refugee teens really needed were practical resources: obtaining citizenship, finding an attorney who can help their parents, getting tutors for SAT or English, or finding a less exploitative part-time job, none of which I can provide.

Eventually, Hyun joined the military. Many of his refugee friends at MUCC have gone into the military because of its practical benefits, including citizenship and health insurance. Before leaving town, he briefly expressed an interest in attending college when he returns. I could not tell him, but it is doubtful that the university would offer him this opportunity again. Dance is bound to physicality. The younger dancers are, the more options they are likely to receive. The dancing body is also ephemeral. It is impossible to guarantee that he will maintain the same body type or level of flexibility, presence, and stamina after a few years have passed.

On that night I heard the news, I cried. As a performance ethnographer, once the performance was over, I could not do anything but wish the best of luck to the young artist. Or, perhaps, it was dance that felt hopeless. Everyone cheered for him when he was dancing under the spotlight. His dancing body was highly visible and adored on stage. Yet, when he needed help the most, it appeared that only a few remained besides him. Dancing is so evanescent that it disappears even before the applause is gone. The structural inequality behind the stage, however, was invisible. The spectacle of the stage hides vulnerability. The transformative, harmonious feeling that I witnessed in theatre felt like an illusion.

Since *Love Means Love*, I have worked with more than 50 refugees from Thailand, China, East Africa, Iraq, Iran, Syria, Turkey, and Poland, and I have presented performance ethnographies across New York, California, and Texas, including the *Refugee Dance Project* (Act 1 & 2 https://www.youtube.com/watch?v=1QBOf2eqLrE & Act 3 https://www.youtube.com/watch?v=PGnfnn_6sRM). Through these projects, I have received multiple awards and been promoted. Looking back, *Love Means Love* was a transition from theory to practice to writing, and it became a turning point in my academic career both as a K-pop dance researcher and performance ethnographer. Dani Snyder-Young wrote that "kinesthetic knowledge, experienced in the gut, can provide the possibility of radical transformation—of real changes of perspective and real shifts in understanding" (Snyder-Young 887). Scholars have emphasized the liberating potential and the "possibility" in performance ethnography, which turns a taken-for-granted daily life into a performative construction (Alexander 110; Denzin 18; Pollock 325). But what do my participants get beyond *my* achievement and transformation *in academia*?

During Q&A sessions, the audience has often asked me about my ethnography project's future direction. Seemingly moved and inspired, they asked, "So what will be the next?" I have never been able to answer the question clearly. I often responded that the performance aims to open the door so marginalized voices could be heard and felt, and kinesthetic empathy in theatre has the potential to change us, and thus, the society we are living in. This would be an ideal answer in a journal paper. However, I realized that all my works over the past five years had still been "opening the door" for further dialogue.

Undoubtedly, performance ethnography values the process. As Della Pollock described, in an ideal performance ethnography, the fieldwork turns the research into a research subject, bringing a process of surprise and disarming transformation (Pollock 328). Such feeling enhances the "fantasies of activist instrumentality, as if we were in possessive charge of the knowledge produced," through which researchers often ask, "now that we know this, what are we going to do with it?" (Pollock 328). Would it be ever possible to see so-called a real result, a palpable change? When can I move from the promising word "possibility" (Warren 318) of performance ethnography to the rhetorically pleasing, theoretically assuring phrase "opening the door"? Judith Hamera said performance is "doing" critical theory (Hamera 208). Ideally, the action-oriented "doing" can directly advocate social change through which theory, method, and practice can converge. But my fieldwork brutally revealed that "doing" performance ethnography is not enough to integrate practice and theory if it truly searching for activism.

In March 2019, I was invited to share my research at a school event. It was a social gathering where the school invited successful alumni and presented select faculty's current research. I was sitting in a nice conference room where waiters served fancy drinks and food for the guests. A notable alumnus was sitting in front of me, a US district court judge nationally known for his advocacy for immigrants. Saying that he received an email from the interim dean about my research on refugees, he asked me about my work. I was deeply honored to be able to share my research but felt guilty somehow. With hesitancy, I confessed my conflicted feeling. I told him that I thought I could make a difference, but the more I work with refugee communities, the more I realize my limitations. Then I shared a story of a woman I met in the *Refugee Dance Project* in San Diego.

After the performance, she asked me if I could introduce her a lawyer who could provide voluntary legal service. Over the next few weeks, I tried to support her, reached out to some local organizations, and asked my colleagues in the law field. I, however, could not offer what she needed. I felt hopeless at the end, as I did after my performance with the refugee teens. After the seemingly beautiful, harmonious performances on stage, there was nothing else I could do. One of the alumni sitting on the same table said empathetically, "If your performance could change at least one person in theatre, I think that's a success." The court judge also encouraged me, saying, "keep doing your work," wearing a supportive smile. However, deep inside of my heart, what I discovered from "doing" the ethnographic fieldwork was dissonance rather than a "utopia in performance" (Dolan 2). One of the reasons ethnographers keep coming back to Dwight Conquergood's "dialogical performance" (Conquergood 9) is that an unfinished work is the only work we can finish. Embracing imperfection can be the only way we can continue.

Searching for a Utopia Beyond Performance

In spring 2019, I sent messages on Facebook to the K-pop dance crew at MUCC, but I have not heard back from them. I believe that, based on his profile photo, one has just returned from the Navy. Other than that, I do not know if they are pursuing their careers in dance. Some might say that I have done enough. I am neither their guardian nor a lifetime civil rights activist. I am a faculty member who conducts ethnographic research, whose schedule is mostly filled with preparing lectures and grading students' assignments during the weekdays, and revising articles submitted to journals during the weekends.

I am still working in academia, a highly safe occupation compared to many others. I know that to Hyun and Way, the performance experiences and regular dance and Korean workshops were the first and perhaps last time they will perform under the spotlight, sharing their stories on the big concert stage. From the audience reception to the choreography process, every single moment in *Love Means Love* was precious. My apprehension has nothing to do with the audience or the community members. It is the sustainability of dance and arts that makes me question its potential. Dancing itself hardly brings an immediate structural change, although a dance piece can discuss political issues through representation.

In November 2019, I delivered the David Sanjek Keynote Lecture in Popular Music at the 64th annual conference of the Society for Ethnomusicology at

Indiana University, Bloomington. My talk focused on K-pop cover dancers and their identity passing, including that of the refugee teens. During the Q&A session, an audience member asked me what was my most meaningful memory from the fieldwork. I responded that I learned how many privileges I have and how much I can still and should share with others. From the page to the stage, performing (auto)ethnography has humbled me to appreciate and respect small things. Answering the question, for a brief moment, I was not happy. I was proud of the progress of my scholarship as a researcher, but ashamed of the fancy Calvin Klein dress I was wearing. I thought of the cold church floor where refugee teens danced wearing worn-out running shoes.

Building on the idea that "there can never be a last definitive word, only penultimate ones," performance ethnography stands with "institutional unfinalizability" and the vitality within it (Hamera 208). Madison wrote, "Theory becomes another way to know performance better; and performance becomes the desired illuminator of theory" (Madison 107). I first learned of what Denzin called "co-performers" (Denzin xi) from theory and built and physically felt empathy dancing with them. We laughed out loud, made mistakes, and encouraged each other throughout the choreography process. I later witnessed their life gradually fading behind the stage.

I wish my "doing" of performance ethnography could be more celebratory. As Randy Martin argued, dance can be a political action with a self-interrogation through which we assess possibilities, continuous allowance, or limitations of dance in given social circumstance (Martin 10). Performance ethnography seeks to involve "going *in* to a social field at risk of going *under* (original emphasis)" (Pollock 327). It demands audacious belief and even naïve hope; even if nothing has changed after a staged performance, the researcher should be ready to go back to her/his desk, reflect, write about the failure, and start another ethnographic journey that never ends.

Thus, I still teach performance ethnography perhaps with even more profound and more genuine passion, but not because it is the tool that makes the ultimate difference. Instead, I teach it because performance ethnography soaks into the fabrics of life, blurring the line across theory, practice, and method, as a way of learning about ourselves and thus, our responsibilities as academics. The more students are educated, the more power they will have in society. The promising framework of "possibility" in performance ethnography resembles a life. Like the refugee teen dancers who were chasing a possibility of being K-pop idols, I have continuously moved forward because life promises me a possibility. I was blinded by my privilege, as much as the teens were blinded by their passion. Nevertheless, even if we will never arrive at the point we dreamed, being blind is better than losing hope.

Merely celebrating hermeneutic approach and "empathy" in performance ethnography could be an act of reinforcing racialized authenticity and nativism (Hamera 327). Essentialism under the name of activism should be avoided at all costs. Nevertheless, without empathy, knowledge could be a sword that takes one's dignity. As Denzin pointed out, "a good performance text must be more than cathartic – it must be political, moving people to action, reflection, or both" (Denzin xi). Building on my "ethnography of failure" (Nayfack 96), I believe that readers of this book include the next generation of academics who will make the fields continuously evolve, until we make a "utopia" not just *in* performance, but also *beyond*, when dreaming and fandoming ourselves through dance is not a complete mirage.

Many of the K-pop fan-dancers discussed in this book go through a process of performing and shaping diasporic identities, symbolically, physically, and culturally through their racial, ethnic, and fandom-oriented identifications, as well as their physical locations and displacements. Within their experiences of diasporic identity, they identify K-pop dance as a "home" from which they, at least temporarily, see their desires and envision their futures. Above all, their intercultural performances become more than individual choices; they are a slice of the manifestations that illuminate fans' audacious hopes and dreams in the (im)possibility of identity passing – a desire that is stronger than the social structure that privileges the privileged.

In winter 2021, I visited my parents' house in Seoul. I found a box of CDs covered with dust. I neither listen to that music, nor use those CDs. Instead of listening to music, in my free time these days, I would rather write a research paper to work toward promotion. Yet, the artifacts made me smile. To some, they would be nothing but electronic trash. But to me, they were full of memories – my first purchase of American pop songs, Madonna's CD *Music*, from saving pennies when I was in high school. I still remember the feeling when I walked into the record shop. I felt like an adult. And the list of artsy CDs that I used for my choreographies in my mid-twenties, the cold dance floor, smell of theatre curtains, my selfish and luxurious struggle as an artist in an ivory tower, and uncountable nostalgic memories of people associated with music and dance.

K-pop cover dancers' videos and K-pop merchandise may or may not be relevant when young fans leave their youth. Yet, the youth does not last forever, but the memories of youth can. Whenever they get a chance to come across a faded K-pop idol poster, handmade keyholder, or their K-pop dance videos, the artifacts will bring memories. Even after their K-pop fandom is over, the memories will remain, because it has been part of who they are, filling their precarious but incompatibly beautiful moments in life. Like dance, fandoming ourselves is as ephemeral as the stars we love, but as persistent as our lives. And the journey can always begin again in a place where it ends.

References

Alexander, Bryant Keith. "Introduction: Performative Rhetorics of Desire, Resistance, and Possibility." *QED: A Journal in GLBTQ Worldmaking*, vol. 2, no. 1, 2015, pp. 109–111. https://doi.org/10.14321/qed.2.1.0109.

Clayton, Michelle, et al. "Inside/Beside Dance Studies: A Conversation Mellon Dance Studies in/and the Humanities." *Dance Research Journal*, vol. 45, no. 3, 2013, pp. 3–28. https://muse.jhu.edu/article/541939.

Conquergood, Dwight. "Performing as a Moral Act: Ethical Dimensions of the Ethnography of Performance." *Literature in Performance*, vol. 5, no. 2, 1985, pp. 1–13. https://doi.org/10.1080/10462938509391578.

Dolan, Jill. *Utopia in Performance: Finding Hope at the Theater*. U of Michigan P, 2010.

Denzin, Norman K. *Performance Ethnography: Critical Pedagogy and the Politics of Culture*. Sage Publications, 2003.

Hamera, Judith. "Performance Ethnography." In *The Sage Handbook of Qualitative Research*, edited by Norman K. Denzin and Yvonna S. Lincoln, SAGE Publications, 2011, pp. 317–330.

Pollock, Della. "Marking New Directions in Performance Ethnography." *Text and Performance Quarterly*, vol. 26, no. 4, 2006, pp. 325–329. https://doi.org/10.1080/10462930600828733.

"Refugee Dance Project: Love Means Love (2017)." YouTube, uploaded by Chuyun Oh, 17 April 2017, https://www.youtube.com/watch?v=5z19y-5Egik.

"Refugee Dance Project: Dance of Home (2018) Act 1 & 2." YouTube, uploaded by Chuyun Oh, 30 October 2018. https://www.youtube.com/watch?v=1QBOf2eqLrE.

"Refugee Dance Project: Dance of Home Act 3 (2018)." YouTube, uploaded by Chuyun Oh, 1 November 2018. https://www.youtube.com/watch?v=PGnfnn_6sRM.

Snyder-Young, Dani. "Beyond 'An Aesthetic of Objectivity': Performance Ethnography, Performance Texts, and Theatricality." *Qualitative Inquiry*, vol. 16, no. 10, 2010, pp. 883–893. https://doi.org/10.1177/1077800410383119.

Thompson, James, and Richard Schechner. "Why "Social Theatre"?" *TDR: The Drama Review*, vol. 48, no. 3, 2004, pp. 11–16. https://muse.jhu.edu/article/172052.

Madison, D. Soyini. "Performing Theory/Embodied Writing." *Text and Performance Quarterly*, vol. 19, no. 2, 1999, pp. 107–124. https://doi.org/10.1080/10462939909366254.

Martin, Randy. *Critical Moves: Dance Studies in Theory and Politics*. Duke UP, 1998.

Nayfack, Shakina. "Dancing Communities: Performance, Difference, and Connection in the Global City (review)." *Dance Research Journal*, vol. 40, pp. 2, 2008, pp. 94–97. https://www.jstor.org/stable/20527612.

Warren, John T. "Introduction: Performance Ethnography: A TPQ Symposium." *Text and Performance Quarterly*, vol. 26, no. 4, 2006, pp. 317–319. https://doi.org/10.1080/10462930600828667.

INDEX

Printed in the United States
by Baker & Taylor Publisher Services